McDougal Littell
LITERATURE

InterActive
READER & WRITER
with *Strategic Reading Support*

Grade 12

McDougal Littell
EVANSTON, ILLINOIS • BOSTON • DALLAS

COVER

RainyEmbankment (1929), Fox Photos. © Hulton Archive / Getty Images; *background* © Getty Images.

ISBN 13: 978-0-618-92048-8   ISBN 10: 0-618-92048-X

Printed in the United States of America.

1 2 3 4 5 6 7 8 9–DOM–12 11 10 09 08

SENIOR PROGRAM CONSULTANTS

Janet Allen
Internationally-known Reading and Literacy Specialist

Arthur N. Applebee
Leading Professor, School of Education, University of Albany, State University of New York; Director of the Center on English Learning and Achievement

Jim Burke
Lecturer, Author, English Teacher, Burlingame, California

Douglas Carnine
Professor of Education, University of Oregon

Yvette Jackson
Executive Director, National Urban Alliance for Effective Education

Robert Jiménez
Professor of Language, Literacy, and Culture, Vanderbilt University

Judith A. Langer
Distinguished Professor, University of Albany, State University of New York; Director of the Center on English Learning and Achievement; Director of the Albany Institute for Research in Education

Robert J. Marzano
Senior Scholar, Mid-Continent Research for Education and Learning (McREL), Denver, Colorado

Donna M. Ogle
Professor of Reading and Language, National-Louis University, Chicago, Illinois; Past President, International Reading Association

Carol Booth Olson
Senior Lecturer, Department of Education, University of California , Irvine

Carol Ann Tomlinson
Professor of Educational Research, Foundations, and Policy, University of Virginia; Co-Director of the University's Institutes on Academic Diversity

ENGLISH LEARNER SPECIALISTS
Mary Lou McCloskey
Past President, TESOL; Director of Teacher Development and Curriculum Design for Educo, Atlanta, Georgia

Lydia Stack
Past President, TESOL; International ESL Consultant

CURRICULUM SPECIALIST
William L. McBride
Nationally-known Speaker, Educator, and Author

TABLE OF CONTENTS

UNIT 4   THE FLOWERING OF ROMANTICISM, 1798–1832

The InterActive Reader & Writer

The InterActive Reader & Writer is a literature book to mark on, write in, and make your own. As you will see, this book helps you become an active reader. It also helps you become a better writer.

An Easy-to-Carry Literature Text

This book won't weigh you down. It fits as comfortably in your hand as it can in your backpack. Yet it is packed with great things to read and do:

- Important works of literature by leading authors
- A rich selection of nonfiction texts—Web pages, magazine articles, and more
- A variety of genres—such as epics, poems, essays, and short stories
- Activities that will help you think more deeply about yourself and the world beyond

Help When You Need It

Many works of literature are challenging the first time you read them. *The InterActive Reader & Writer* helps you understand these works. Here's how:

BEFORE READING ACTIVITIES

Big Question The first activity in each unit gets you thinking about a real-life question that the literature addresses.

Learn the Terms A brief skill lesson helps you understand the most important features of the literature and teaches terms you will need in order to talk and write about the selection.

DURING READING ACTIVITIES

Focus Each section is broken into smaller sections. A "Focus" box tells you what to look for as you read.

Pause & Reflect At the end of each section, a quick question or two helps you check your understanding.

Mark It Up These features invite you to mark your own notes and answers—right on the page!

VOCABULARY SUPPORT

Words to Know Important words are underlined and boldfaced in blue. Their definitions appear nearby in the side column.

Specialized Vocabulary Vocabulary notes in nonfiction selections explain special words used in certain careers or fields of study.

Special Features

TEST PREPARATION

No one likes tests, but everyone likes doing well on them. *The Interactive Reader & Writer* will help you become a better test-taker.

TestSmart TestSmart questions appear right next to the text you are reading. These give you an opportunity to practice answering multiple-choice questions about literature—without worrying about being scored!

Test Tips You'll be given helpful strategies to use when answering test questions.

Assessment Practice Multiple-choice test items help you focus on how well you've read the texts provided. They also help you prepare for real tests.

Written Responses Many tests ask you to write one or more paragraphs about a reading passage. This book gives you the opportunity to write about each selection you read. A **Test-Taker's Toolkit** shows you how to develop each written response, step-by-step.

NONFICTION READING

Each main literature selection in *The InterActive Reader & Writer* is paired with a nonfiction selection that is related in some way to the literature. You will learn many different strategies for getting the most out of the nonfiction you read. These strategies will help you on tests, in other classes, and in the world outside of school. For example, you will learn how to:

- Identify text features
- Summarize
- Determine author's purpose
- Analyze cause-and-effect relationships

LINKS TO

McDougal Littell Literature

If you are using *McDougal Littell Literature,* you will find the *InterActive Reader & Writer* to be the perfect companion. *The InterActive Reader & Writer* helps you read certain core selections from *McDougal Littell Literature* more carefully and with more understanding.

Read on to learn more!

User's Guide

The InterActive Reader & Writer with Strategic Reading Support has an easy-to-follow organization, as shown by these sample pages from the essay "A Modest Proposal" by Jonathan Swift.

1 Anchor Selection
Each lesson is made up of a cluster of readings. The main literature selection is called the **anchor selection.** You will read this first.

2 Related Nonfiction
The title in smaller type is the **Related Nonfiction** piece. As you preview each lesson, read the title and think about how this piece might relate to the anchor selection.

UNIT 3

THE RESTORATION AND THE 18TH CENTURY

LESSON 3A

1 *A Modest Proposal*
BY JONATHAN SWIFT

RELATED NONFICTION
Children Sink to the Bottom: Thousands in Haiti Subsist on Nation's Leavings **2**

JUST-STARVE-US.
WORKHOUSE

Tell Ah! Tell us can aught be worse?
Than hungry Maw & empty Purse!!
MERCY SHOW & PITY US,
GREAT OVERSEER.

98

How can we fight INJUSTICE?

There's an old proverb that states, "The pen is mightier than the sword." Jonathan Swift wielded his pen like a rapier, using it to slash away at injustice. Though some may claim that the power of the pen is greatly diminished these days, people still fight injustice with words—in speeches, in newspapers and magazines, and on the Internet.

CHART IT With a small group, brainstorm some contemporary examples of injustice. Write three of them down in the chart. For each example, identify some tactics that people can use to fight the injustice.

Examples of Injustice	Tactics for Fighting Injustice

ASSESSMENT GOALS

By the end of this lesson, you will be able to . . .

- analyze satire
- use active reading strategies to comprehend text
- analyze descriptive details in nonfiction
- analyze a writing prompt and plan a problem-solution essay

A MODEST PROPOSAL **99**

③ Big Question
Each lesson begins with an activity that gets you thinking about a real-life question that the literature addresses. Sometimes you'll work in a group to complete this activity. After reading, you'll return to this question. Don't be surprised if you have a different perspective.

④ Assessment Goals
This box sums up the lesson's main learning goals. The first goal names the **literature skill.** The second goal is your overall **reading objective.** The third goal names the skill you'll be learning with the **nonfiction** selections. The last goal names the **writing activity** you'll complete at the end of the lesson.

1 **Learn the Terms: Academic Vocabulary**
Talking and writing about literature is a lot easier when you have the right words for the job. This page presents important terms and explains what to look for in the literature you read.

2 You will come back to these academic terms several times during the unit. For example, in this lesson you will come across the term *irony* in the side notes of the main selection.

Satire

SATIRE is a literary technique in which behaviors or institutions are ridiculed for the purpose of improving society. What sets satire apart from other forms of social and political protest is humor. For example, Swift used his savage wit to attack prominent British politicians and to protest unjust policies in Ireland.

The following chart shows three types of IRONY that Swift used in his satires. Look for examples of these techniques as you read "A Modest Proposal."

TECHNIQUE	EXAMPLE
SITUATIONAL IRONY a contrast between what is expected and what actually occurs	After safely completing a dangerous mountain climb, a climber slips in the shower and hurts herself.
VERBAL IRONY when a writer or character says one thing but means the opposite	A football player fumbles the ball and loses the game. When he reaches the sideline, his coach tells him, "Nice play!"
UNDERSTATEMENT a form of irony that creates emphasis by saying less than what is true or appropriate	Reporting from a town that was hit by a hurricane, a reporter describes the place as "a bit messy."

A Modest Proposal

FOR PREVENTING THE CHILDREN OF POOR PEOPLE IN IRELAND
FROM BEING A BURDEN TO THEIR PARENTS OR COUNTRY,
AND FOR MAKING THEM BENEFICIAL TO THE PUBLIC

JONATHAN SWIFT

(5) BACKGROUND By 1700, Ireland was completely dominated by England. The Catholic majority could not vote, hold public office, buy land, or receive an education—policies that reduced most Irish people to poverty. When crops failed, many faced starvation. Jonathan Swift, outraged by England's treatment of Ireland, wrote a satirical attack on this injustice in "A Modest Proposal."

I t is a melancholy object to those who walk through this great town[1] or travel in the country, when they see the streets, the roads, and cabin doors, crowded with beggars of the female sex, followed by three, four, or six children, all in rags and importuning every passenger for an alms.[2] These mothers, instead of being able to work for their honest livelihood, are forced to employ all their time in strolling to beg **sustenance** for their helpless infants, who, as they grow up, either turn thieves for want[3] of work, or leave their dear native country to fight for the Pretender[4] in Spain, or sell themselves to the Barbadoes.[5]

10   I think it is agreed by all parties that this prodigious number of children in the arms, or on the backs, or at the heels of their mothers, and

---

1. **this great town:** Dublin, Ireland.
2. **importuning** (ĭm'pôr-tōōn'ĭng) **. . . alms** (ämz): begging from every passerby for a charitable handout.
3. **want:** lack; need.
4. **Pretender:** James Edward Stuart, who claimed the English throne, from which his now deceased father, James II, had been removed in 1688. Because James II and his son were Roman Catholic, the common people of Ireland were loyal to them.
5. **sell . . . Barbadoes:** To escape poverty, some Irish migrated to the West Indies, obtaining money for their passage by agreeing to work as slaves on plantations there for a set period.

A MODEST PROPOSAL   **101**

---

(3) MARK IT UP
Use these marks to monitor your reading:
* This is important.
? I don't understand.
! This is a surprise.

(4) When you see this pencil ✏, you'll be asked to mark up the text. You can also write in this book in any way you find useful.

(6) FOCUS
In this section, the speaker describes the terrible poverty that afflicts Ireland, and he proposes a solution to this problem.

sustenance (sŭs'tə-nəns) *n.* a means of support or nourishment

---

(3) MARK IT UP
This easy-to-use marking system helps you track your understanding. You will see it at the beginning of every literature selection in this book.

(4) You'll mark up the text in other ways, too. The pencil symbol ✏ appears whenever you are being asked to circle, underline, or mark the text in other ways.

(5) BACKGROUND
This paragraph gives important information about the selection you are about to read. Always read this section before starting the main text.

(6) FOCUS
Every selection is broken down into parts or "bites." A Focus box introduces each part and tells you what to look for as you read.

① ▶

When you come to the arrow symbol, follow the arrow to the side column. Answer the question. Then read on.

② 💡 **TestSmart**

TestSmart questions will give you practice answering multiple-choice questions typically found on tests.

Some **TestSmart** questions will ask about words found in the selection. The **TIP** that follows will help strengthen your word-attack skills in testing situations.

A **TIP** may ask you to underline things in the text. The blue line shows how one student did the mark-up. The underlined context clue suggests one answer—A.

CLARIFY

Reread lines 10–21. What problem does the speaker hope to solve with his proposal?

_____

_____

_____

TESTSMART **②**

VOCABULARY

What does the word *raiment* mean in line 31?

Ⓐ clothing
Ⓑ weather
Ⓒ indignation
Ⓓ optimism

TIP Use **context clues** to figure out the best meaning of an unfamiliar word. Reread lines 28–32, and underline any words or phrases that provide clues to the meaning of the word *raiment.* ✏

---

frequently of their fathers, is in the present deplorable state of the kingdom a very great additional grievance; and therefore whoever could find out a fair, cheap, and easy method of making these children sound, useful members of the commonwealth would deserve so well of the public as to have his statue set up for a preserver of the nation.

But my intention is very far from being confined to provide only for the children of professed beggars; it is of a much greater extent, and shall take in the whole number of infants at a certain age who are born of
20 parents in effect as little able to support them as those who demand our charity in the streets. ◀ **①**

As to my own part, have turned my thoughts for many years upon this important subject, and maturely weighed the several schemes of other projectors,[6] I have always found them grossly mistaken in their computation. It is true, a child just dropped from its dam[7] may be supported by her milk for a solar year, with little other nourishment; at most not above the value of two shillings, which the mother may certainly get, or the value in scraps, by her lawful occupation of begging; and it is exactly at one year old that I propose to provide for them in such a manner
30 as instead of being a charge upon their parents or the parish, or wanting food and raiment for the rest of their lives, they shall on the contrary contribute to the feeding, and partly to the clothing, of many thousands. ◀

There is likewise another great advantage in my scheme, that it will prevent those voluntary abortions, and that horrid practice of women murdering their bastard children, alas, too frequent among us, sacrificing the poor innocent babes, I doubt,[8] more to avoid the expense than the shame, which would move tears and pity in the most savage and inhuman breast.

The number of souls in this kingdom being usually reckoned one
40 million and a half, of these I calculate there may be about two hundred thousand couple whose wives are breeders; from which number I subtract thirty thousand couples who are able to maintain their own children, although I apprehend there cannot be so many under the present distresses of the kingdom; but this being granted, there will remain an hundred and seventy thousand breeders. I again subtract fifty thousand for those women who miscarry, or whose children die by accident or disease within the year. There only remain an hundred and twenty thousand children of poor parents annually born. The question therefore is, how this number

---

6. **projectors:** persons who propose public projects or plans.
7. **dam** (dăm): female parent. The term is used mostly for farm animals.
8. **doubt:** suspect.

shall be reared and provided for, which, as I have already said, under the present situation of affairs, is utterly impossible by all the methods hitherto proposed. For we can neither employ them in handicraft or agriculture; we neither build houses (I mean in the country) nor cultivate land. They can very seldom pick up a livelihood by stealing till they arrive at six years old, except where they are of towardly parts;[9] although I confess they learn the __rudiments__ much earlier, during which time they can however be looked upon only as probationers, as I have been informed by a principal gentleman in the county of Cavan, who protested to me that he never knew above one or two instances under the age of six, even in a part of the kingdom so renowned for the quickest proficiency in that art. ▶

I am assured by our merchants that a boy or girl before twelve years old is no salable commodity; and even when they come to this age they will not yield above three pounds, or three pounds and half a crown at most on the Exchange; which cannot turn to account[10] either to the parents or the kingdom, the charge of nutriment and rags having been at least four times that value.

I shall now therefore humbly propose my own thoughts, which I hope will not be liable to the least objection.

I have been assured by a very knowing American of my acquaintance in London, that a young healthy child well nursed is at a year old a most delicious, nourishing, and wholesome food, whether stewed, roasted, baked, or boiled; and I make no doubt that it will equally serve in a fricassee or a ragout.[11]

I do therefore humbly offer it to public consideration that of the hundred and twenty thousand children, already computed, twenty thousand may be reserved for breed,[12] whereof only one fourth part to be males, which is more than we allow to sheep, black cattle, or swine; and my reason is that these children are seldom the fruits of marriage, a circumstance not much regarded by our savages, therefore one male will be sufficient to serve four females. That the remaining hundred thousand may at a year old be offered in sale to the persons of quality and fortune through the kingdom, always advising the mother to let them suck plentifully in the last month, so as to render them plump and fat for a good table. A child will make two dishes at an entertainment for friends; and when the family dines alone, the fore or hind quarter will make a

9. __are of towardly__ (tôrd′lē) __parts:__ have a promising talent.
10. __turn to account:__ earn a profit; benefit; prove useful.
11. __fricassee__ (frĭk′ə-sē′) . . . __ragout__ (ră-gōō′): types of meat stews.
12. __reserved for breed:__ kept for breeding (instead of being slaughtered).

3 __rudiment__ (rōō′də-mənt) _n._ a basic principle or element

ANALYZE
Reread the boxed text. What is **ironic** about the speaker's discussion of stealing?

_____
_____
_____

3 **Vocabulary**
Important vocabulary words are underlined and boldfaced in the text. A definition and a respelling appear in the side column.

4 **Footnotes**
Some selections in this book include definitions of special words and phrases. When you see a number in the text, look down at the bottom of the page for an explanation of the meaning.

Pause & Reflect

Whenever you see this signal, stop reading. Go to the side column and answer the questions. They'll give you a quick check of your understanding. Then move ahead to the next **Focus** and continue your reading.

SUMMARIZE

What plan does the speaker propose for Ireland's children?

_____

_____

_____

collateral (kə-lăt′ər-əl) *adj.*
accompanying as a parallel or subordinate factor; related

PAUSE & REFLECT

1. What was your reaction to the speaker's proposal? Underline phrases that helped create this reaction. *MAKE JUDGMENTS*

_____

_____

_____

2. What attitude does the speaker have toward the poor of Ireland? *DRAW CONCLUSIONS*

_____

_____

_____

---

reasonable dish, and seasoned with a little pepper or salt will be very good boiled on the fourth day, especially in winter. ◄

I have reckoned upon a medium that a child just born will weigh twelve pounds, and in a solar year if tolerably nursed increaseth to twenty eight pounds.

90   I grant this food will be somewhat dear, and therefore very proper for landlords, who, as they have already devoured most of the parents, seem to have the best title to the children.

Infant's flesh will be in season throughout the year, but more plentiful in March, and a little before and after. For we are told by a grave author, an eminent French physician,[13] that fish being a prolific[14] diet, there are more children born in Roman Catholic countries about nine months after Lent[15] than at any other season; therefore, reckoning a year after Lent, the markets will be more glutted than usual, because the number of popish infants is at least three to one in this kingdom; and therefore it will have

100   one other **collateral** advantage, by lessening the number of Papists[16] among us.

I have already computed the charge of nursing a beggar's child (in which list I reckon all cottagers, laborers, and four fifths of the farmers), to be about two shillings per annum, rags included; and I believe no gentleman would repine to give ten shillings for the carcass of a good fat child, which, as I have said, will make four dishes of excellent nutritive meat, when he hath only some particular friend or his own family to dine with him. Thus the squire will learn to be a good landlord, and grow popular among the tenants; the mother will have eight shillings net profit

110   and be fit for work till she produces another child.

Those who are more thrifty (as I must confess the times require) may flay the carcass; the skin of which artificially dressed will make admirable gloves for ladies, and summer boots for fine gentlemen.

As to our city of Dublin, shambles[17] may be appointed for this purpose in the most convenient parts of it, and butchers we may be assured will not be wanting; although I rather recommend buying the children alive, and dressing them hot from the knife as we do roasting pigs.

PAUSE & REFLECT ①

---

13. **grave . . . physician:** François Rabelais (răb′ə-lā′), a 16th-century French satirist.
14. **prolific:** promoting fertility.
15. **Lent:** Catholics traditionally do not eat meat during Lent, the 40 days leading up to Easter, and instead eat a lot of fish.
16. **popish** (pō′pĭsh) **. . . Papists:** hostile or contemptuous terms referring to Roman Catholics.
17. **shambles:** slaughterhouses.

A very worthy person, a true lover of his country, and whose virtues I highly esteem, was lately pleased in discoursing on this matter to offer
120 a refinement upon my scheme. He said that many gentlemen of this kingdom, having of late destroyed their deer, he conceived that the want of venison might be well supplied by the bodies of young lads and maidens, not exceeding fourteen years of age nor under twelve, so great a number of both sexes in every county being now ready to starve for want of work and service; and these to be disposed of by their parents, if alive, or otherwise by their nearest relations. But with due <u>deference</u> to so excellent a friend and so deserving a patriot, I cannot be altogether in his sentiments; for as to the males, my American acquaintance assured me from frequent experience that their flesh was generally tough and lean, like that of our
130 schoolboys, by continual exercise, and their taste disagreeable; and to fatten them would not answer the charge. Then as to the females, it would, I think with humble submission, be a loss to the public, because they soon would become breeders themselves; and besides, it is not improbable that some scrupulous people might be apt to censure such a practice (although indeed very unjustly) as a little bordering upon cruelty; which, I confess, hath always been with me the strongest objection against any project, how well soever intended.

But in order to justify my friend, he confessed that this <u>expedient</u> was put into his head by the famous Psalmanazar, a native of the island
140 Formosa,[18] who came from thence to London above twenty years ago, and in conversation told my friend that in his country when any young person happened to be put to death, the executioner sold the carcass to persons of quality as a prime dainty; and that in his time the body of a plump girl of fifteen, who was crucified for an attempt to poison the emperor, was sold to his Imperial Majesty's prime minister of state, and other great mandarins of the court, in joints from the gibbet,[19] at four hundred crowns. Neither indeed can I deny that if the same use were made of several plump young girls in this town, who without one single groat[20] to their fortunes cannot stir abroad without a chair,[21] and appear at the playhouse and assemblies in
150 foreign fineries which they never will pay for, the kingdom would not be the worse.

---

18. **Psalmanazar** (săl′mə-năz′ər) . . . **Formosa** (fôr-mō′sə): a French imposter in London who called himself George Psalmanazar and pretended to be from Formosa (now Taiwan), where, he said, cannibalism was practiced.
19. **gibbet** (jĭb′ĭt): gallows.
20. **groat:** an old British coin worth four pennies.
21. **cannot stir . . . chair:** cannot go outside without using an enclosed chair carried on poles by two men.

FOCUS
In the next section, the speaker responds to an alternative proposal and lays out the advantages of his own.

deference (děf′ər-əns) *n.* a yielding or courteous regard toward the opinion, judgment, or wishes of others; respect

expedient (ĭk-spē′dē-ənt) *n.* something useful in achieving the desired effect; a convenience; an advantage

2 Many older British literature selections, like this one, contain challenging vocabulary words. Always read the definitions provided at least twice, and look for context clues. Try reading the sentence with a simpler word in place of the more challenging word. If you still feel confused by the meaning, read on.

The selection continues . . .

earth. Therefore let no man talk to me of other expedients: of taxing our absentees at five shillings a pound: of using neither clothes nor household furniture except what is of our own growth and manufacture: of utterly rejecting the materials and instruments that promote foreign luxury: of curing the expensiveness of pride, vanity, idleness, and gaming in our
230 women: of introducing a vein of parsimony,[25] prudence, and temperance: of learning to love our country, in the want of which we differ even from Laplanders and the inhabitants of Topinamboo:[26] of quitting our animosities and factions, nor acting any longer like the Jews, who were murdering one another at the very moment their city was taken:[27] of being a little cautious not to sell our country and conscience for nothing: of teaching landlords to have at least one degree of mercy toward their tenants: lastly, of putting a spirit of honesty, industry, and skill into our shopkeepers; who, if a resolution could now be taken to buy only our native goods, would immediately unite to cheat and exact upon us in the
240 price, the measure, and the goodness, nor could ever yet be brought to make one fair proposal of just dealing, though often and earnestly invited to it. ◄

Therefore I repeat, let no man talk to me of these and the like expedients,[28] till he hath at least some glimpse of hope that there will ever be some hearty and sincere attempt to put them in practice.

But as to myself, having been wearied out for many years with offering vain, idle, visionary thoughts, and at length utterly despairing of success, I fortunately fell upon this proposal, which, as it is wholly new, so it hath something solid and real, of no expense and little trouble, full in our own
250 power, and whereby we can incur no danger in disobliging England. For this kind of commodity will not bear exportation, the flesh being of too tender a consistence to admit a long continuance in salt, although perhaps I could name a country which would be glad to eat up our whole nation without it.

After all, I am not so violently bent upon my own opinion as to reject any offer proposed by wise men, which shall be found equally innocent, cheap, easy, and effectual. But before something of that kind shall be

---

25. **parsimony** (pär'sə-mō'nē): frugality; thrift.
26. **Topinamboo** (tŏp'ĭ-năm'bōō): an area in Brazil supposedly inhabited by wild savages.
27. **Jews . . . taken:** In A.D. 70, during a Jewish revolt against Roman rule, the inhabitants of Jerusalem, by fighting among themselves, made it easier for the Romans to capture the city.
28. **let no man . . . expedients:** In his writings, Swift had suggested "other expedients" without success.

1 TestSmart

Here is another **TestSmart** question. The **TIP** discusses one way that questions are often worded on tests.

TESTSMART   1

Which of the following words *best* characterizes the "other expedients" that the speaker rejects as solutions to Ireland's poverty?

(A) optimistic
(B) reasonable
(C) illogical
(D) passionate

TIP Notice that the question asks which is the **best answer.** This tells you that more than one answer may be possible, so you need to look for the one that is strongest or most accurate. Reread lines 225–242 and read all of the answer choices to decide which one best describes the other expedients.

advanced in contradiction to my scheme, and offering a better, I desire the
author or authors will be pleased maturely to consider two points. First, as
things now stand, how they will be able to find food and raiment for an
hundred thousand useless mouths and backs. And secondly, there being
a round million of creatures in human figure throughout this kingdom,
whose sole subsistence put into a common stock[29] would leave them in
debt two millions of pounds sterling, adding those who are beggars by
profession to the bulk of farmers, cottagers, and laborers, with their wives
and children who are beggars in effect; I desire those politicians who
dislike my overture, and may perhaps be so bold to attempt an answer,
that they will first ask the parents of these mortals whether they would not
at this day think it a great happiness to have been sold for food at a year
old in the manner I prescribe, and thereby have avoided such a perpetual
scene of misfortunes as they have since gone through by the oppression
of landlords, the impossibility of paying rent without money or trade, the
want of common sustenance, with neither house nor clothes to cover them
from the inclemencies of the weather, and the most inevitable prospect of
entailing the like or greater miseries upon their breed forever.

I profess, in the sincerity of my heart, that I have not the least personal
interest in endeavoring to promote this necessary work, having no other
motive than the public good of my country, by advancing our trade,
providing for infants, relieving the poor, and giving some pleasure to the
rich. I have no children by which I can propose to get a single penny; the
youngest being nine years old, and my wife past childbearing.

PAUSE & REFLECT

PAUSE & REFLECT

What idea does Swift suggest
with the speaker's challenge
to "politicians who dislike my
overture" in lines 266–275?
MAKE INFERENCES

_____

_____

_____

2 **Big Question** ⚡?

Think about the
contemporary examples
of injustice that you listed
on page 99. How effective
would a **satire** similar to
"A Modest Proposal" be in
fighting these injustices?
Explain your answer.

_____

_____

_____

2 **Big Question** ⚡?

At the end of each main
literature selection, you'll
be asked to think again
about the **Big Question** you
discussed before reading.

29. **common stock:** ordinary stock in a company or business venture.

1 Assessment Practice I: Reading Comprehension

After reading each main literature selection, you'll have an opportunity to practice your test-taking skills and strategies by answering questions about the selection. The direction line will tell you how to mark the answers.

2 Literary Skills

Certain test items will ask questions that are related to the literary skills. You can review these skills by turning back to **Learn the Terms,** page 100.

3 Test Strategies

Other test items will give you a chance to use the **TestSmart TIPs** from earlier in the lesson. Here, notice how the **TIP** on page 108 can help answer test item 6. The **TIP** on page 102 can help answer test item 7.

4 Vocabulary

The last two test items focus on vocabulary. Remember to use the line numbers to help locate and reread the sentences in which the words appear.

Assessment Practice I — 1

Reading Comprehension

DIRECTIONS *Answer these questions about "A Modest Proposal" by filling in the correct ovals.*

1. Which of the following benefits will *not* result from the speaker's proposal?
   - (A) Ireland's poor will have more money.
   - (B) More Irish people will get married.
   - (C) The Catholic population will decrease.
   - (D) Absentee landlords will return to Ireland.

2. According to the speaker, his proposal will benefit the wealthier people of Ireland by
   - (A) making them fonder of their spouses
   - (B) lowering their taxes
   - (C) adding variety to their diet
   - (D) making money from the sale of babies

3. Which of the following is an example of verbal irony?
   - (A) the title of the essay
   - (B) the speaker's description of mothers begging for food
   - (C) the estimate of 200,000 "breeders" in Ireland
   - (D) the argument that the proposal will encourage marriage

4. What technique does Swift use to create satire in lines 133–137, where the speaker suggests that some people might consider slaughtering and eating girls 12 to 14 years old "a little bordering upon cruelty"?
   - (A) situational irony
   - (B) verbal irony
   - (C) understatement
   - (D) hyperbole

5. Why does the speaker lack faith in the alternative solutions listed near the end of the essay?
   - (A) Similar proposals have been ignored in the past.
   - (B) These solutions have been tried and they didn't work.
   - (C) He is jealous of the people who have proposed these solutions.
   - (D) He thinks his own proposal is the most humane.

6. Which word *best* describes the effect that Swift wanted to have on his readers?
   - (A) exciting
   - (B) persuasive
   - (C) convincing
   - (D) horrifying

7. The word *prodigious* in line 10 means
   - (A) impoverished
   - (B) athletic
   - (C) enormous
   - (D) insignificant

8. What does the word *procure* mean in line 189?
   - (A) heal
   - (B) obtain
   - (C) prohibit
   - (D) cook

For help, use the **Test-Taker's Toolkit** below.

Responding in Writing

9. **Short Response** Does the real message of "A Modest Proposal" come across clearly, or could Swift's use of irony confuse readers into mistaking the satire for a sincere proposal? Write a brief evaluation of the essay, referring to at least two examples of irony to support your opinion.

_____

_____

_____

_____

_____

_____

TEST-TAKER'S TOOLKIT

- ⊗ **ACADEMIC VOCABULARY** Remember that **situational irony** is a contrast between what is expected and what actually occurs; **verbal irony** occurs when a writer says one thing but means the opposite; and **understatement** is saying less than what is true or appropriate.

- ⊗ **GRAPHIC ORGANIZER** Use the chart below to help you plan your response.

Example of Irony	How It Relates to Swift's Message

A MODEST PROPOSAL **111**

5 Responding in Writing

After each main literature selection, you'll write a short response. This activity might ask you to use some of the literary terms you have learned.

6 Test-Taker's Toolkit

The **Test-Taker's Toolkit** helps you plan your response. Completing the graphic organizer will give you the ideas you'll use in your writing.

1 Related Nonfiction

Once you've completed the literature section, you'll get ready to read the **Related Nonfiction.**

2 What's the Connection?

This activity gets you thinking and talking about the nonfiction selection you are about to read. It also explains how they connect to the literature selection.

3 Learn the Skill

Before you read the **Related Nonfiction,** you will learn a useful skill or strategy. You will encounter the boldfaced terms later as you are reading and as you complete the practice test.

---

① Related Nonfiction

Children Sink to the Bottom: Thousands in Haiti Subsist on Nation's Leavings
NEWSPAPER ARTICLE

Use with "A Modest Proposal," p. 98

What's the Connection? ②

In his satirical essay, Swift describes children whom society does not value—a condition that remains true for millions of children today. This article describes the poverty and misery of Haiti's street children.

CHART IT In the K-W-L chart, write down what you know about children who are living on the street, either in the United States or abroad and then write down what you want to find out. After you read the article, complete the chart by writing down important information you have learned.

Street Children

K What I Know	W What I Want to Find Out	L What I Learned

③

LEARN THE SKILL: ANALYZE DESCRIPTIVE DETAILS

Although news articles are usually written in a concise manner, some journalists skillfully use **descriptive details** to create a mood or convey a tone (the writer's attitude toward a subject). As you read "Children Sink to the Bottom," pay attention to the following:

- **imagery**—words that describe sensory experiences
- **figurative language**—language that goes beyond the literal meaning
- **diction**—a writer's choice of words and word order

For more on descriptive details, see the Author's Craft entry in the Nonfiction Skills Handbook beginning on page R2.

Children Sink to the Bottom: Thousands in Haiti Subsist on Nation's Leavings

by Ian James

A child searches through garbage for food in Port-au-Prince, Haiti.

On the edge of town, dozens of boys congregate below a statue of Jesus. It's their home as they scratch out lives on the town's littered streets noisy with trucks and motorcycles.

Forced from their homes by poverty and broken families, the children load and sweep buses for 10 meager tips. They don't attend school, their clothes are ragged, and fellow citizens largely regard them as a nuisance.

"I don't know my age," says a barefoot Jean-Claude George, who has the body of a 10-year-old but the gaze of a man who has known years of suffering. "I've been on the street a long time." ▶

20 Like others among the children who sleep on buses or near the white statue, Jean-Claude fled an abusive home in the countryside for this town on Haiti's southern coast, 100 miles from the capital of Port-au-Prince.

He earns small change on the buses to pay for food and shoes, but the sandals often disappear in 30 the company he keeps. "The other kids keep an eye on me all night,"

he says. "Once I go to sleep, they steal them."

Street children struggle in cities around the globe, from São Paulo to Bombay. But in this Caribbean nation, the Western Hemisphere's poorest, the problem of homelessness among children is especially 40 severe. Some experts say the situation has worsened in recent years amid Haiti's political turmoil. Thousands of children wander the cities, looking for odd jobs, begging or stealing to eat.

CLOSE READD

4 SET A PURPOSE

to learn about Haiti's street children

5 DESCRIPTIVE DETAILS

Why might the author have included the metaphor that Jean-Claude has "the gaze of a man who has known years of suffering" (lines 17–18)?

_____

_____

_____

_____

RELATED NONFICTION **113**

4 Set a Purpose
You will begin each nonfiction selection by setting a purpose for reading. When you set a purpose, you give yourself a reason for reading. Your purpose helps you stay focused on the text. One student's purpose for reading appears on the lines provided. Yours may be different.

5 Descriptive Details
Some notes ask you to apply the skill or strategy you learned before reading.

1 Specialized Vocabulary

When a nonfiction selection contains a term that is unique to a certain area of study, a note is provided that will help you figure out the term's meaning.

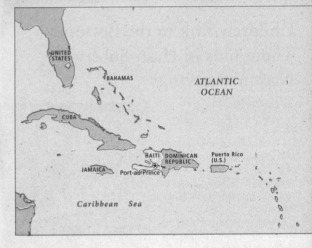

SPECIALIZED Vocabulary 1

The phrase *political agenda* in line 72 may be unfamiliar to you. Look for clues to the phrase's meaning in the context. Write a definition below. *WORD ANALYSIS*

_____

_____

_____

CHILDREN REMAIN ON STREET

President Jean-Bertrand Aristide, a former Roman Catholic priest,
50 tried to make children's issues a cornerstone of his presidency, but government efforts have failed to bring the children off the streets.

In 1986, before he was president, Aristide founded the Family Is Life orphanage. His political involvement eventually made it a target for opponents. In 1991, the same year he was ousted in a coup, five
60 children died in a suspicious fire at the facility. In 1992, some children were wounded when Aristide opponents stormed the building and began shooting. The orphanage eventually closed in 1999 amid protests by orphans who said promises of jobs weren't kept.

Dominique Esperant, the former regional head of the social
70 affairs ministry in Les Cayes hopes to put street children back on the political agenda. "Everyone seems to think the best way to deal with this is to kick these kids out of town," Esperant says. "I believe they can become good citizens like anyone else if someone is there to help them out." ◄

CENTER WOULD
80 HOUSE CHILDREN

Frustrated by a lack of government funds, Esperant is trying to raise money independently to start a center to house street children.

He meets with the children below the statue of Jesus, drawing a crowd as he writes their names on a list. At last count, the list had 57 names.

"There is no work back home," says Lesene Souverain, 17, who says he left home when he was 9 because his parents couldn't pay for school. "At least on the streets, there are people who can help me."

In the nearby hills, deforested land is turning into desert. Curls of smoke rise as farmers use remaining trees to make charcoal for cooking. Esperant says most of Les Cayes' street children come from this wasteland.

"They don't have any arable land to plant anymore," he says. "So they came to the city to look for life, to look for a way to survive." ▶

CHILD LABOR IS COMMON

110 Child labor is common even for those who stay at home. Boys in Les Cayes sell crackers and muffins from trays on their heads. In Port-au-Prince, some young girls work as prostitutes to augment family earnings.

Sometimes, poor parents give away children to be servants for better-off families. It's widely accepted in Haiti to keep a child 120 servant, or *restavek*, a Creole term that means "staying with." The children often are mistreated, and human rights groups criticize the practice as child slavery.

This boy carrying a heavy container of water is a *restavek*, a poor Haitian child handed over to a family to be a servant.

1 **Assessment Practice II: Reading Comprehension**
In this second practice test, you'll answer test items about both selections you have read in the lesson.

2 **Connecting Texts**
Test items such as numbers 5 and 6 ask you to connect, compare, or contrast information from the anchor selection and the Related Nonfiction. You can look back at the selections if you need to.

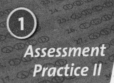

1
Assessment Practice II

Reading Comprehension

DIRECTIONS *Answer these questions about the two selections in this lesson by filling in the correct ovals.*

1. Which word *best* describes the way Haitians generally react to the street children?
   (A) alarmed
   (B) sympathetic
   (C) annoyed
   (D) desperate

2. Why did Jean-Claude leave the countryside?
   (A) He wanted a better education.
   (B) His family was abusing him.
   (C) He needed to support his family.
   (D) He got into trouble with the police.

3. What factor explains why homeless children are more common in Haiti than in most neighboring countries?
   (A) climate
   (B) population growth
   (C) illegal immigration
   (D) poverty

4. What has been the effect of farmers cutting down trees to make charcoal for cooking?
   (A) The loss of farmland has increased unemployment.
   (B) Children are finding jobs in restaurants.
   (C) Haiti has become less dependent on foreign oil.
   (D) Farmers have more income to care for children.

5. What does Dominique Esperant have in common with Jonathan Swift?
   (A) running an orphanage
   (B) writing satirical essays about poverty
   (C) concern about deforestation
   (D) drawing attention to neglected children

2

6. Which statement is supported by both selections?
   (A) The needs of poor children are often overlooked.
   (B) Children should be made to work hard.
   (C) Poor people should not have children.
   (D) Rural children are worse off than urban children.

7. The word *arable* in line 103 of "Children Sink to the Bottom" refers to land that is
   (A) well-irrigated
   (B) fit for growing crops
   (C) ready to be plowed
   (D) hardened from drought

8. The word *augment* in line 114 means
   (A) implement
   (B) replace
   (C) supplement
   (D) expend

Timed Writing Practice

PROMPT

Swift wasn't serious about the plan he outlined in "A Modest Proposal," but he took the problem of Irish poverty very seriously. Write a problem-solution essay in which you propose one step that should be taken to help the poor. Narrow the focus of your essay to (address a specific example of poverty). You can focus on the conditions described in one of the selections you have read, or you can choose another example of poverty that you are familiar with. Provide at least three reasons for your solution, and one or two details to support each reason.

④

BUDGET YOUR TIME

You have **45 minutes** to respond. Decide how much time to spend on each step.

Analyze ____5____
Plan _____10_____
Write _____20_____
Review _____10_____

TEST-TAKER'S TOOLKIT

• ANALYZE THE PROMPT

a. Underline the type of writing you are being asked to do.

b. Circle any key words that describe what should be included in your writing. One example has been circled for you.

• PLAN YOUR RESPONSE

Make notes Decide which example of poverty you will focus on, and brainstorm a list of possible solutions. Choose the solution you will propose in your essay. In the chart here, list three reasons why your solution will help the poor, and list details to support your reasons.

Organize your information In the introductory paragraph, describe the specific problem of poverty that you will address in the essay, and clearly state a solution. Then you can write a paragraph for each reason you noted in your chart. Use your details to support each reason. End the essay with a conclusion in which you sum up your ideas.

Reason 1	Detail(s)
Reason 2	Detail(s)
Reason 3	Detail(s)

• WRITE AND REVIEW

Capture your readers' attention by including a vivid description or a striking question in your introduction.

Be sure to leave time to check your spelling and grammar.

RELATED NONFICTION **117**

---

③ Timed Writing Practice
This writing activity is an opportunity to practice responding to a prompt on a writing test—without the stress of test-taking!

④ Budget Your Time
Responding to a writing prompt is easier when you break it into steps. This feature helps you plan how much time to spend on each step. The blue text shows how one student budgeted her time.

⑤ Test-Taker's Toolkit
The **Test-Taker's Toolkit** shows you how to break the writing process into three easy steps. Fill in the graphic organizer provided. This will help you gather the information you'll need to write your full response. (You may want to copy the graphic organizer onto a larger sheet of paper.)

Keeping Track of Your Understanding

Here are the basic skills and strategies you will use most often as you read the selections in this book. They are important because they help you keep track of your understanding as you read. They also help you stay involved as a reader.

Preview
Get your bearings before you read.

- Scan the title, graphics, and subheadings.
- Skim the first paragraph to get a sense of what the text is about.

Set a Purpose
Think about *why* you are reading a text.

- Ask: Am I reading to learn, to be entertained, or for another reason?
- Decide how this purpose affects your reading.

Connect
Take the text personally.

- Think about whether any situations described remind you of experiences in your own life.
- Ask: If I were this character, how would I feel?

Predict
Guess what will happen next.

- Note details that give hints.
- Read on to find out if you guessed correctly.

Visualize
Picture in your mind what is being described.

- Note descriptions of characters and settings.
- Use these details to help you form a clear mental image.

Question
Ask yourself questions as you read.

- Question what is happening and why.
- Search for answers in the text.

Clarify
Stop to review important pieces of information.

- Watch for answers to questions you had earlier.
- Reread difficult parts as needed.

Monitor
Check your understanding as you read.

- Ask: How well am I understanding the text?
- Ask for help if you need it.

Summarize
Restate what you've read.

- Use your own words to describe events.
- Take notes if necessary.

Digging Deeper

From time to time you will encounter questions that ask you to think a little harder about what you're reading. Questions like these are more difficult because the answers are usually not directly stated. But you will find that tackling tough questions is worth the extra brain power it takes to answer them. That's because the deeper you dig into a text, the more you get out of it. Here are some of the higher-level skills and strategies you will encounter in this book:

Make Inferences
Make logical guesses based on details in the text and your own experiences.

- Keep track of important details in your reading.
- Ask: How can what I already know help me "read between the lines"?

Interpret
Find deeper meaning in what you read.

- Think about what the author is trying to tell the reader.
- Consider the outcome of events and what they might mean.

Draw Conclusions
Decide what's happening based on evidence, experience, and reasoning.

- Start by making inferences as you read.
- Then combine your inferences to reach a logical conclusion.

Evaluate
Examine something to decide its value or worth.

- You can decide to evaluate the actions of a particular character, for example.
- You can also decide on the value of what you are reading.

Analyze
Break things down to gain a better understanding.

- Consider the experiences and feelings that make a character act a certain way.
- In nonfiction, look for details to help you learn how something works or is defined.

Make Judgments
Form an opinion based on information given.

- Gather evidence from the text.
- Be ready to support your opinion.

UNIT 1

THE ANGLO-SAXON AND MEDIEVAL PERIODS

LESSON 1A

from *Beowulf*
BY THE BEOWULF POET

RELATED NONFICTION
The Years of the Dragon

Where do MONSTERS lurk?

Unlike the monsters in *Beowulf*, those in our world are not always easy to identify. Evil can hide in the most unexpected places: behind a smiling face, between the lines of a law, in otherwise noble-sounding words. Even when evil is clearly exposed, people may disagree on how to confront it.

LIST IT With a small group of classmates, list examples of real-life or fictional monsters. Discuss what the monsters on your list have in common, and then come up with a definition of the word. Share your list and definition with other groups.

Examples of Monsters
1. Jack the Ripper
2. Adolf Hitler

Definition

ASSESSMENT GOALS

By the end of this lesson, you will be able to...

- analyze the characteristics of an epic
- use active reading strategies to comprehend text
- identify text features to help you navigate nonfiction
- analyze a writing prompt and plan an analytical essay

Characteristics of an Epic

An **EPIC** is a long narrative poem that depicts the adventures of a great hero. *Beowulf* is the only surviving epic written in Old English—the language of the Anglo-Saxon people, who lived in England in the early Middle Ages. Although it was composed in England, *Beowulf* describes legendary events involving Scandinavian ancestors of the Anglo-Saxons. The poem was originally intended to be chanted aloud in public.

Beowulf reflects the culture and values of the Anglo-Saxons, but it has characteristics that are common to most epic poetry. Review the characteristics in the graphic below to help you analyze the poem.

EPIC

Hero

The hero, who is of noble birth or high position, performs deeds requiring incredible courage and strength.

Character Traits

The hero embodies character traits that reflect important ideals of society.

Diction and Tone

The poem uses formal diction (the writer's choice of words and sentence structure) and a serious tone (the expression of the writer's attitude toward a subject).

Universal Themes

The poem reflects universal themes (themes common to most cultures and periods) and timeless values.

BEOWULF

BACKGROUND *Beowulf* is set in Scandinavia around the 500s among two groups: the Danes of what is now Denmark and the Geats (gēts) of what is now Sweden. The Geat warrior Beowulf crosses the sea to defeat Grendel, a monster who is terrorizing the Danes. He later returns to his homeland to succeed his uncle as king of the Geats.

Hrothgar (hrôth′gär′) *is king of the Danes. He has built a wonderful mead hall called Herot* (hĕr′ət), *where his subjects congregate and make merry. As this selection opens, a fierce and powerful monster named Grendel is about to invade the mead hall.*

GRENDEL

A powerful monster, living down
In the darkness, growled in pain, impatient
As day after day the music rang
Loud in that hall, the harp's rejoicing
5 Call and the poet's clear songs, sung
Of the ancient beginnings of us all, recalling
The Almighty making the earth, shaping
These beautiful plains marked off by oceans,
Then proudly setting the sun and moon
10 To glow across the land and light it;
The corners of the earth were made lovely with trees
And leaves, made quick with life, with each
Of the nations who now move on its face. And then
As now warriors sang of their pleasure:

CLOSE READ

MARK IT UP

Use these marks to monitor your reading:

* This is important.

? I don't understand.

! This is a surprise.

When you see this pencil ✎, you'll be asked to mark up the text. You can also write in this book in any way you find useful.

F)ocus

In this section, the poet describes life in a mead hall, a large wooden building used for rest and entertainment. Read to find out what happens when the monster Grendel invades the mead hall where Danish warriors are gathered.

15 So Hrothgar's men lived happy in his hall
   Till the monster stirred, that demon, that fiend,
   Grendel, who haunted the moors,[1] the wild
   Marshes, and made his home in a hell
   Not hell but earth. He was spawned[2] in that slime,
20 Conceived by a pair of those monsters born
   Of Cain,[3] murderous creatures banished
   By God, punished forever for the crime
   Of Abel's death. The Almighty drove
   Those demons out, and their exile was bitter,
25 Shut away from men; they split
   Into a thousand forms of evil—spirits
   And fiends, goblins, monsters, giants,
   A brood forever opposing the Lord's
   Will, and again and again defeated.

30   Then, when darkness had dropped, Grendel
   Went up to Herot, wondering what the warriors
   Would do in that hall when their drinking was done.
   He found them sprawled in sleep, suspecting
   Nothing, their dreams undisturbed. The monster's
35 Thoughts were as quick as his greed or his claws:
   He slipped through the door and there in the silence
   Snatched up thirty men, smashed them
   Unknowing in their beds and ran out with their bodies,
   The blood dripping behind him, back
40 To his **lair**, delighted with his night's slaughter. ◄
       At daybreak, with the sun's first light, they saw
   How well he had worked, and in that gray morning
   Broke their long feast with tears and laments
   For the dead. Hrothgar, their lord, sat joyless
45 In Herot, a mighty prince mourning
   The fate of his lost friends and companions,
   Knowing by its tracks that some demon had torn
   His followers apart. He wept, fearing
   The beginning might not be the end. And that night

lair (lâr) n. the den or resting place of a wild animal

VISUALIZE

Underline words and phrases in the boxed text that help you picture Grendel's attack on the warriors. ✎

---

1. **moors** (mŏŏrz): broad, open regions with patches of bog.
2. **spawned:** given birth to.
3. **Cain:** the eldest son of Adam and Eve. According to the Bible (Genesis 4), he murdered his younger brother Abel.

50   Grendel came again, so set
     On murder that no crime could ever be enough,
     No savage assault quench his lust
     For evil. Then each warrior tried
     To escape him, searched for rest in different
55   Beds, as far from Herot as they could find,
     Seeing how Grendel hunted when they slept.
     Distance was safety; the only survivors
     Were those who fled him. Hate had triumphed. ▶
          So Grendel ruled, fought with the righteous,
60   One against many, and won; so Herot
     Stood empty, and stayed deserted for years,
     Twelve winters of grief for Hrothgar, king
     Of the Danes, sorrow heaped at his door
     By hell-forged hands. His misery leaped
65   The seas, was told and sung in all
     Men's ears: how Grendel's hatred began,
     How the monster relished his savage war
     On the Danes, keeping the bloody feud
     Alive, seeking no peace, offering
70   No truce, accepting no settlement, no price
     In gold or land, and paying the living
     For one crime only with another. No one
     Waited for reparation⁴ from his plundering claws:
     That shadow of death hunted in the darkness,
75   Stalked Hrothgar's warriors, old
     And young, lying in waiting, hidden
     In mist, invisibly following them from the edge
     Of the marsh, always there, unseen.
          So mankind's enemy continued his crimes,
80   Killing as often as he could, coming
     Alone, bloodthirsty and horrible. Though he lived
     In Herot, when the night hid him, he never
     Dared to touch king Hrothgar's glorious
     Throne, protected by God—God,⁵
85   Whose love Grendel could not know. But Hrothgar's ▶

PREDICT

How do you think life will change for Hrothgar and his warriors now that Grendel is on the loose?

_____

_____

_____

_____

CLARIFY

Reread lines 79–85. Why is Grendel unable to attack Hrothgar directly?

_____

_____

_____

_____

---

4. **reparation:** something done to make amends for loss or suffering. In Germanic society, someone who killed another person was generally expected to make a payment to the victim's family as a way of restoring peace.

5. The reference to God shows the influence of Christianity on the Beowulf Poet.

Heart was bent. The best and most noble
Of his council debated remedies, sat
In secret sessions, talking of terror
And wondering what the bravest of warriors could do.
90 And sometimes they sacrificed to the old stone gods,
Made heathen[6] vows, hoping for Hell's
Support, the Devil's guidance in driving
Their **affliction** off. That was their way,
And the heathen's only hope, Hell
95 Always in their hearts, knowing neither God
Nor His passing as He walks through our world, the Lord
Of Heaven and earth; their ears could not hear
His praise nor know His glory. Let them
Beware, those who are thrust into danger,
100 Clutched at by trouble, yet can carry no solace
In their hearts, cannot hope to be better! Hail
To those who will rise to God, drop off
Their dead bodies and seek our Father's peace! ✋ **PAUSE & REFLECT**

BEOWULF
    So the living sorrow of Healfdane's son[7]
105 Simmered, bitter and fresh, and no wisdom
Or strength could break it: that agony hung
On king and people alike, harsh
And unending, violent and cruel, and evil.
    In his far-off home Beowulf, Higlac's
110 Follower[8] and the strongest of the Geats—greater
And stronger than anyone anywhere in this world—
Heard how Grendel filled nights with horror
And quickly commanded a boat fitted out,
Proclaiming that he'd go to that famous king,
115 Would sail across the sea to Hrothgar,
Now when help was needed. None

6. **heathen** (hē′thən): pagan; non-Christian. Though the Beowulf Poet was a Christian, he recognized that the characters in the poem lived before the Germanic tribes were converted to Christianity, when they still worshiped "the old stone gods."

7. **Healfdane's son:** Hrothgar.

8. **Higlac's follower:** a warrior loyal to Higlac (hĭg′lăk′), king of the Geats (and Beowulf's uncle).

Of the wise ones regretted his going, much
As he was loved by the Geats: the omens were good,
And they urged the adventure on. So Beowulf
120 Chose the mightiest men he could find,
The bravest and best of the Geats, fourteen
In all, and led them down to their boat;
He knew the sea, would point the prow
Straight to that distant Danish shore. . . .

*Beowulf and his men sail over the sea to the land of the Danes to offer help
to Hrothgar. They are escorted by a Danish guard to Herot, where Wulfgar,
one of Hrothgar's soldiers, tells the king of their arrival. Hrothgar knows of
Beowulf and is ready to welcome the young prince and his men.*

125   Then Wulfgar went to the door and addressed
The waiting seafarers with soldier's words:
    "My lord, the great king of the Danes, commands me
To tell you that he knows of your noble birth
And that having come to him from over the open
130 Sea you have come bravely and are welcome.
Now go to him as you are, in your armor and helmets,
But leave your battle-shields here, and your spears,
Let them lie waiting for the promises your words
May make." ▶
        Beowulf arose, with his men
135 Around him, ordering a few to remain
With their weapons, leading the others quickly
Along under Herot's steep roof into Hrothgar's
Presence. Standing on that prince's own hearth,
Helmeted, the silvery metal of his mail shirt[9]
140 Gleaming with a smith's high art,[10] he greeted
The Danes' great lord:
                "Hail, Hrothgar!
Higlac is my cousin[11] and my king; the days
Of my youth have been filled with glory. Now Grendel's
Name has echoed in our land: sailors

MAKE INFERENCES

Why might Wulfgar have
asked Beowulf and his men to
leave their weapons outside
of Herot?

_____

_____

_____

_____

_____

---

9. **mail shirt:** flexible body armor made of metal links or overlapping metal scales.
10. **smith's high art:** the skilled craft of a blacksmith (a person who fashions objects from iron).
11. **cousin:** here, a general term for a relative. Beowulf is actually Higlac's nephew.

_____

_____

_____

_____

purge (pûrj) *v.* to cleanse or rid of something undesirable

MAKE INFERENCES

Why does Beowulf want to fight Grendel with only his bare hands?

_____

_____

_____

_____

_____

gorge (gôrj) *v.* to stuff with food; glut

145 Have brought us stories of Herot, the best
Of all mead-halls, deserted and useless when the moon
Hangs in skies the sun had lit,
Light and life fleeing together.
My people have said, the wisest, most knowing
150 And best of them, that my duty was to go to the Danes'
Great king. They have seen my strength for themselves,
Have watched me rise from the darkness of war,
Dripping with my enemies' blood. I drove
Five great giants into chains, chased
155 All of that race from the earth. I swam
In the blackness of night, hunting monsters
Out of the ocean, and killing them one
By one; death was my errand and the fate
They had earned. Now Grendel and I are called ◀
160 Together, and I've come. Grant me, then,
Lord and protector of this noble place,
A single request! I have come so far,
Oh shelterer of warriors and your people's loved friend,
That this one favor you should not refuse me—
165 That I, alone and with the help of my men,
May **purge** all evil from this hall. I have heard,
Too, that the monster's scorn of men
Is so great that he needs no weapons and fears none.
Nor will I. My lord Higlac
170 Might think less of me if I let my sword
Go where my feet were afraid to, if I hid
Behind some broad linden shield:[12] my hands
Alone shall fight for me, struggle for life
Against the monster.[13] God must decide ◀
175 Who will be given to death's cold grip.
Grendel's plan, I think, will be
What it has been before, to invade this hall
And **gorge** his belly with our bodies. If he can,
If he can. And I think, if my time will have come,
180 There'll be nothing to mourn over, no corpse to prepare
For its grave: Grendel will carry our bloody
Flesh to the moors, crunch on our bones

---

12. **linden shield:** a shield made from the wood of a linden tree.
13. Beowulf insists on fighting Grendel without weapons.

And smear torn scraps of our skin on the walls
Of his den. No, I expect no Danes
185 Will fret about sewing our shrouds,[14] if he wins.
And if death does take me, send the hammered
Mail of my armor to Higlac, return
The inheritance I had from Hrethel,[15] and he
From Wayland.[16] Fate will unwind as it must!"

190   Hrothgar replied, protector of the Danes:
    "Beowulf, you've come to us in friendship, and because
Of the reception your father found at our court.
Edgetho[17] had begun a bitter feud,
Killing Hathlaf, a Wulfing[18] warrior:
195 Your father's countrymen were afraid of war,
If he returned to his home, and they turned him away.
Then he traveled across the curving waves
To the land of the Danes. I was new to the throne,
Then, a young man ruling this wide
200 Kingdom and its golden city: Hergar,
My older brother, a far better man
Than I, had died and dying made me,
Second among Healfdane's sons, first
In this nation. I bought the end of Edgetho's
205 Quarrel, sent ancient treasures through the ocean's
Furrows to the Wulfings; your father swore
He'd keep that peace. My tongue grows heavy, ▶
And my heart, when I try to tell you what Grendel
Has brought us, the damage he's done, here
210 In this hall. You see for yourself how much smaller
Our ranks have become, and can guess what we've lost
To his terror. Surely the Lord Almighty
Could stop his madness, smother his lust!
How many times have my men, glowing
215 With courage drawn from too many cups
Of ale, sworn to stay after dark

---

14. **shrouds:** cloths in which dead bodies are wrapped.
15. **Hrethel** (hrĕth'əl): a former king of the Geats—Higlac's father and Beowulf's grandfather.
16. **Wayland:** a famous blacksmith and magician.
17. **Edgetho** (ĕj'thō): Beowulf's father.
18. **Wulfing:** a member of another Germanic tribe.

PAUSE & REFLECT

1. How does Beowulf's response to Grendel differ from Hrothgar's response? *COMPARE AND CONTRAST*

_____

_____

_____

_____

2. Reread lines 225–232. What effect does the arrival of Beowulf and his men have on the Danes? *DRAW CONCLUSIONS*

_____

_____

FOCUS

In the next section, Grendel returns to Herot to attack the Danes. Read to find out how Beowulf surprises Grendel.

And stem that horror with a sweep of their swords.
And then, in the morning, this mead-hall glittering
With new light would be drenched with blood, the benches
220 Stained red, the floors, all wet from that fiend's
Savage assault—and my soldiers would be fewer
Still, death taking more and more.
But to table, Beowulf, a banquet in your honor:
Let us toast your victories, and talk of the future."
225   Then Hrothgar's men gave places to the Geats,
Yielded benches to the brave visitors
And led them to the feast. The keeper of the mead
Came carrying out the carved flasks,
And poured that bright sweetness. A poet
230 Sang, from time to time, in a clear
Pure voice. Danes and visiting Geats
Celebrated as one, drank and rejoiced. . . .   **PAUSE & REFLECT**

THE BATTLE WITH GRENDEL

After the banquet, Hrothgar and his followers leave Herot, and Beowulf and his warriors remain to spend the night. Beowulf reiterates his intent to fight Grendel without a sword and, while his followers sleep, lies waiting, eager for Grendel to appear.

Out from the marsh, from the foot of misty
Hills and bogs, bearing God's hatred,
235 Grendel came, hoping to kill
Anyone he could trap on this trip to high Herot.
He moved quickly through the cloudy night,
Up from his swampland, sliding silently
Toward that gold-shining hall. He had visited Hrothgar's
240 Home before, knew the way—
But never, before nor after that night,
Found Herot defended so firmly, his reception
So harsh. He journeyed, forever joyless,
Straight to the door, then snapped it open,
245 Tore its iron fasteners with a touch
And rushed angrily over the threshold.[19]
He strode quickly across the inlaid
Floor, snarling and fierce: his eyes

---

19. **threshold:** the strip of wood or stone at the bottom of a doorway.

Gleamed in the darkness, burned with a gruesome
250 Light. Then he stopped, seeing the hall
Crowded with sleeping warriors, stuffed
With rows of young soldiers resting together.
And his heart laughed, he relished the sight,
Intended to tear the life from those bodies
255 By morning; the monster's mind was hot
With the thought of food and the feasting his belly
Would soon know. But fate, that night, intended
Grendel to gnaw the broken bones
Of his last human supper. Human
260 Eyes were watching his evil steps,
Waiting to see his swift hard claws.
Grendel snatched at the first Geat
He came to, ripped him apart, cut
His body to bits with powerful jaws,
265 Drank the blood from his veins and bolted ▶
Him down, hands and feet; death
And Grendel's great teeth came together,
Snapping life shut. Then he stepped to another
Still body, clutched at Beowulf with his claws,
270 Grasped at a strong-hearted wakeful sleeper
—And was instantly seized himself, claws
Bent back as Beowulf leaned up on one arm.
    That shepherd of evil, guardian of crime,
Knew at once that nowhere on earth
275 Had he met a man whose hands were harder;
His mind was flooded with fear—but nothing
Could take his **talons** and himself from that tight
Hard grip. Grendel's one thought was to run
From Beowulf, flee back to his marsh and hide there:
280 This was a different Herot than the hall he had emptied.
But Higlac's follower remembered his final
Boast and, standing erect, stopped
The monster's flight, fastened those claws
In his fists till they cracked, clutched Grendel
285 Closer. The **infamous** killer fought
For his freedom, wanting no flesh but retreat,
Desiring nothing but escape; his claws
Had been caught, he was trapped. That trip to Herot
Was a miserable journey for the writhing monster!  **PAUSE & REFLECT**

talon (tăl′ən) *n.* a claw

infamous (ĭn′fə-məs) *adj.* having a very bad reputation

PAUSE & REFLECT

Circle the words in lines 233–289 that describe Grendel's feelings before Beowulf seizes him. Underline the words that describe Grendel's reaction to Beowulf. 🖊

What changes does Grendel experience in this scene? *ANALYZE*

_____

_____

_____

_____

Focus

In the next section, Beowulf fights with Grendel. Read to find out the outcome of their battle.

290   The high hall rang, its roof boards swayed,
      And Danes shook with terror. Down
      The aisles the battle swept, angry
      And wild. Herot trembled, wonderfully
      Built to withstand the blows, the struggling
295   Great bodies beating at its beautiful walls;
      Shaped and fastened with iron, inside
      And out, artfully worked, the building
      Stood firm. Its benches rattled, fell
      To the floor, gold-covered boards grating
300   As Grendel and Beowulf battled across them.
      Hrothgar's wise men had fashioned Herot
      To stand forever; only fire,
      They had planned, could shatter what such skill had put
      Together, swallow in hot flames such splendor
305   Of ivory and iron and wood. Suddenly
      The sounds changed, the Danes started
      In new terror, cowering in their beds as the terrible
      Screams of the Almighty's enemy sang
      In the darkness, the horrible shrieks of pain
310   And defeat, the tears torn out of Grendel's
      Taut throat, hell's captive caught in the arms
      Of him who of all the men on earth
      Was the strongest.

                     That mighty protector of men
      Meant to hold the monster till its life
315   Leaped out, knowing the fiend was no use
      To anyone in Denmark. All of Beowulf's
      Band had jumped from their beds, ancestral
      Swords raised and ready, determined
      To protect their prince if they could. Their courage
320   Was great but all wasted: they could hack at Grendel
      From every side, trying to open
      A path for his evil soul, but their points
      Could not hurt him, the sharpest and hardest iron
      Could not scratch at his skin, for that sin-stained demon
325   Had bewitched all men's weapons, laid spells
      That blunted every mortal man's blade. ◄

      And yet his time had come, his days
      Were over, his death near; down

ANALYZE

Throughout time, many poets have described battles as conflicts between good and evil. Reread the boxed text, and circle words that relate to this **universal theme.**

To hell he would go, swept groaning and helpless
330 To the waiting hands of still worse fiends.
Now he discovered—once the afflictor
Of men, tormentor of their days—what it meant
To feud with Almighty God: Grendel
Saw that his strength was deserting him, his claws
335 Bound fast, Higlac's brave follower tearing at
His hands. The monster's hatred rose higher,
But his power had gone. He twisted in pain,
And the bleeding sinews[20] deep in his shoulder
Snapped, muscle and bone split
340 And broke. The battle was over, Beowulf
Had been granted new glory: Grendel escaped,
But wounded as he was could flee to his den,
His miserable hole at the bottom of the marsh,
Only to die, to wait for the end
345 Of all his days. And after that bloody
Combat the Danes laughed with delight.
He who had come to them from across the sea,
Bold and strong-minded, had driven affliction
Off, purged Herot clean. He was happy,
350 Now, with that night's fierce work; the Danes
Had been served as he'd boasted he'd serve them; Beowulf,
A prince of the Geats, had killed Grendel,
Ended the grief, the sorrow, the suffering
Forced on Hrothgar's helpless people
355 By a bloodthirsty fiend. No Dane doubted
The victory, for the proof, hanging high
From the rafters where Beowulf had hung it, was the monster's
Arm, claw and shoulder and all. ▶

And then, in the morning, crowds surrounded
360 Herot, warriors coming to that hall
From faraway lands, princes and leaders
Of men hurrying to behold the monster's
Great staggering tracks. They gaped with no sense
Of sorrow, felt no regret for his suffering,
365 Went tracing his bloody footprints, his beaten
And lonely flight, to the edge of the lake

CLARIFY

Why does Beowulf hang
Grendel's arm from the
rafters?

_____

_____

_____

---

20. **sinews** (sĭn′yo͞oz): the tendons that connect muscles to bones.

PAUSE & REFLECT

1. What characteristics of an **epic hero** does Beowulf show in his battle with Grendel? *ANALYZE*

_____

_____

_____

_____

_____

2. Reread lines 389–396. Why might the Beowulf poet have chosen to include this description in the poem? *MAKE INFERENCES*

_____

_____

_____

_____

_____

Where he'd dragged his corpselike way, doomed
And already weary of his vanishing life.
The water was bloody, steaming and boiling
370 In horrible pounding waves, heat
Sucked from his magic veins; but the swirling
Surf had covered his death, hidden
Deep in murky darkness his miserable
End, as hell opened to receive him.
375   Then old and young rejoiced, turned back
From that happy pilgrimage, mounted their hard-hooved
Horses, high-spirited stallions, and rode them
Slowly toward Herot again, retelling
Beowulf's bravery as they jogged along.
380 And over and over they swore that nowhere
On earth or under the spreading sky
Or between the seas, neither south nor north,
Was there a warrior worthier to rule over men.
(But no one meant Beowulf's praise to belittle
385 Hrothgar, their kind and gracious king!)
        And sometimes, when the path ran straight and clear,
They would let their horses race, red
And brown and pale yellow backs streaming
Down the road. And sometimes a proud old soldier
390 Who had heard songs of the ancient heroes
And could sing them all through, story after story,
Would weave a net of words for Beowulf's
Victory, tying the knot of his verses
Smoothly, swiftly, into place with a poet's
395 Quick skill, singing his new song aloud
While he shaped it, and the old songs as well. . . .  **PAUSE & REFLECT**

GRENDEL'S MOTHER

Although one monster has died, another still lives. From her lair in a cold and murky lake, where she has been brooding over her loss, Grendel's mother emerges, bent on revenge.

FOCUS

In the next section, Grendel's mother comes to Herot to seek revenge for her son's death. As you read, notice the effect she has on the Danes.

　　　　So she reached Herot,
Where the Danes slept as though already dead;
Her visit ended their good fortune, reversed
400　The bright vane[21] of their luck. No female, no matter
How fierce, could have come with a man's strength,
Fought with the power and courage men fight with,
Smashing their shining swords, their bloody,
Hammer-forged blades onto boar-headed helmets,[22]
405　Slashing and stabbing with the sharpest of points.
The soldiers raised their shields and drew
Those gleaming swords, swung them above
The piled-up benches, leaving their mail shirts
And their helmets where they'd lain when the terror took hold of them.
410　To save her life she moved still faster,
Took a single victim and fled from the hall,
Running to the moors, discovered, but her supper
Assured, sheltered in her dripping claws.
She'd taken Hrothgar's closest friend,
415　The man he most loved of all men on earth;
She'd killed a glorious soldier, cut
A noble life short. No Geat could have stopped her:
Beowulf and his band had been given better
Beds; sleep had come to them in a different
420　Hall. Then all Herot burst into shouts:
She had carried off Grendel's claw. Sorrow
Had returned to Denmark. They'd traded deaths,
Danes and monsters, and no one had won,
Both had lost! . . . ▶

SUMMARIZE

What happens after Grendel's mother reaches Herot?

_____

_____

_____

_____

_____

---

21. **vane:** a device that turns to show the direction the wind is blowing—here associated metaphorically with luck, which is as changeable as the wind.

22. **boar-headed helmets:** Germanic warriors often wore helmets bearing the images of wild pigs or other fierce creatures in the hope that the images would increase their ferocity and protect them against their enemies.

Devastated by the loss of his friend, Hrothgar sends for Beowulf and recounts
what Grendel's mother has done. Then Hrothgar describes the dark lake where
Grendel's mother has dwelt with her son.

PAUSE & REFLECT

1. Reread lines 425–443.
What effect does the long
description of the lake have on
the reader? *ANALYZE*

_____

_____

_____

_____

2. Is Grendel's mother simply
an evil monster? Explain why
or why not. *MAKE JUDGMENTS*

_____

_____

_____

_____

425 "They live in secret places, windy
     Cliffs, wolf-dens where water pours
     From the rocks, then runs underground, where mist
     Steams like black clouds, and the groves of trees
     Growing out over their lake are all covered
430 With frozen spray, and wind down snakelike
     Roots that reach as far as the water
     And help keep it dark. At night that lake
     Burns like a torch. No one knows its bottom,
     No wisdom reaches such depths. A deer,
435 Hunted through the woods by packs of hounds,
     A stag with great horns, though driven through the forest
     From faraway places, prefers to die
     On those shores, refuses to save its life
     In that water. It isn't far, nor is it
440 A pleasant spot! When the wind stirs
     And storms, waves splash toward the sky,
     As dark as the air, as black as the rain
     That the heavens weep. Our only help,
     Again, lies with you. Grendel's mother
445 Is hidden in her terrible home, in a place
     You've not seen. Seek it, if you dare! Save us,
     Once more, and again twisted gold,
     Heaped-up ancient treasure, will reward you
     For the battle you win!"[23] . . . **PAUSE & REFLECT**

THE BATTLE WITH GRENDEL'S MOTHER

*Beowulf accepts Hrothgar's challenge, and the king and his men accompany the
hero to the dreadful lair of Grendel's mother. Fearlessly, Beowulf prepares to
battle the terrible creature.*

FOCUS
In the next section,
Beowulf dives into the
lake. Read to find out what
happens when Grendel's
mother finds him.

450   He leaped into the lake, would not wait for anyone's
         Answer; the heaving water covered him
         Over. For hours he sank through the waves;

---

23. Germanic warriors placed great importance on amassing treasure as a way of
    acquiring fame and temporarily defeating fate.

At last he saw the mud of the bottom.
And all at once the greedy she-wolf

455 Who'd ruled those waters for half a hundred
Years discovered him, saw that a creature
From above had come to explore the bottom
Of her wet world. She welcomed him in her claws,
Clutched at him savagely but could not harm him,

460 Tried to work her fingers through the tight
Ring-woven mail on his breast, but tore
And scratched in vain. Then she carried him, armor
And sword and all, to her home; he struggled
To free his weapon, and failed. The fight

465 Brought other monsters swimming to see
Her catch, a host of sea beasts who beat at
His mail shirt, stabbing with tusks and teeth
As they followed along. Then he realized, suddenly,
That she'd brought him into someone's battle-hall,

470 And there the water's heat could not hurt him,
Nor anything in the lake attack him through
The building's high-arching roof. A brilliant
Light burned all around him, the lake
Itself like a fiery flame.

        Then he saw

475 The mighty water witch, and swung his sword,
His ring-marked blade,[24] straight at her head;
The iron sang its fierce song,
Sang Beowulf's strength. But her guest
Discovered that no sword could slice her evil

480 Skin, that Hrunting[25] could not hurt her, was useless
Now when he needed it. They wrestled, she ripped
And tore and clawed at him, bit holes in his helmet,
And that too failed him; for the first time in years
Of being worn to war it would earn no glory;

485 It was the last time anyone would wear it. But Beowulf ▶
Longed only for fame, leaped back
Into battle. He tossed his sword aside,

---

24. **his ring-marked blade:** For the battle with Grendel's mother, Beowulf has been given an heirloom sword with an intricately etched blade.

25. **Hrunting** (hrŭn'tǐng): the name of Beowulf's sword. (Germanic warriors' swords were possessions of such value that they were often given names.)

TESTSMART

Reread lines 474–485. Which word *best* describes the mood of this passage?

(A) mysterious

(B) suspenseful

(C) mournful

(D) tranquil

TIP When a test question asks you to describe a poem's mood, **think about your own emotional response** to the imagery and figurative language as well as the sound and rhythm of the verse. In a narrative poem such as *Beowulf*, you should also think about what is happening in the story. What feeling do you have as you read this passage? Decide which answer choice is closest to your feeling. Then make sure you can support your answer with evidence from the text. For this question, underline the words in lines 474–485 that help create a distinct mood.

Angry; the steel-edged blade lay where
He'd dropped it. If weapons were useless he'd use
490 His hands, the strength in his fingers. So fame
Comes to the men who mean to win it
And care about nothing else! He raised
His arms and seized her by the shoulder; anger
Doubled his strength, he threw her to the floor.
495 She fell, Grendel's fierce mother, and the Geats'
Proud prince was ready to leap on her. But she rose
At once and repaid him with her clutching claws,
Wildly tearing at him. He was weary, that best
And strongest of soldiers; his feet stumbled
500 And in an instant she had him down, held helpless.
Squatting with her weight on his stomach, she drew
A dagger, brown with dried blood, and prepared
To avenge her only son. But he was stretched
On his back, and her stabbing blade was blunted
505 By the woven mail shirt he wore on his chest.
The hammered links held; the point
Could not touch him. He'd have traveled to the bottom of the earth,
Edgetho's son, and died there, if that shining
Woven metal had not helped—and Holy
510 God, who sent him victory, gave judgment
For truth and right, Ruler of the Heavens,
Once Beowulf was back on his feet and fighting.

Then he saw, hanging on the wall, a heavy
Sword, hammered by giants, strong
515 And blessed with their magic, the best of all weapons
But so massive that no ordinary man could lift
Its carved and decorated length. He drew it
From its scabbard, broke the chain on its hilt,
And then, savage, now, angry
520 And desperate, lifted it high over his head
And struck with all the strength he had left,
Caught her in the neck and cut it through,
Broke bones and all. Her body fell
To the floor, lifeless, the sword was wet
525 With her blood, and Beowulf rejoiced at the sight. ✋ **PAUSE & REFLECT**

✋ **PAUSE & REFLECT**

1. What saves Beowulf's life in his battle with Grendel's mother? *CLARIFY*

_____

_____

_____

2. Who is more difficult for Beowulf to defeat, Grendel or his mother? Explain your response. *COMPARE AND CONTRAST*

_____

_____

_____

_____

_____

The brilliant light shone, suddenly,
As though burning in that hall, and as bright as Heaven's
Own candle, lit in the sky. He looked
At her home, then following along the wall
530 Went walking, his hands tight on the sword,
His heart still angry. He was hunting another
Dead monster, and took his weapon with him
For final revenge against Grendel's vicious
Attacks, his nighttime raids, over
535 And over, coming to Herot when Hrothgar's
Men slept, killing them in their beds,
Eating some on the spot, fifteen
Or more, and running to his **loathsome** moor
With another such sickening meal waiting
540 In his pouch. But Beowulf repaid him for those visits,
Found him lying dead in his corner,
Armless, exactly as that fierce fighter
Had sent him out from Herot, then struck off
His head with a single swift blow. The body
545 Jerked for the last time, then lay still.
　　The wise old warriors who surrounded Hrothgar,
Like him staring into the monsters' lake,
Saw the waves surging and blood
Spurting through. They spoke about Beowulf,
550 All the graybeards,[26] whispered together
And said that hope was gone, that the hero
Had lost fame and his life at once, and would never
Return to the living, come back as triumphant
As he had left; almost all agreed that Grendel's
555 Mighty mother, the she-wolf, had killed him.
The sun slid over past noon, went further
Down. The Danes gave up, left
The lake and went home, Hrothgar with them.
The Geats stayed, sat sadly, watching,
560 Imagining they saw their lord but not believing
They would ever see him again. ▶
　　　　　　　　　　　　　—Then the sword
Melted, blood-soaked, dripping down
Like water, disappearing like ice when the world's

FOCUS
During Beowulf's battle with Grendel's mother, the Danes and the Geats wait for him to emerge from the lake. As you read the next section, notice their responses to his long absence and his return.

loathsome (lōth′səm) *adj.* disgusting

MAKE INFERENCES

Reread the boxed text. Why do the Danes give up hope and leave while the Geat warriors continue to wait for Beowulf?

_____

_____

_____

_____

_____

_____

26. **graybeards:** old men.

Eternal Lord loosens invisible
565 Fetters and unwinds icicles and frost
As only He can, He who rules
Time and seasons, He who is truly
God. The monsters' hall was full of
Rich treasures, but all that Beowulf took
570 Was Grendel's head and the hilt of the giants' ◄
Jeweled sword; the rest of that ring-marked
Blade had dissolved in Grendel's steaming
Blood, boiling even after his death.
And then the battle's only survivor
575 Swam up and away from those silent corpses;
The water was calm and clean, the whole
Huge lake peaceful once the demons who'd lived in it
Were dead.
                    Then that noble protector of all seamen[27]
Swam to land, rejoicing in the heavy
580 Burdens he was bringing with him. He
And all his glorious band of Geats
Thanked God that their leader had come back unharmed;
They left the lake together. The Geats
Carried Beowulf's helmet, and his mail shirt.
585 Behind them the water slowly thickened
As the monsters' blood came seeping up.
They walked quickly, happily, across
Roads all of them remembered, left
The lake and the cliffs alongside it, brave men
590 Staggering under the weight of Grendel's skull,
Too heavy for fewer than four of them to handle—
Two on each side of the spear jammed through it—
Yet proud of their ugly load and determined
That the Danes, seated in Herot, should see it.
595 Soon, fourteen Geats arrived
At the hall, bold and warlike, and with Beowulf,
Their lord and leader, they walked on the mead-hall
Green. Then the Geats' brave prince entered
Herot, covered with glory for the daring
600 Battles he had fought; he sought Hrothgar

---

27. **that noble protector of all seamen:** Beowulf, who will be buried in a tower that will serve as a navigational aid to sailors.

To salute him and show Grendel's head.
He carried that terrible trophy by the hair,
Brought it straight to where the Danes sat,
Drinking, the queen[28] among them. It was a weird
605 And wonderful sight, and the warriors stared. . . . **PAUSE & REFLECT**

PAUSE & REFLECT

Why is Grendel's severed head so important to the Geats and the Danes? *MAKE INFERENCES*

_____

_____

_____

_____

BEOWULF'S LAST BATTLE

With Grendel's mother destroyed, peace is restored to the land of the Danes, and Beowulf, laden with Hrothgar's gifts, returns to the land of his own people, the Geats. After his uncle and cousin die, Beowulf becomes king of the Geats and rules in peace and prosperity for 50 years. One day, however, a fire-breathing dragon that has been guarding a treasure for hundreds of years is disturbed by a thief, who enters the treasure tower and steals a cup. The dragon begins terrorizing the Geats, and Beowulf, now an old man, takes on the challenge of fighting it.

Focus
The next section takes place in the land of the Geats, where Beowulf has been king for 50 years. Read to learn about a new monster he must confront in his old age.

And Beowulf uttered his final boast:
"I've never known fear, as a youth I fought
In endless battles. I am old, now,
But I will fight again, seek fame still,
610 If the dragon hiding in his tower dares
To face me."
                Then he said farewell to his followers,
Each in his turn, for the last time:
"I'd use no sword, no weapon, if this beast
Could be killed without it, crushed to death
615 Like Grendel, gripped in my hands and torn
Limb from limb. But his breath will be burning
Hot, poison will pour from his tongue.
I feel no shame, with shield and sword
And armor, against this monster: when he comes to me
620 I mean to stand, not run from his shooting
Flames, stand till fate decides
Which of us wins. My heart is firm,
My hands calm: I need no hot
Words. Wait for me close by, my friends.
625 We shall see, soon, who will survive
This bloody battle, stand when the fighting

---

28. **queen:** Welthow, wife of Hrothgar.

Reread lines 613–632.
Underline statements in
Beowulf's speech that express
his feelings about the new
danger he faces.

Has Beowulf's character
changed over the years, or is
he essentially the same as he
was when he battled Grendel?

☐ changed
☐ the same

Support your answer with
details.

_____

_____

_____

_____

_____

_____

Is done. No one else could do
What I mean to, here, no man but me
Could hope to defeat this monster. No one
630 Could try. And this dragon's treasure, his gold
And everything hidden in that tower, will be mine
Or war will sweep me to a bitter death!" ◀
    Then Beowulf rose, still brave, still strong,
And with his shield at his side, and a mail shirt on his breast,
635 Strode calmly, confidently, toward the tower, under
The rocky cliffs: no coward could have walked there!
And then he who'd endured dozens of desperate
Battles, who'd stood boldly while swords and shields
Clashed, the best of kings, saw
640 Huge stone arches and felt the heat
Of the dragon's breath, flooding down
Through the hidden entrance, too hot for anyone
To stand, a streaming current of fire
And smoke that blocked all passage. And the Geats'
645 Lord and leader, angry, lowered
His sword and roared out a battle cry,
A call so loud and clear that it reached through
The hoary[29] rock, hung in the dragon's
Ear. The beast rose, angry,
650 Knowing a man had come—and then nothing
But war could have followed. Its breath came first,
A steaming cloud pouring from the stone,
Then the earth itself shook. Beowulf
Swung his shield into place, held it
655 In front of him, facing the entrance. The dragon
Coiled and uncoiled, its heart urging it
Into battle. Beowulf's ancient sword
Was waiting, unsheathed, his sharp and gleaming
Blade. The beast came closer; both of them
660 Were ready, each set on slaughter. The Geats'
Great prince stood firm, unmoving, prepared
Behind his high shield, waiting in his shining
Armor. The monster came quickly toward him,
Pouring out fire and smoke, hurrying
665 To its fate. Flames beat at the iron

---

29. **hoary** (hôr′ē): gray with age.

Shield, and for a time it held, protected
Beowulf as he'd planned; then it began to melt,
And for the first time in his life that famous prince
Fought with fate against him, with glory
670 Denied him. He knew it, but he raised his sword
And struck at the dragon's scaly hide.
The ancient blade broke, bit into
The monster's skin, drew blood, but cracked
And failed him before it went deep enough, helped him
675 Less than he needed. The dragon leaped
With pain, thrashed and beat at him, spouting
Murderous flames, spreading them everywhere.
And the Geats' ring-giver[30] did not boast of glorious
Victories in other wars: his weapon
680 Had failed him, deserted him, now when he needed it
Most, that excellent sword. Edgetho's
Famous son stared at death,
Unwilling to leave this world, to exchange it
For a dwelling in some distant place—a journey
685 Into darkness that all men must make, as death
Ends their few brief hours on earth. ▶

      Quickly, the dragon came at him, encouraged
As Beowulf fell back; its breath flared,
And he suffered, wrapped around in swirling
690 Flames—a king, before, but now
A beaten warrior. None of his comrades
Came to him, helped him, his brave and noble
Followers; they ran for their lives, fled
Deep in a wood. And only one of them
695 Remained, stood there, miserable, remembering,
As a good man must, what kinship should mean.
      His name was Wiglaf, he was Wexstan's son
And a good soldier; his family had been Swedish,
Once. Watching Beowulf, he could see
700 How his king was suffering, burning. Remembering
Everything his lord and cousin had given him,
Armor and gold and the great estates

ANALYZE

Reread lines 663–686. How do
you interpret the statement
that Beowulf is fighting "with
fate against him"?

_____

_____

_____

_____

Underline details that support
your interpretation. ✏

30. **ring-giver:** king; lord. When a man swore allegiance to a Germanic lord in return
    for his protection, the lord typically bestowed a ring on his follower to symbolize
    the bond.

Wexstan's family enjoyed, Wiglaf's
Mind was made up; he raised his yellow
705 Shield and drew his sword. . . .
      And Wiglaf, his heart heavy, uttered
The kind of words his comrades deserved:
      "I remember how we sat in the mead-hall, drinking
And boasting of how brave we'd be when Beowulf
710 Needed us, he who gave us these swords
And armor: all of us swore to repay him,
When the time came, kindness for kindness
   —With our lives, if he needed them. He allowed us to join him,
Chose us from all his great army, thinking
715 Our boasting words had some weight, believing
Our promises, trusting our swords. He took us
For soldiers, for men. He meant to kill
This monster himself, our mighty king,
Fight this battle alone and unaided,
720 As in the days when his strength and daring dazzled
Men's eyes. But those days are over and gone
And now our lord must lean on younger
Arms. And we must go to him, while angry
Flames burn at his flesh, help
725 Our glorious king! By almighty God,
I'd rather burn myself than see
Flames swirling around my lord.
And who are we to carry home
Our shields before we've slain his enemy
730 And ours, to run back to our homes with Beowulf
So hard-pressed here? I swear that nothing
He ever did deserved an end
Like this, dying miserably and alone,
Butchered by this savage beast: we swore
735 That these swords and armor were each for us all!" . . .

✋ **PAUSE & REFLECT**

✋ **PAUSE & REFLECT**

1. What social value is reflected in Wiglaf's decision to stand by Beowulf? *MAKE INFERENCES*

_____

_____

_____

_____

2. Beowulf's actions in the battle against the dragon

☐ increase his heroic stature

☐ decrease his heroic stature

Explain your choice. *EVALUATE*

_____

_____

_____

_____

_____

THE DEATH OF BEOWULF

Wiglaf joins Beowulf, who again attacks the dragon single-handed; but the remnant of his sword shatters, and the monster wounds him in the neck. Wiglaf then strikes the dragon, and he and Beowulf together finally succeed in killing the beast. Their triumph is short-lived, however, because Beowulf's wound proves to be mortal.

Beowulf spoke, in spite of the swollen,
Livid wound, knowing he'd unwound
His string of days on earth, seen
As much as God would grant him; all worldly
740 Pleasure was gone, as life would go,
Soon:
      "I'd leave my armor to my son,
Now, if God had given me an heir,
A child born of my body, his life
Created from mine. I've worn this crown
745 For fifty winters: no neighboring people
Have tried to threaten the Geats, sent soldiers
Against us or talked of terror. My days
Have gone by as fate willed, waiting
For its word to be spoken, ruling as well
750 As I knew how, swearing no unholy oaths,
Seeking no lying wars. I can leave
This life happy; I can die, here,
Knowing the Lord of all life has never
Watched me wash my sword in blood
755 Born of my own family. Belovèd
Wiglaf, go, quickly, find
The dragon's treasure: we've taken its life,
But its gold is ours, too. Hurry,
Bring me ancient silver, precious
760 Jewels, shining armor and gems,
Before I die. Death will be softer,
Leaving life and this people I've ruled
So long, if I look at this last of all prizes." ▶

Then Wexstan's son went in, as quickly
765 As he could, did as the dying Beowulf
Asked, entered the inner darkness
Of the tower, went with his mail shirt and his sword.

(F)OCUS
Although Beowulf and Wiglaf defeat the dragon, their victory comes at a terrible cost. Read the next section to learn about Beowulf's final moments.

livid (lĭv′ĭd) *adj.* discolored from being bruised

TESTSMART

Reread lines 741–763. In his speech to Wiglaf, Beowulf is *most* proud that he has

(A) ruled in peace
(B) been loved by his children
(C) lived a long life
(D) grown wealthy

TIP Some test questions ask you to select the most important option from a number of choices. To answer such questions, you will need to **evaluate** the different choices. If specific line numbers are mentioned, be sure to reread that section, underlining clues that point you toward the best answer. ✏

Flushed with victory he groped his way,
A brave young warrior, and suddenly saw
770 Piles of gleaming gold, precious
Gems, scattered on the floor, cups
And bracelets, rusty old helmets, beautifully
Made but rotting with no hands to rub
And polish them. They lay where the dragon left them;
775 It had flown in the darkness, once, before fighting
Its final battle. (So gold can easily
Triumph, defeat the strongest of men,
No matter how deep it is hidden!) And he saw,
Hanging high above, a golden
780 Banner, woven by the best of weavers
And beautiful. And over everything he saw
A strange light, shining everywhere,
On walls and floor and treasure. Nothing
Moved, no other monsters appeared;
785 He took what he wanted, all the treasures
That pleased his eye, heavy plates
And golden cups and the glorious banner,
Loaded his arms with all they could hold.
Beowulf's dagger, his iron blade,
790 Had finished the fire-spitting terror
That once protected tower and treasures
Alike; the gray-bearded lord of the Geats
Had ended those flying, burning raids
Forever.
           Then Wiglaf went back, anxious
795 To return while Beowulf was alive, to bring him
Treasure they'd won together. He ran,
Hoping his wounded king, weak
And dying, had not left the world too soon.
Then he brought their treasure to Beowulf, and found
800 His famous king bloody, gasping
For breath. But Wiglaf sprinkled water
Over his lord, until the words
Deep in his breast broke through and were heard.
Beholding the treasure he spoke, haltingly:
805   "For this, this gold, these jewels, I thank
Our Father in Heaven, Ruler of the Earth—
For all of this, that His grace has given me,

Allowed me to bring to my people while breath
Still came to my lips. I sold my life
810 For this treasure, and I sold it well. Take
What I leave, Wiglaf, lead my people,
Help them; my time is gone. Have
The brave Geats build me a tomb,
When the funeral flames have burned me, and build it
815 Here, at the water's edge, high
On this spit[31] of land, so sailors can see
This tower, and remember my name, and call it
Beowulf's tower, and boats in the darkness
And mist, crossing the sea, will know it." ▶

820   Then that brave king gave the golden
Necklace from around his throat to Wiglaf,
Gave him his gold-covered helmet, and his rings,
And his mail shirt, and ordered him to use them well:
    "You're the last of all our far-flung family.
825 Fate has swept our race away,
Taken warriors in their strength and led them
To the death that was waiting. And now I follow them."
    The old man's mouth was silent, spoke
No more, had said as much as it could;
830 He would sleep in the fire, soon. His soul
Left his flesh, flew to glory. . . .
    And when the battle was over Beowulf's followers
Came out of the wood, cowards and traitors,
Knowing the dragon was dead. Afraid,
835 While it spit its fires, to fight in their lord's
Defense, to throw their javelins[32] and spears,
They came like shamefaced jackals,[33] their shields
In their hands, to the place where the prince lay dead,
And waited for Wiglaf to speak. He was sitting
840 Near Beowulf's body, wearily sprinkling
Water in the dead man's face, trying
To stir him. He could not. No one could have kept
Life in their lord's body, or turned

MAKE INFERENCES

Reread the boxed text. What do Beowulf's instructions for the building of his tomb suggest about his concern for the future?

_____

_____

_____

_____

_____

---

31. **spit:** a narrow point of land extending into a body of water.
32. **javelins** (jăv′lĭnz): light spears used as weapons.
33. **jackals** (jăk′əlz): doglike animals that sometimes feed on the flesh of dead beasts.

_____

_____

_____

_____

_____

_____

_____

_____

_____

FOCUS
In the next section, Beowulf's ashes are buried in his tomb. Read to find out how the Geats honor his memory.

Aside the Lord's will: world
845 And men and all move as He orders,
And always have, and always will.
      Then Wiglaf turned and angrily told them
What men without courage must hear.
Wexstan's brave son stared at the traitors,
850 His heart sorrowful, and said what he had to:
      "I say what anyone who speaks the truth
Must say. . . .
      Too few of his warriors remembered
To come, when our lord faced death, alone.
855 And now the giving of swords, of golden
Rings and rich estates, is over,
Ended for you and everyone who shares
Your blood: when the brave Geats hear
How you bolted[34] and ran none of your race
860 Will have anything left but their lives. And death
Would be better for them all, and for you, than the kind
Of life you can lead, branded with disgrace!". . .
      Then the warriors rose,
Walked slowly down from the cliff, stared
865 At those wonderful sights, stood weeping as they saw
Beowulf dead on the sand, their bold
Ring-giver resting in his last bed;
He'd reached the end of his days, their mighty
War-king, the great lord of the Geats,
870 Gone to a glorious death. . . . **PAUSE & REFLECT**

MOURNING BEOWULF
      Then the Geats built the tower, as Beowulf
Had asked, strong and tall, so sailors
Could find it from far and wide; working
For ten long days they made his monument,
875 Sealed his ashes in walls as straight
And high as wise and willing hands
Could raise them. And the riches he and Wiglaf
Had won from the dragon, rings, necklaces,
Ancient, hammered armor—all
880 The treasures they'd taken were left there, too,

---

34. **bolted:** ran away; fled.

Silver and jewels buried in the sandy
Ground, back in the earth, again
And forever hidden and useless to men.
And then twelve of the bravest Geats
885 Rode their horses around the tower,
Telling their sorrow, telling stories
Of their dead king and his greatness, his glory,
Praising him for heroic deeds, for a life
As noble as his name. So should all men
890 Raise up words for their lords, warm
With love, when their shield and protector leaves
His body behind, sends his soul
On high. And so Beowulf's followers
Rode, mourning their belovèd leader,
895 Crying that no better king had ever
Lived, no prince so mild,[35] no man
So open to his people, so deserving of praise. ✋ **PAUSE & REFLECT**

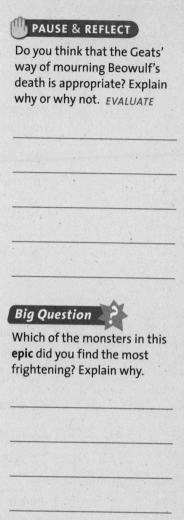

✋ **PAUSE & REFLECT**

Do you think that the Geats' way of mourning Beowulf's death is appropriate? Explain why or why not. *EVALUATE*

_____

_____

_____

_____

_____

Big Question ?

Which of the monsters in this **epic** did you find the most frightening? Explain why.

_____

_____

_____

_____

35. **mild:** gentle or kindly.

Reading Comprehension

DIRECTIONS *Answer these questions about* Beowulf *by filling in the correct ovals.*

1. Why does Beowulf journey to the land of the Danes?

   (A) He plans to overthrow Hrothgar.

   (B) Hrothgar pleaded with him for help.

   (C) He has heard about Grendel's attacks on Herot.

   (D) He wants to retrace his father's footsteps.

2. Which character trait is demonstrated by Beowulf's decision to fight Grendel with his bare hands?

   (A) cleverness

   (B) bravery

   (C) caution

   (D) cruelty

3. Reread lines 425–443. Which word *best* describes the mood conveyed in this description of the lake?

   (A) menacing

   (B) solemn

   (C) humid

   (D) tranquil

4. What trophy does Beowulf take after killing Grendel's mother?

   (A) Grendel's head

   (B) Grendel's claw

   (C) Grendel's mother's head

   (D) Grendel's mother's treasure

5. After killing the fire-breathing dragon, why does Beowulf ask Wiglaf to bring him the dragon's treasure?

   (A) He plans to give the treasure to his children.

   (B) He is afraid that the Geats will steal the treasure.

   (C) He wants to test Wiglaf's bravery.

   (D) He will get comfort from seeing his last prize.

6. Which of the following characteristics does *Beowulf* have in common with most epic poems?

   (A) a hero who slays dragons

   (B) a cold, northern setting

   (C) a serious tone

   (D) a lack of female characters

7. What does the word *fret* mean in line 185?

   (A) wear away

   (B) create a hole

   (C) worry

   (D) decorate

8. From the description in lines 513–523, you can tell that the word *scabbard* in line 518 refers to a

   (A) sea creature

   (B) handle

   (C) wound

   (D) case

Responding in Writing

9. Short Response Write a character sketch of Beowulf in the form of a speech to be delivered at his funeral. Focus on three traits that make Beowulf an epic hero.

For help, use the *Test-Taker's Toolkit* below.

_____

_____

_____

_____

_____

_____

TEST-TAKER'S TOOLKIT

- ⊗ **ACADEMIC VOCABULARY** When you're asked to write a **character sketch,** you should briefly describe the character's important traits. You may need to infer these traits from details in the story, such as the character's words, thoughts, and actions, as well as the comments of other characters.

- ⊗ **GRAPHIC ORGANIZER** Use the chart below to help you plan your response. Look back at the epic to help you remember details about Beowulf.

Trait 1	Supporting Details
Trait 2	Supporting Details
Trait 3	Supporting Details

Use with Beowulf, p. 2

What's the Connection?

In his final battle, Beowulf confronts a fire-breathing dragon that has terrorized the Geats. Dragons appear in the literature and art of many cultures around the world. "The Years of the Dragon" is a newspaper article that describes a variety of dragons and the heroes who do battle with them.

CHART IT In the K-W-L chart, write down what you know about dragons and what you would like to learn about them. Then after you read the article, complete the chart by writing down important information you have learned.

DRAGONS		
K What I Know	**W** What I Want to Find Out	**L** What I Learned

LEARN THE SKILL: IDENTIFY TEXT FEATURES

Many nonfiction writers use design elements called **text features** to organize text and to point out key ideas and important information. Here are the most common text features:

- A **title** suggests an article's topic.
- A **subheading** indicates the start of a new section and identifies its focus.
- **Bulleted lists** show items of equal importance. Some lists use boldface type instead of bullets.
- **Graphic aids** such as charts, diagrams, and photographs often clarify ideas in the text.
- **Captions** give information about photos or other graphics.

For more on text features, see the Nonfiction Skills Handbook beginning on page R2.

The Years of the Dragon

by Bill Reed

For a mythical creature, the dragon boasts a real history. From dragons drawn in China 5,000 years ago to Puff the Magic Dragon to the dragon of Cheyenne Mountain, this beast has lurked in the human imagination for centuries.

Don't think the long dance with
10 dragons is over. Most recently, the dragon has been in the limelight in the fantasy world of Alagaesia, thanks to author Christopher Paolini's three-part trilogy, *The Inheritance*. His first book, *Eragon*, was made into a film that was released on DVD. . . .

But dragons can be far more than light entertainment. Most
20 dragon myths have deep links to the spiritual and magical.

They burn through the pages of a vast array of sacred literature— there's the Hindu mythology of Indra, god of the sky and giver of rain, and the biblical description of a fire-breathing leviathan in Job 41:18–19: "His snorting throws out flashes of light; his eyes are
30 like the rays of dawn. Firebrands stream from his mouth; sparks of fire shoot out."

"It's obviously a topic that intrigues people," said Heather Lyle, librarian and storyteller at the Pikes Peak Library District. "And dragons certainly intrigue children."

Lyle has been collecting dragon
40 stories for years. Like most dragon lovers, she's discovered that there's no shortage of such stories, and they come from all over.

TEXT FEATURES

Scan the **title** and image. What do they tell you the article will be about?

SPECIALIZED
Vocabulary

The word *amalgam* in line
58 might be new to you.
Reread the sentence in which
it appears and underline
possible context clues to its
meaning.

Then jot down a definition of
the word. *WORD ANALYSIS*

_____

_____

TESTSMART

Reread lines 61–70. What
is the main idea of this
paragraph?

Ⓐ Asian dragons are
powerful.

Ⓑ European dragons
often live in caves.

Ⓒ Dragons will defend
treasure with their
lives.

Ⓓ Dragons can represent
different qualities.

TIP When you think you've
identified the **main idea,**
try **underlining details** that
support it. If only one detail
supports your answer, then
it probably isn't the correct
choice.

Dragon myths seem to have popped up independently across the globe—Europe, Asia, North America, Africa. We even have a hometown myth, as the queer shapes atop Cheyenne Mountain
50 gave rise to a dragon myth among the Ute Indians.

Theories abound as to why dragon myths are so widespread. Perhaps it's because the discovery of dinosaur bones fueled visions of giant reptiles for ancient peoples. Perhaps what we call "the dragon" is an amalgam of basic human fears that crop up in every culture: rep-
60 tiles, teeth, great size and fire. ◀

What the dragon myths mean is as ever-changing as the dragons themselves. In Asia, dragons often symbolized power and vitality, a symbol many emperors in China used to represent themselves. In Europe, most dragons were malevolent, a dangerous creature deep in a cave that must be slain by the
70 hero to gain a great treasure. ◀

Master myth collector Joseph Campbell discussed dragons with Bill Moyers in their book *The Power of Myth*. He concluded that the European dragon, sitting in his cave on a hoard of gold that he'll never use, represents the part of us that keeps us from getting the most out of life, the part of us
80 that must be slain.

Like the multiheaded Hydra in Greek mythology, however,

for every dragon slain, two more seem to appear. The dragons in *The Hobbit*, Dungeons & Dragons and video games are carrying an ancient myth into a new age.

DRAGONS FROM
90 ## AROUND THE WORLD

Greece: The Lernean (or Lernaean) Hydra sprouted new heads when one was cut off. In Greek mythology, Hercules fought and killed the Hydra. Also in Greek mythology, Jason killed a Hydra to get the Golden Fleece.

Vikings: They often had dragon figureheads on the prow of their
100 ships to endow their warriors with good sight and cunning.

Mexico: Quetzalcoatl (kĕt-säl′kō-ät′l) is the winged and feathered serpent from Aztec legends. Some think the myth of Quetzalcoatl started with a bird with long tail feathers that looked like a flying serpent, the Quetzal.

Africa: Amphisbaena (ăm′ fĭs-
110 bē′ nə) is a dragon with two heads, one at the tip of its tail. It is usually portrayed with scales on its body, feathered wings and feet of a rooster, and if one head holds the tail in its mouth it can roll around like a hoop. . . .

North America: The Piasa was a legend created by the Illini

Indians in modern-day Illinois. The birdlike creature had the body of a dragon, the head of a person and a long tail, and lived near the Mississippi River. This dragon did not bother humans until one day when it found dead bodies and tasted the meat. It liked the taste and started hunting humans.

WHAT IS A DRAGON?

Here are the common characteristics of dragons:

- reptilian
- breathes or spits fire or poison
- guards treasure, knowledge or another resource and will fight to the death for it
- lives in or is associated with water
- influences storms, rain or wind
- can fly, even if it doesn't have wings
- magical powers
- most are smart and speak in riddles

WELL-KNOWN DRAGONS

You may recognize these fire-breathing denizens of lore.

Puff the Magic Dragon. Made famous by the Peter, Paul & Mary song, Puff is powerful but gentle, and represents the childhood of Jackie Paper. When the boy stops believing in him, it quiets his "fearless roar."

Smaug. The dragon in J.R.R. Tolkien's *The Hobbit* is a wily old beast with a magnificent hoard of treasure, but Bilbo Baggins finds his weak spot.

Dragon from *Shrek*. The girl dragon, who somehow mates with Eddie Murphy's donkey character and gives birth to a "dronkey."

Saphira. The dragon that Eragon finds and befriends in the *Eragon* novel and movie.

Draco the constellation. A far northern constellation. The most famous myth about the constellation holds that Draco represents Ladon, the hundred-headed dragon that guarded the golden apples of the Hesperides and was slain by Hercules. . . .

Beowulf and the Dragon. After the evil dragon sears the countryside in rage, King Beowulf decides to take him on. Neither combatant survives the fight. . . .

St. George and the Dragon. The patron saint of England slew a mighty dragon and saved a virgin princess who was about to be sacrificed. Although the story is thought to have been brought back from Asia by crusaders, the Christian retelling cast the dragon as paganism, and St. George's victory becomes the victory of the faithful over heathens. St. George's feast day is April 23.

TEXT FEATURES

Do you consider the **lists** under the three **subheadings** an effective way to organize information in the article? Explain why or why not.

Reading Comprehension

DIRECTIONS *Answer these questions about the two selections in this lesson by filling in the correct ovals.*

1. What does the author of "The Years of the Dragon" mean when he says, "Don't think the long dance with dragons is over" (lines 9–10)?

   Ⓐ "Dragon dances" are common in China.

   Ⓑ Not all dragons are extinct.

   Ⓒ Dragons are still part of popular culture.

   Ⓓ There are many myths about dancing dragons.

2. According to the author, which of the following may have inspired dragon myths?

   Ⓐ dinosaur fossils

   Ⓑ fireworks

   Ⓒ thunderstorms

   Ⓓ video games

3. Joseph Campbell believed that European dragons represent

   Ⓐ the power of emperors

   Ⓑ negative thoughts and feelings

   Ⓒ a fear of reptiles

   Ⓓ the cruelty of nature

4. Which statement would the author of "The Years of the Dragon" most likely agree with?

   Ⓐ Dragons don't have the same meaning for everyone.

   Ⓑ Dragon myths all come from the same source.

   Ⓒ Most dragon myths were inspired by real events.

   Ⓓ All dragons are frightening.

5. Which section of the article does *not* offer support for the idea that dragons have "lurked in the human imagination for centuries" (lines 6–8)?

   Ⓐ introductory section

   Ⓑ Dragons from Around the World

   Ⓒ What Is a Dragon?

   Ⓓ Well-Known Dragons

6. The dragon in *Beowulf* is typical of European rather than Asian dragons because it

   Ⓐ has wings

   Ⓑ breathes fire

   Ⓒ guards treasure

   Ⓓ uses magical powers

7. From its context in lines 22–28 of the article, you can tell that the word *array* in line 23 means

   Ⓐ bonfire

   Ⓑ group

   Ⓒ poem

   Ⓓ fantasy

8. What does the word *malevolent* mean in lines 67–68 of the article?

   Ⓐ vulnerable

   Ⓑ ancient

   Ⓒ selfish

   Ⓓ evil

Timed Writing Practice

PROMPT

Both of the selections you have read describe (monsters). Why are stories about monsters so popular? What do they reveal about the world and about human nature? Write an analytical essay in which you discuss two or three monster stories and examine their meanings. You may write about monsters depicted in literature, movies, and other media.

TEST-TAKER'S TOOLKIT

1. ANALYZE THE PROMPT

A. Identify the type of writing you are asked to do.

B. Circle key words that indicate the topic of your writing. One has been circled for you.

C. Restate the prompt in your own words on the lines to the right.

I am being asked to _____

_____

_____

_____

_____

2. PLAN YOUR RESPONSE

A. **Make notes** Brainstorm a list of monster stories you might want to write about. Choose two or three for which you can provide the most details. Then create a chart that will help you compile and organize your details.

B. **Organize your information** An analytical essay should begin with an introduction of the topic and a statement of your main idea. Then you can write one or two paragraphs about each of the monster stories you will discuss in your essay. Be sure to end with a conclusion that summarizes your key points.

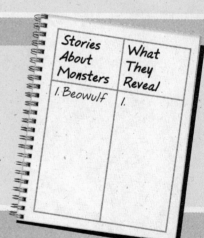

Stories About Monsters	What They Reveal
1. Beowulf	1.

3. WRITE AND REVIEW

A. A strong opener can help your essay get a good score. Try beginning with a quotation or a shocking detail from a monster story to grab your readers' attention.

B. Be sure to leave time to check your spelling and grammar.

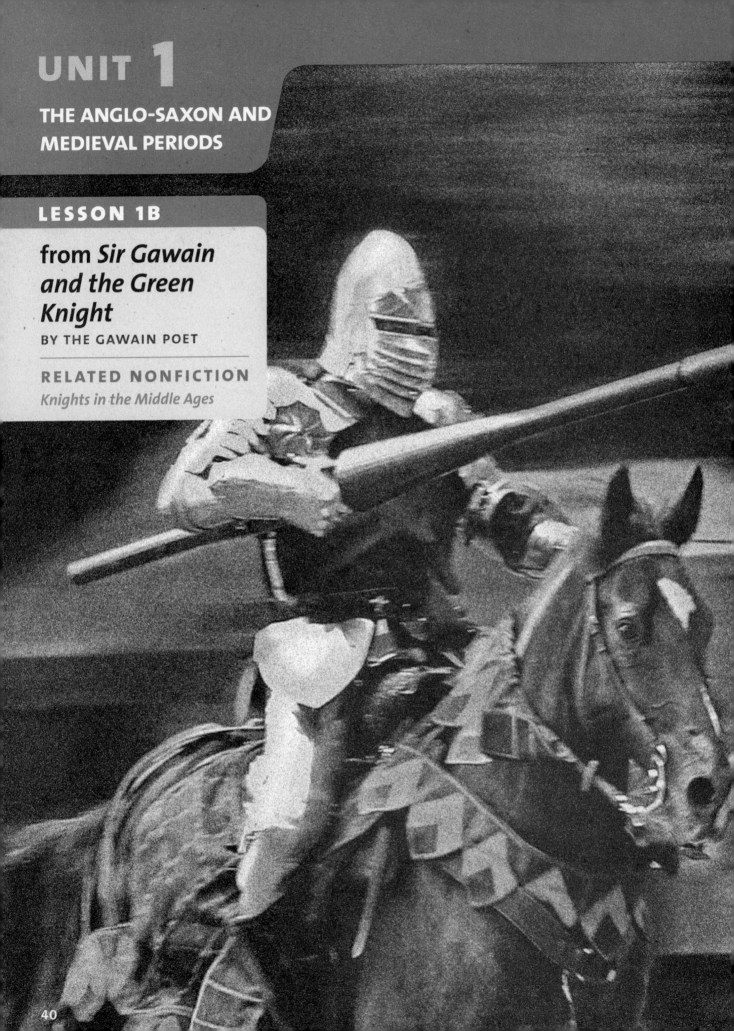

LESSON 1B

from *Sir Gawain and the Green Knight*

BY THE GAWAIN POET

RELATED NONFICTION

Knights in the Middle Ages

Is HONOR worth dying for?

For the knights of the Middle Ages, honor came with heavy obligations. According to the code of chivalry, a knight was supposed to be brave, modest, courteous, loyal, and honest. His role was to protect the weak and battle evildoers, including anyone who threatened his king or his church. If necessary, he had to sacrifice his life to uphold these ideals.

DISCUSS What ideals are important for your own sense of honor? Record your thoughts in a word web. Then, with a partner, discuss the sacrifices you would be willing to make to defend your honor.

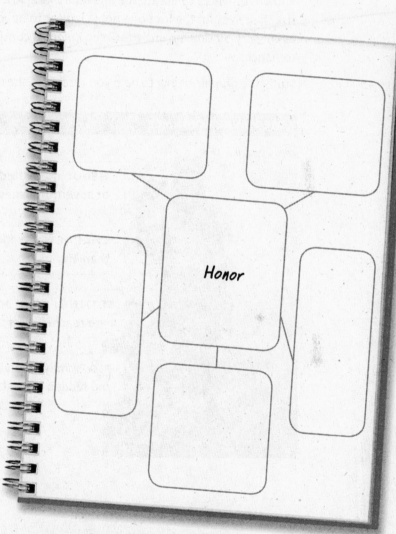

ASSESSMENT GOALS

By the end of this lesson, you will be able to...

• analyze a medieval romance

• use active reading strategies to comprehend text

• summarize information in a nonfiction text

• analyze a writing prompt and plan a short story

Medieval Romance

A **MEDIEVAL ROMANCE** is a verse or prose narrative that usually involves adventurous heroes, idealized love, exotic places, and supernatural events. Romances first appeared in France during the 12th century, and they soon spread to England. Many of the best-known romances celebrate the legendary King Arthur and his knights, who often risk their lives for the love of a noble lady or to uphold the code of behavior known as chivalry. *Sir Gawain and the Green Knight* is considered one of the finest Arthurian romances.

Study the graphic below to help you recognize the characteristics of medieval romance.

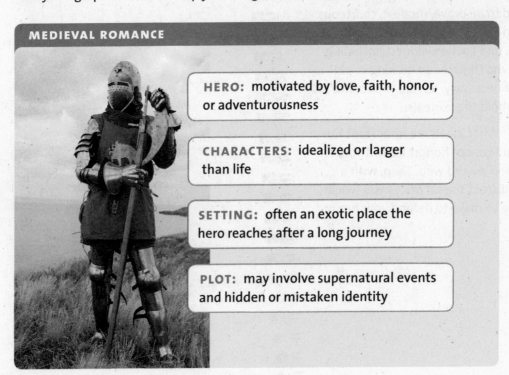

MEDIEVAL ROMANCE

HERO: motivated by love, faith, honor, or adventurousness

CHARACTERS: idealized or larger than life

SETTING: often an exotic place the hero reaches after a long journey

PLOT: may involve supernatural events and hidden or mistaken identity

Sir Gawain
AND THE
Green Knight

MARK IT UP
Use these marks to monitor your reading:

✳ This is important.

❓ I don't understand.

❗ This is a surprise.

When you see this pencil ✏, you'll be asked to mark up the text. You can also write in this book in any way you find useful.

BACKGROUND Like many of the Arthurian romances, *Sir Gawain and the Green Knight* starts off in Camelot, where King Arthur rules over the knights of the Round Table. Gawain is the king's nephew and one of the greatest knights in his court.

As the poem begins, Arthur and his knights are gathered to celebrate Christmas and the new year with feasting and revelry. In the midst of their festivities, an enormous man—who is entirely green—bounds through the door.

ⒻOCUS
In this section, a stranger interrupts a feast at King Arthur's court. Read to find out about his surprising challenge.

Splendid that knight errant stood in a splay[1] of green,
And green, too, was the mane of his mighty destrier;[2]
Fair fanning tresses enveloped the fighting man's shoulders,
And over his breast hung a beard as big as a bush;
5 The beard and the huge mane burgeoning[3] forth from his head
Were clipped off clean in a straight line over his elbows,
And the upper half of each arm was hidden underneath
As if covered by a king's chaperon,[4] closed round the neck.
The mane of the marvelous horse was much the same,
10 Well crisped and combed and carefully pranked with knots,[5]

---

1. **knight errant** (ĕr´ənt): a knight who wanders about, searching for adventure in order to prove his chivalry; **splay:** display.
2. **destrier** (dĕs´trē-ər): war horse.
3. **burgeoning** (bûr´jə-nĭng): growing.
4. **chaperon** (shăp´ə-rōn´): hood.
5. **pranked with knots:** decorated with bows.

Threads of gold interwoven with the glorious green,
Now a thread of hair, now another thread of gold;
The tail of the horse and the forelock[6] were tricked the same way,
And both were bound up with a band of brilliant green
15   Adorned with glittering jewels the length of the dock,[7]
Then caught up tight with a thong in a criss-cross knot
Where many a bell tinkled brightly, all burnished gold.
So monstrous a mount, so mighty a man in the saddle
Was never once encountered on all this earth
                    till then;
20   His eyes, like lightning, flashed,
        And it seemed to many a man,
        That any man who clashed
        With him would not long stand. ◀

But the huge man came unarmed, without helmet or hauberk,[8]
25   No breastplate or gorget or iron cleats[9] on his arms;
He brought neither shield nor spearshaft to shove or to smite,
But instead he held in one hand a bough of the holly
That grows most green when all the groves are bare
And held in the other an ax, immense and unwieldy,
30   A pitiless battleblade terrible to tell of. . . .
King Arthur stared down at the stranger before the high dais[10]
And greeted him nobly, for nothing on earth frightened him.
And he said to him, "Sir, you are welcome in this place;[11]
I am the head of this court. They call me Arthur.
35   Get down from your horse, I beg you, and join us for dinner,
And then whatever you seek we will gladly see to."
But the stranger said, "No, so help me God on high,
My errand is hardly to sit at my ease in your castle!
But friend, since your praises are sung so far and wide,
40   Your castle the best ever built, people say, and your barons
The stoutest men in steel armor that ever rode steeds,

ANALYZE

Reread lines 1–23. Underline details that give the impression that the Green Knight is a larger-than-life figure. ✏

6. **forelock:** the part of a horse's mane that falls between the ears.
7. **dock:** the fleshy part of an animal's tail.
8. **hauberk** (hô′bərk): a coat of chain mail (a type of armor).
9. **breastplate or gorget** (gôr′jĭt) **or iron cleats:** armor for the chest, the throat, or the shoulders and elbows.
10. **dais** (dā′ĭs): a raised platform where honored guests are seated.
11. **this place:** Camelot, Arthur's favorite castle and the site of his court of the Round Table.

Most mighty and most worthy of all mortal men

And tough devils to toy with in tournament games,[12]

And since courtesy is in flower[13] in this court, they say,

45 All these tales, in truth, have drawn me to you at this time.

You may be assured by this holly branch I bear

That I come to you in peace, not spoiling for[14] battle.

If I'd wanted to come in finery, fixed up for fighting,

I have back at home both a helmet and a hauberk,

50 A shield and a sharp spear that shines like fire,

And other weapons that I know pretty well how to use.

But since I don't come here for battle, my clothes are mere cloth.

Now if you are truly as bold as the people all say,

You will grant me gladly the little game that I ask

           as my right."

55   Arthur gave him answer

   And said, "Sir noble knight,

   If it's a duel you're after,

   We'll furnish you your fight."

"Good heavens, I want no such thing! I assure you, Sire,

60 You've nothing but beardless babes about this bench!

If I were hasped[15] in my armor and high on my horse,

You haven't a man that could match me, your might is so feeble. ▶

And so all I ask of this court is a Christmas game,

For the Yule is here, and New Year's, and here sit young men;

65 If any man holds himself, here in this house, so hardy,

So bold in his blood—and so brainless in his head—

That he dares to stoutly exchange one stroke for another,

I shall let him have as my present this lovely gisarme,[16]

This ax, as heavy as he'll need, to handle as he likes,

70 And I will abide the first blow, bare-necked as I sit.

If anyone here has the daring to try what I've offered,

Leap to me lightly, lad; lift up this weapon;

I give you the thing forever—you may think it your own;

---

12. In medieval tournaments, knights on horseback fought one another for sport.

13. **courtesy is in flower:** the high standards of behavior expected in a king's court are currently flourishing.

14. **spoiling for:** eager for.

15. **hasped:** fastened.

16. **gisarme** (gĭ-zärm'): a battle-ax with a long shaft and a two-edged blade.

MONITOR

The Green Knight assures King Arthur that he hasn't come to Camelot for a duel. Underline statements in his speech that support this claim.

PAUSE & REFLECT

What challenge does
the Green Knight issue
to King Arthur and his
knights? *CLARIFY*

_____

_____

_____

_____

FOCUS

In this section of the poem,
King Arthur and his knights
respond to the Green
Knight's challenge. As you
read, notice the character
traits that they display.

MAKE INFERENCES

Reread the boxed text. Why
does the Green Knight taunt
Arthur and his knights?

_____

_____

_____

_____

And I will stand still for your stroke, steady on the floor,
75 Provided you honor my right, when my inning comes,
           to repay.
    But let the respite be
    A twelvemonth and a day;[17]
    Come now, my boys, let's see
    What any here can say." **PAUSE & REFLECT**

80 If they were like stone before, they were stiller now,
Every last lord in the hall, both the high and the low;
The stranger on his destrier stirred in the saddle
And ferociously his red eyes rolled around;
He lowered his grisly eyebrows, glistening green,
85 And waved his beard and waited for someone to rise;
When no one answered, he coughed, as if embarrassed,
And drew himself up straight and spoke again:
"What! Can this be King Arthur's court?" said the stranger,
"Whose renown runs through many a realm, flung far and wide?
90 What has become of your chivalry and your conquest,
Your greatness-of-heart and your grimness and grand words?
Behold the radiance and renown of the mighty Round Table
Overwhelmed by a word out of one man's mouth!
You shiver and blanch before a blow's been shown!"
95 And with that he laughed so loud that the lord was distressed;
In chagrin, his blood shot up in his face and limbs
          so fair;
    More angry he was than the wind,
    And likewise each man there;
    And Arthur, bravest of men,
100   Decided now to draw near.

And he said, "By heaven, sir, your request is strange;
But since you have come here for folly,[18] you may as well find it.
I know no one here who's aghast of your great words.
Give me your gisarme, then, for the love of God,
105 And gladly I'll grant you the gift you have asked to be given."
Lightly the King leaped down and clutched it in his hand;

---

17. **let the respite . . . day:** let the period of delay be a year and a day.
18. **folly:** dangerous and foolish activity.

Then quickly that other lord alighted on his feet.
Arthur lay hold of the ax, he gripped it by the handle,
And he swung it up over him sternly, as if to strike.
110 The stranger stood before him, in stature higher
By a head or more than any man here in the house;
Sober and thoughtful he stood there and stroked his beard,
And with patience like a priest's he pulled down his collar,
No more unmanned[19] or dismayed by Arthur's might
115 Than he'd be if some baron on the bench had brought him a glass
        of wine.
    Then Gawain, at Guinevere's[20] side,
    Made to the King a sign:
    "I beseech you, Sire," he said,
    "Let this game be mine.

120 "Now if you, my worthy lord," said Gawain to the King,
"Would command me to step from the dais and stand with you there,
That I might without bad manners move down from my place
(Though I couldn't, of course, if my liege lady[21] disliked it)
I'd be deeply honored to advise you before all the court;
125 For I think it unseemly, if I understand the matter,
That challenges such as this churl[22] has chosen to offer
Be met by Your Majesty—much as it may amuse you—
When so many bold-hearted barons sit about the bench:
No men under Heaven, I am sure, are more hardy in will
130 Or better in body on the fields where battles are fought;
I myself am the weakest, of course, and in wit the most feeble;
My life would be least missed, if we let out the truth.
Only as you are my uncle have I any honor,
For excepting your blood, I bear in my body slight virtue.
135 And since this affair that's befallen us here is so foolish,
And since I have asked for it first, let it fall to me.
If I've reasoned incorrectly, let all the court say,
      without blame." ▶

ANALYZE

Underline words and phrases in the boxed text that give you insight into Gawain's personality.

Put a check mark by the words you would use to describe his character.

☐ loyal
☐ headstrong
☐ courteous
☐ ambitious
☐ modest
☐ brave

---

19. **unmanned:** deprived of manly courage.
20. **Guinevere:** King Arthur's wife.
21. **liege** (lēj) **lady:** a lady to whom one owes loyalty and service; here used by Gawain to refer to Queen Guinevere.
22. **churl:** rude, uncouth person.

The nobles gather round
And all advise the same:
140 "Let the King step down
And give Sir Gawain the game!" . . .

Arthur grants Gawain's request to take on the Green Knight's challenge. The Green Knight asks Gawain to identify himself, and the two agree on their pact. Gawain then prepares to strike his blow against the Green Knight.

On the ground, the Green Knight got himself into position,
His head bent forward a little, the bare flesh showing,
His long and lovely locks laid over his crown
145 So that any man there might note the naked neck.
Sir Gawain laid hold of the ax and he hefted it high,
His pivot foot thrown forward before him on the floor,
And then, swiftly, he slashed at the naked neck;
The sharp of the battleblade shattered asunder[23] the bones
150 And sank through the shining fat and slit it in two,
And the bit of the bright steel buried itself in the ground.
The fair head fell from the neck to the floor of the hall
And the people all kicked it away as it came near their feet.
The blood splashed up from the body and glistened on the green,
155 But he never faltered or fell for all of that,
But swiftly he started forth upon stout shanks[24]
And rushed to reach out, where the King's retainers[25] stood,
Caught hold of the lovely head, and lifted it up,
And leaped to his steed and snatched up the reins of the bridle,
160 Stepped into stirrups of steel and, striding aloft,
He held his head by the hair, high, in his hand;
And the stranger sat there as steadily in his saddle
As a man entirely unharmed, although he was headless
            on his steed. ◀
He turned his trunk about,
165 That baleful[26] body that bled,
And many were faint with fright
When all his say was said.

---

23. **asunder:** into pieces.
24. **shanks:** legs.
25. **retainers:** servants or attendants.
26. **baleful:** threatening evil; sinister.

He held his head in his hand up high before him,
Addressing the face to the dearest of all on the dais;
170 And the eyelids lifted wide, and the eyes looked out,
And the mouth said just this much, as you may now hear:
"Look that you go, Sir Gawain, as good as your word,
And seek till you find me, as loyally, my friend,
As you've sworn in this hall to do, in the hearing of the knights.
175 Come to the Green Chapel, I charge you, and take
A stroke the same as you've given, for well you deserve
To be readily requited on New Year's morn.
Many men know me, the Knight of the Green Chapel;
Therefore if you seek to find me, you shall not fail.
180 Come or be counted a coward, as is fitting."
Then with a rough jerk he turned the reins
And haled away through the hall-door, his head in his hand,
And fire of the flint flew out from the hooves of the foal.
To what kingdom he was carried no man there knew,
185 No more than they knew what country it was he came from.
What then?
The King and Gawain there
Laugh at the thing and grin;
And yet, it was an affair
Most marvelous to men. 🤚 **PAUSE & REFLECT**

🤚 **PAUSE & REFLECT**

Reread lines 186–189. What can you infer about Arthur's and Gawain's reaction to their encounter with the Green Knight? *MAKE INFERENCES*

_____

_____

_____

_____

FOCUS
In the next section, Gawain stops to rest at a castle on his way to meet the Green Knight. Read to find out about his experiences with the lady of the castle.

As the end of the year approaches, Gawain leaves on his quest to find the Green Chapel and fulfill his pledge. After riding through wild country and encountering many dangers, he comes upon a splendid castle. The lord of the castle welcomes Gawain and invites him to stay with him and his lady for a few days.

The lord proposes that he will go out to hunt each day while Gawain stays at the castle. At the end of the day, they will exchange what they have won. While the lord is out hunting, the lady attempts to seduce Gawain. Gawain resists her, however, and on the first two days accepts only kisses, which he gives to the lord at the end of each day in exchange for what the lord has gained in the hunt. On the third day Gawain continues to resist the lady, but she presses him to accept another gift.

190 She held toward him a ring of the yellowest gold
And, standing aloft on the band, a stone like a star

Why does Gawain refuse to accept gifts from the lady until her husband has "granted him some end to his adventure"?

(A) He feels that the gifts she offers are too expensive.

(B) He has promised her husband not to accept any gifts.

(C) He doesn't want to deceive her husband about the gift.

(D) He wants to avoid being in debt to the lady.

TIP On some test questions, the answer is not stated directly in the text. You will have to **infer the answer** by combining clues from the text with your own knowledge. To help you answer this question, underline information about the agreement between Gawain and the lord of the castle in the summaries at the beginning of this section. ✐

Then decide which answer choice makes the most sense.

From which flew splendid beams like the light of the sun;
And mark you well, it was worth a rich king's ransom.
But right away he refused it, replying in haste,
195 "My lady gay, I can hardly take gifts at the moment;
Having nothing to give, I'd be wrong to take gifts in turn."
She implored[27] him again, still more earnestly, but again
He refused it and swore on his knighthood that he could take nothing.
Grieved that he still would not take it, she told him then:
200 "If taking my ring would be wrong on account of its worth,
And being so much in my debt would be bothersome to you,
I'll give you merely this sash that's of slighter value."
She swiftly unfastened the sash that encircled her waist,
Tied around her fair tunic, inside her bright mantle;[28]
205 It was made of green silk and was marked of gleaming gold
Embroidered along the edges, ingeniously stitched.
This too she held out to the knight, and she earnestly begged him
To take it, trifling as it was, to remember her by.
But again he said no, there was nothing at all he could take,
210 Neither treasure nor token, until such time as the Lord
Had granted him some end to his adventure.
"And therefore, I pray you, do not be displeased,
But give up, for I cannot grant it, however fair
        or right.
    I know your worth and price,
215   And my debt's by no means slight;
    I swear through fire and ice
    To be your humble knight." ◀

"Do you lay aside this silk," said the lady then,
"Because it seems unworthy—as well it may?
220 Listen. Little as it is, it seems less in value,
But he who knew what charms are woven within it
Might place a better price on it, perchance.
For the man who goes to battle in this green lace,
As long as he keeps it looped around him,
225 No man under Heaven can hurt him, whoever may try,
For nothing on earth, however uncanny, can kill him."
The knight cast about in distress, and it came to his heart

---

27. **implored:** begged.
28. **tunic . . . mantle:** shirtlike garment worn under a sleeveless cloak.

This might be a treasure indeed when the time came to take
The blow he had bargained to suffer beside the Green Chapel.
230 If the gift meant remaining alive, it might well be worth it;
So he listened in silence and suffered the lady to speak,
And she pressed the sash upon him and begged him to take it,
And Gawain did, and she gave him the gift with great pleasure
And begged him, for her sake, to say not a word,
235 And to keep it hidden from her lord. And he said he would,
That except for themselves, this business would never be known
          to a man.
      He thanked her earnestly,
      And boldly his heart now ran;
      And now a third time she
240   Leaned down and kissed her man.

*When the lord returns at the end of the third day, Gawain gives him a kiss but
does not reveal the gift of the sash.* ✋ **PAUSE & REFLECT**

*On New Year's Day Gawain must go to meet the Green Knight. Wearing the
green sash, he sets out before dawn. Gawain arrives at a wild, rugged place,
where he sees no chapel but hears the sound of a blade being sharpened. Gawain
calls out, and the Green Knight appears with a huge ax. The Green Knight
greets Gawain, who, with pounding heart, bows his head to take his blow.*

Quickly then the man in the green made ready,
Grabbed up his keen-ground ax to strike Sir Gawain;
With all the might in his body he bore it aloft
And sharply brought it down as if to slay him;
245 Had he made it fall with the force he first intended
He would have stretched out the strongest man on earth.
But Sir Gawain cast a side glance at the ax
As it glided down to give him his Kingdom Come,[29]
And his shoulders jerked away from the iron a little,
250 And the Green Knight caught the handle, holding it back,
And mocked the prince with many a proud reproof:
"*You* can't be Gawain," he said, "who's thought so good,
A man who's never been daunted on hill or dale!

---

29. **his Kingdom Come:** his death and entry into the afterlife; a reference to the
sentence "Thy kingdom come" in the Lord's Prayer.

1. How do Gawain's actions
on the third day differ from
his actions on the previous
two days? *COMPARE AND
CONTRAST*

_____

_____

_____

2. What is your opinion of
Gawain's decision to accept
the sash from the lady?
MAKE JUDGMENTS

_____

_____

FOCUS
In this section, Gawain has
found the Green Knight and
is ready to receive a blow
from his ax. Read to find out
what happens to him.

For look how you flinch for fear before anything's felt!
255   I never heard tell that Sir Gawain was ever a coward!
I never moved a muscle when *you* came down;
In Arthur's hall I never so much as winced.
My head fell off at my feet, yet I never flickered;
But you! You tremble at heart before you're touched!
260   I'm bound to be called a better man than you, then,
                    my lord."[30]
          Said Gawain, "I shied once:
          No more. You have my word.
          But if my head falls to the stones
          It cannot be restored.

265   "But be brisk, man, by your faith, and come to the point!
Deal out my doom if you can, and do it at once,
For I'll stand for one good stroke, and I'll start no more
Until your ax has hit—and that I swear."
"Here goes, then," said the other, and heaves it aloft
270   And stands there waiting, scowling like a madman;
He swings down sharp, then suddenly stops again,
Holds back the ax with his hand before it can hurt,
And Gawain stands there stirring not even a nerve;
He stood there still as a stone or the stock of a tree
275   That's wedged in rocky ground by a hundred roots.
O, merrily then he spoke, the man in green:
"Good! You've got your heart back! Now I can hit you.
May all that glory the good King Arthur gave you
Prove efficacious now—if it ever can—
280   And save your neck." In rage Sir Gawain shouted,
"*Hit* me, hero! I'm right up to here with your threats!
Is it *you* that's the cringing coward after all?" ◀
"Whoo!" said the man in green, "he's wrathful, too!
No pauses, then; I'll pay up my pledge at once,
                    I vow!"
285   He takes his stride to strike
          And lifts his lip and brow;
          It's not a thing Gawain can like,
          For nothing can save him now!

MAKE INFERENCES

Reread lines 265–282. Why has
Gawain become angry?

_____

_____

_____

_____

_____

_____

---

30. The Green Knight has proclaimed himself a better man than Gawain.

He raises that ax up lightly and flashes it down,
290 And that blinding bit bites in at the knight's bare neck—
But hard as he hammered it down, it hurt him no more
Than to nick the nape of his neck, so it split the skin;
The sharp blade slit to the flesh through the shiny hide,
And red blood shot to his shoulders and spattered the ground.
295 And when Gawain saw his blood where it blinked in the snow
He sprang from the man with a leap to the length of a spear;
He snatched up his helmet swiftly and slapped it on,
Shifted his shield into place with a jerk of his shoulders,
And snapped his sword out faster than sight; said boldly—
300 And, mortal born of his mother that he was,
There was never on earth a man so happy by half—
"No more strokes, my friend; you've had your swing!
I've stood one swipe of your ax without resistance;
If you offer me any more, I'll repay you at once
305 With all the force and fire I've got—as you
          will see.
     I take one stroke, that's all,
     For that was the compact³¹ we
     Arranged in Arthur's hall;
     But now, no more for me!"  **PAUSE & REFLECT**

PAUSE & REFLECT

Do you think that the Green Knight intended to give Gawain only a slight injury, or was his aim off? Explain. *DRAW CONCLUSIONS*

310 The Green Knight remained where he stood, relaxing on his ax—
Settled the shaft on the rocks and leaned on the sharp end—
And studied the young man standing there, shoulders hunched,
And considered that staunch and doughty³² stance he took,
Undaunted yet, and in his heart he liked it;
315 And then he said merrily, with a mighty voice—
With a roar like rushing wind he reproved the knight—
"Here, don't be such an ogre on your ground!
Nobody here has behaved with bad manners toward you
Or done a thing except as the contract said.
320 I owed you a stroke, and I've struck; consider yourself
Well paid. And now I release you from all further duties.
If I'd cared to hustle, it may be, perchance, that I might

FOCUS
In this final section, the Green Knight explains how he tested Gawain. As you read, notice Gawain's reaction.

---

31. **compact**: binding agreement.
32. **staunch**: firm; **doughty** (dou'tē): brave.

Have hit somewhat harder, and then you might well be cross!
The first time I lifted my ax it was lighthearted sport,
325 I merely feinted[33] and made no mark, as was right,
For you kept our pact of the first night with honor
And abided by your word and held yourself true to me,
Giving me all you owed as a good man should.
I feinted a second time, friend, for the morning
330 You kissed my pretty wife twice and returned me the kisses;
And so for the first two days, mere feints, nothing more
                        severe.
        A man who's true to his word,
        There's nothing he needs to fear;
        You failed me, though, on the third
335   Exchange, so I've tapped you here.

"That sash you wear by your scabbard[34] belongs to me;
My own wife gave it to you, as I ought to know.
I know, too, of your kisses and all your words
And my wife's advances, for I myself arranged them.
340 It was I who sent her to test you. I'm convinced
You're the finest man that ever walked this earth.
As a pearl is of greater price than dry white peas,
So Gawain indeed stands out above all other knights.
But you lacked a little, sir; you were less than loyal;
345 But since it was not for the sash itself or for lust
But because you loved your life, I blame you less." ◄

Sir Gawain stood in a study a long, long while,
So miserable with disgrace that he wept within,
And all the blood of his chest went up to his face
350 And he shrank away in shame from the man's gentle words.
The first words Gawain could find to say were these:
"Cursed be cowardice and covetousness both,
Villainy and vice that destroy all virtue!"
He caught at the knots of the girdle[35] and loosened them
355 And fiercely flung the sash at the Green Knight.

---

33. **feinted** (fān'tĭd): pretended to attack.
34. **scabbard** (skăb'ərd): a sheath for a dagger or sword.
35. **girdle**: sash.

"There, there's my fault! The foul fiend vex[36] it!
Foolish cowardice taught me, from fear of your stroke,
To bargain, covetous, and abandon my kind,
The selflessness and loyalty suitable in knights;
360 Here I stand, faulty and false, much as I've feared them,
Both of them, untruth and treachery; may they see sorrow
           and care!
     I can't deny my guilt;
     My works shine none too fair!
     Give me your good will
365 And henceforth I'll beware." ▶

At that, the Green Knight laughed, saying graciously,
"Whatever harm I've had, I hold it amended
Since now you're confessed so clean, acknowledging sins
And bearing the plain penance[37] of my point;[38]
370 I consider you polished as white and as perfectly clean
As if you had never fallen since first you were born.[39]
And I give you, sir, this gold-embroidered girdle,
For the cloth is as green as my gown. Sir Gawain, think
On this when you go forth among great princes;
375 Remember our struggle here; recall to your mind
This rich token. Remember the Green Chapel.
And now, come on, let's both go back to my castle
And finish the New Year's revels with feasting and joy,
           not strife,
     I beg you," said the lord,
380 And said, "As for my wife,
     She'll be your friend, no more
     A threat against your life."

"No, sir," said the knight, and seized his helmet
And quickly removed it, thanking the Green Knight,
385 "I've reveled too well already; but fortune be with you;
May He who gives all honors honor you well." . . .

MAKE INFERENCES

What does Gawain's response to the Green Knight suggest about his character?

_____

_____

_____

_____

---

36. **vex:** harass; torment.
37. **penance:** punishment accepted by a person to show sorrow for wrongdoing.
38. **point:** blade.
39. The Green Knight is saying that Gawain has paid for his fault by admitting it and offering his head to the ax.

PAUSE & REFLECT

Did you find the outcome of the **medieval romance** satisfying? Why or why not? *EVALUATE*

_____

_____

_____

_____

Big Question ?

Look back at the word web you created on page 41. Which of the ideals you listed are most important to Gawain? Explain your answer.

_____

_____

_____

_____

And so they embraced and kissed and commended each other
To the Prince of Paradise, and parted then
    in the cold;
 Sir Gawain turned again
390 To Camelot and his lord;
 And as for the man of green,
 He went wherever he would. **PAUSE & REFLECT**

Reading Comprehension

DIRECTIONS *Answer these questions about* Sir Gawain and the Green Knight *by filling in the correct ovals.*

1. The Green Knight comes to Camelot because he wants to

   Ⓐ seize the throne from King Arthur

   Ⓑ test the reputation of Arthur and his knights

   Ⓒ fight a duel with King Arthur

   Ⓓ get revenge against his wife's lover

2. What is the "Christmas game" the Green Knight refers to in line 63?

   Ⓐ riding on his green horse

   Ⓑ keeping his identity a secret

   Ⓒ an exchange of gifts

   Ⓓ an exchange of blows with an ax

3. Why does Gawain volunteer to take on the Green Knight's challenge?

   Ⓐ He thinks Arthur is too important for the task.

   Ⓑ He has a long-standing grudge against the Green Knight.

   Ⓒ He wants to impress Queen Guinevere.

   Ⓓ He thinks he is the only one who can defeat the Green Knight.

4. Why does Gawain accept the sash from the lady of the castle?

   Ⓐ He needs to prove his love for her.

   Ⓑ She says that it will protect him.

   Ⓒ Her husband asked her to offer it.

   Ⓓ He wants a souvenir of his travels.

5. Which characteristic of medieval romance is reflected in lines 336–340?

   Ⓐ hero motivated by honor

   Ⓑ idealized characters

   Ⓒ exotic setting

   Ⓓ hidden identify

6. The Green Knight cut Gawain's neck on his third swing because Gawain

   Ⓐ boasted about King Arthur's greatness

   Ⓑ seduced the Green Knight's wife

   Ⓒ kept the gift of the sash a secret

   Ⓓ made insulting remarks about the Green Knight

7. Which word *best* describes Gawain's reaction when the Green Knight reveals why he cut his neck?

   Ⓐ shame   Ⓒ fear

   Ⓑ anger   Ⓓ confusion

8. Reread lines 377–388. Why does Gawain turn down the Green Knight's offer to come back to his castle?

   Ⓐ He promised Arthur to return home quickly.

   Ⓑ He is still ashamed of his own behavior.

   Ⓒ He fears another trick from the Green Knight.

   Ⓓ He is angry with the Green Knight.

For help, use the **Test-Taker's Toolkit** below.

Responding in Writing

9. Short Response What message does *Sir Gawain and the Green Knight* convey about the ideals of chivalry? Write a paragraph analyzing the way chivalry is portrayed in this medieval romance.

_____

_____

_____

_____

_____

_____

_____

TEST-TAKER'S TOOLKIT

⊗ **GRAPHIC ORGANIZER** Use the chart below to help you plan your response. Look back at the romance to help you remember details about how well Gawain lives up to the code of behavior known as chivalry.

	Element of Chivalry	Gawain's Actions
Bravery		
Modesty		
Courtesy		
Loyalty		
Honesty		

What's the Connection?

Sir Gawain was one of the greatest knights of the Round Table. The legends of King Arthur and his knights were inspired by the practices of real warriors during the Middle Ages. In the online article "Knights in the Middle Ages," you will read about the training and arming of knights.

ASK QUESTIONS As you read the article, turn the title and each section heading into a question and write it in the first column of the notetaking chart. After you finish each section, answer the question in the second column.

Related Nonfiction

Knights in the Middle Ages
ONLINE ARTICLE

Use with Sir Gawain and the Green Knight, *p. 40*

Question	Answer
What was a knight in the Middle Ages?	

LEARN THE SKILL: SUMMARIZE

When you **summarize** a nonfiction text, you briefly restate the text's main ideas and important information. Summarizing can help you understand and remember what you read. When you summarize, you should

- present ideas and information in the same order in which they appear in the text
- leave out examples and details that are not essential for understanding the writer's key points

For more on summarizing, see the Nonfiction Skills Handbook beginning on page R2.

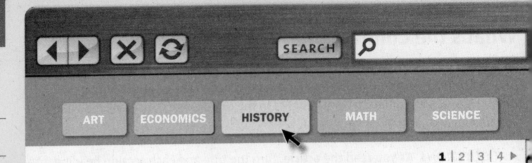

ART   ECONOMICS   **HISTORY**   MATH   SCIENCE

SEARCH 🔍

1 | 2 | 3 | 4 ▶

KNIGHTS IN THE MIDDLE AGES

Knighthoods are now handed out as titles of honor. You might even hear about rock musicians or movie stars being knighted. But during the Middle Ages, the only people eligible to become knights were highly trained soldiers who rode on horseback and wore armor. They formed a separate social class with distinct customs and values.

Knights had to provide their own equipment, which was very expensive. A knight needed several warhorses that were
10 specially bred to carry the weight of an armored rider. Each horse was worth more than ten times the price of an ordinary horse. Armor and weapons were also costly. Even the horses required armor to protect them in battle.

In return for military service, some knights were granted fiefs from their feudal lords. Others held no land but received payment for service. Knights also profited
20 by ransacking conquered cities and by ransoming knights they captured. As knights grew wealthier and more settled on their estates, they began to pay "shield money" to avoid serving in the king's army. Kings used these funds to hire mercenary fighters. ◀

SPECIALIZED

Vocabulary

The word _fief_ in line 17 is related to the word _feudalism_, which refers to the medieval social system that governed relations between a lord and his subordinates. Underline context clues in lines 16–26 that help you figure out the meaning of _fief_. ✏

SEARCH 🔍

THE PATH TO KNIGHTHOOD

A knight's training began at age seven or eight, when he was sent to the castle of a lord. As a
30 page, he performed simple household chores. In addition, he started learning how to ride horses and handle a sword.

The boy became a squire in his early teens and was apprenticed to a knight. He served the knight at table, looked after his horses and equipment, and helped him into his armor before tournaments and battles. While providing these services, the squire developed skills he would need as a warrior.
40 Learning how to fight with swords and other weapons was difficult enough, but then he had to practice these skills while wearing armor. Finally, he mastered them on horseback. As he grew older, he would take part in battles.

Because a knight's equipment was so heavy, it was especially important for squires to build up strength and endurance. But not all of their training was physical. They also learned the values of knighthood and the good manners that would be required at court.

Most squires, if they could afford it, became knights when they were about 20 years old. Sometimes a squire might be given the title of knight right on
50 the battlefield as a reward for bravery. But more often, squires received a full dubbing ceremony after their training was completed.

The day before the ceremony, the squire fasted and took a ritual bath. He spent the evening in church, where he heard a sermon on the responsibilities of knighthood. The next morning, he was dressed in symbolic clothing, such as a white robe to symbolize cleanliness and a red cloak to symbolize the willingness to shed his own blood.

In the ceremony, he kneeled down and took an oath to serve his lord and uphold a strict code of conduct. Then a knight or lord dubbed him by tapping him lightly on the shoulders with the flat side of a sword. This ritual, called
60 an accolade, signaled that the squire was now a knight. Attendants helped him put on his armor, and he was given a sword and gold spurs, which only knights were allowed to wear. From that point on, the knight would be addressed as "Sir."

After the ceremony, the new knight handed out gifts, and there was a celebration that included a feast. The next day a tournament was usually held

SUMMARIZE

What training was required before a squire could become a knight?

_____

_____

_____

_____

_____

_____

in honor of the new knight so that he and the other knights of the castle could demonstrate their skills.

THE CODE OF CHIVALRY

During his dubbing ceremony, a knight committed himself to uphold the ideals
70 of chivalry. The young man promised to be honest and loyal, to treat women courteously and protect them from harm, to go to mass every day, and to fast on Fridays in memory of Jesus Christ. Knights were also supposed to be brave, modest, and merciful.

Though knights often made great sacrifices in the name of chivalry, they tended to behave brutally while waging war. They might spare the lives of enemy knights who could be ransomed, but they seldom showed any mercy to soldiers beneath their class. And if they were courteous toward noble ladies, they could abuse peasant women with impunity.

Mercenary knights were especially feared because they had no estates and
80 no loyalty to a particular region. When they were laid off during times of peace, they sometimes banded together and went on looting sprees, leaving behind a trail of death and destruction. ◀

THE TOOLS OF A KNIGHT

The earliest form of body armor was chain mail, which consisted of thousands of small rings linked together to form a metal fabric. A full suit of chain mail weighed 30–50 pounds, and all of this weight hung directly from the shoulders. Knights wore padded cloth garments under the mail to help cushion blows. Chain mail gave knights a great advantage in battle, but the armor could be pierced by a lance or arrows launched from powerful longbows or crossbows.
90 Knights also wore metal helmets and carried shields.

In the 14th century, knights began to wear steel plates for greater protection. At first the plates only covered the chest and shoulders. But by the 15th century, full suits of plate armor were common. Plate armor could be even heavier than chain mail, although the weight was more evenly distributed across the body. Heat buildup was also a big problem. However, the armor was nearly indestructible. ◀

In addition to armor, a knight relied on his weapons to succeed in battle. The two main weapons of the medieval knight were the sword and the lance, a long thrusting spear. Stirrups allowed a knight to stay in his saddle as he charged
100 into an opponent with the full impact of his galloping horse. Knights also fought with daggers, axes, and clubs.

By the 16th century, knights had become obsolete on the battlefield due

---

CLARIFY

Reread lines 69–82. In what ways did knights often fail to live up to the ideals of chivalry?

_____

_____

_____

_____

SUMMARIZE

What developments in body armor occurred during the Middle Ages?

_____

_____

_____

_____

to improved military tactics and the development of firearms. Yet some of the most beautiful armor dates from the late Middle Ages, when noblemen would display heavily decorated armor as a sign of wealth and prestige.

SHOWING OFF IN TOURNAMENTS

Tournaments were events in which knights demonstrated their fighting skills before an audience. They could last as long as a week and involve several thousand knights.

110   The highlight of a tournament was the jousting competition. Two knights would gallop on horseback toward each other at top speed, each attempting to knock the opponent off his horse with a lance. Teams of knights also participated in competitions called melees.

In the early Middle Ages, tournaments were especially chaotic and violent. Eventually, measures were taken to help prevent knights from getting badly injured or killed. Knights wore special tournament armor with extra padding underneath. Lances and swords were blunted. Umpires watched the combat to enforce rules. But even with these safeguards, many knights were injured and died while participating in tournaments.

120   A successful competitor could win prizes and fame. By the end of the Middle Ages, the contests resembled modern-day rodeos. There were tournament stars who toured the circuit. People who came to see them perform could look forward to a festival, complete with dancing, singing, and feasting. ▶

TESTSMART

Which statement is *not* true of medieval tournaments?

Ⓐ Knights sometimes fought in teams.

Ⓑ Rules of competition were enforced by umpires.

Ⓒ Knights tried to knock each other off their horses.

Ⓓ The contests eventually became safe.

TIP Sometimes a question will require you to choose an answer that contradicts information in a selection. **Use the process of elimination** to choose the right answer. In this case, reread lines 107–124. If you find an answer choice that accurately describes information in this passage, you can eliminate it from the list of possible correct answers. Keep in mind that the answer choices may not be worded exactly the same as statements in the selection.

Reading Comprehension

DIRECTIONS *Answer these questions about the two selections in this lesson by filling in the correct ovals.*

1. Why did someone need to be well off to become a knight?

   (A) Knights had to pay large fees for their dubbing ceremonies.

   (B) The expense of training a knight was very high.

   (C) Knights provided their own horses, armor, and weapons.

   (D) Kings demanded "shield money" from knights.

2. Which of the following is *not* true of squires?

   (A) They helped knights put on armor.

   (B) They received land for their military service.

   (C) They practiced fighting on horseback.

   (D) They were taught good manners.

3. What was the most important reason why knights needed to own horses?

   (A) They used horses in their dubbing ceremonies.

   (B) Horses were associated with valor.

   (C) Their armor was too heavy for them to walk far in.

   (D) Tournament audiences were impressed by horses.

4. What brought an end to the dominance of knights as warriors?

   (A) the development of firearms

   (B) improvements in plate armor

   (C) the invention of stirrups

   (D) safety measures in tournaments

5. Which statement is supported by both selections?

   (A) Knights were allowed to plunder cities they captured.

   (B) Knights did not always live up to their ideals.

   (C) Knights had to be strong enough to carry heavy armor and weapons.

   (D) Knights sought to impress women at tournaments.

6. Which detail from "Knights in the Middle Ages" is most relevant to the outcome of *Sir Gawain and the Green Knight*?

   (A) Knights were supposed to be courteous to women.

   (B) By the 16th century, knights had become obsolete.

   (C) Tournaments could make knights famous.

   (D) Knights vowed to be honest and loyal.

7. From its context in lines 19–21, you can tell that the word *ransacking* means

   (A) plundering   (C) fleeing

   (B) covering with cloth   (D) governing

8. The word *mercenary* is used in line 25 to describe

   (A) people who lack mercy

   (B) sons rejected by their families

   (C) disloyal soldiers

   (D) soldiers who only fight for money

Timed Writing Practice

PROMPT

Chivalry may be dead, as the saying goes, but the world of medieval knighthood is still a popular subject for fiction. Write a short story about a knight who faces an important challenge. The knight can be a famous hero such as Gawain or a new character you create, such as a young person training to become a knight. Use details from both selections to help you portray the story's setting and characters.

BUDGET YOUR TIME

You have **45 minutes** to respond. Decide how much time to spend on each step.

Analyze _____

Plan _____

Write _____

Review _____

TEST-TAKER'S TOOLKIT

1. ANALYZE THE PROMPT

A. Identify the type of writing you are asked to do.

B. Circle key words that indicate the topic of your writing. One phrase has been circled for you.

C. Restate the prompt in your own words on the lines to the right.

I am being asked to _____

_____

_____

_____

_____

2. PLAN YOUR RESPONSE

A. **Make notes** Think about interesting characters, settings (such as a castle or a forest), plots, and conflicts. Write down whatever comes into your mind. Circle the ideas that interest you the most.

B. **Organize your information** Fill out this chart to help you organize your ideas.

Characters
Setting
Main Conflict

3. WRITE AND REVIEW

A. Make sure that you provide clues at the beginning of the story to let readers know that your story is set in the Middle Ages. For example, you might include sensory details to create a vivid description of a knight's armor.

B. Be sure to leave time to check your spelling and grammar.

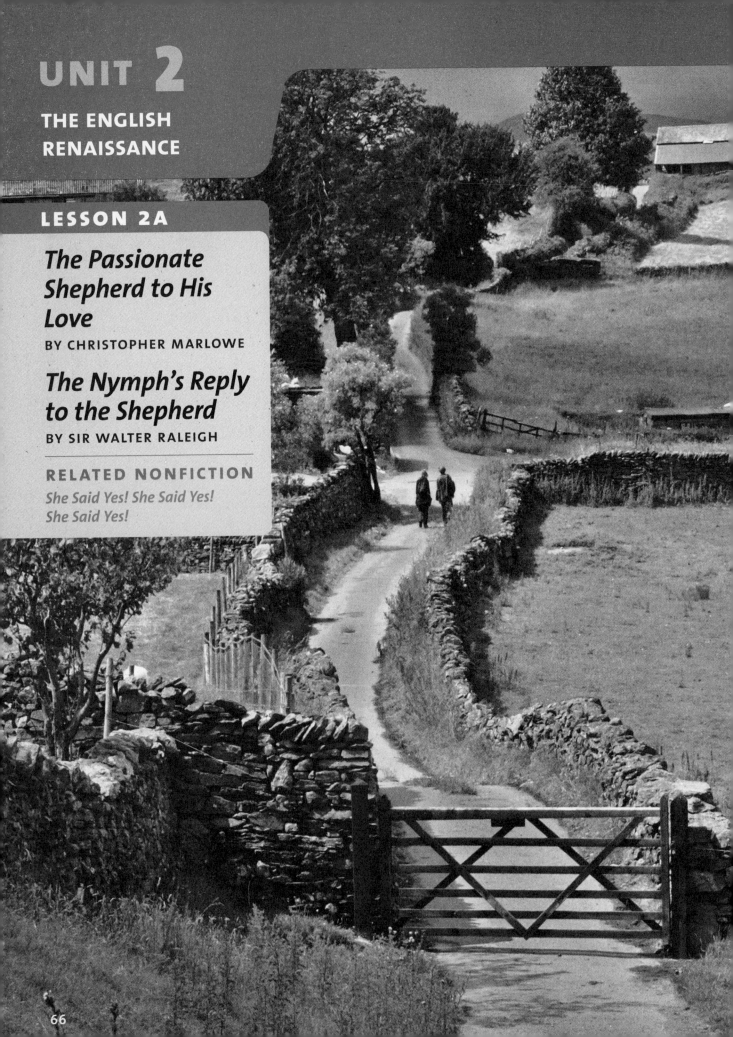

UNIT 2

THE ENGLISH RENAISSANCE

LESSON 2A

The Passionate Shepherd to His Love
BY CHRISTOPHER MARLOWE

The Nymph's Reply to the Shepherd
BY SIR WALTER RALEIGH

RELATED NONFICTION
She Said Yes! She Said Yes! She Said Yes!

Is PASSION *overrated?*

Throughout the ages, writers have composed poems and songs describing the passion of new love. But have people placed too much emphasis on intensely romantic love? Are other aspects of love more important?

LIST IT Which of the qualities listed here are most important for love to thrive? Which ones do you value less? Number the list of qualities from 1 to 10, with 1 being the most important and 10 being the least. Then share reasons for your opinions with a partner.

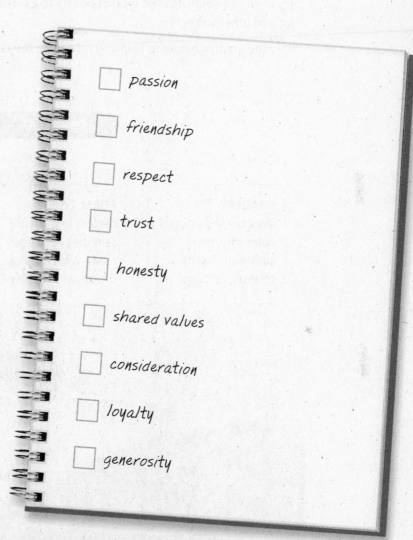

☐ passion

☐ friendship

☐ respect

☐ trust

☐ honesty

☐ shared values

☐ consideration

☐ loyalty

☐ generosity

ASSESSMENT GOALS

By the end of this lesson, you will be able to . . .

• analyze the characteristics of pastoral poetry

• use active reading strategies to comprehend text

• determine author's purpose in a nonfiction text

• analyze a writing prompt and plan an opinion essay

Pastoral

A **PASTORAL** is a poem that presents shepherds in idealized rural settings. Pastorals were very popular during the English Renaissance. Poets like Marlowe and Raleigh did not write pastorals to show how people in the country really lived and spoke. Instead, they used this sophisticated type of poetry to express their feelings and thoughts about love and other subjects.

Study the graphic below to help you recognize the characteristics of pastoral poetry.

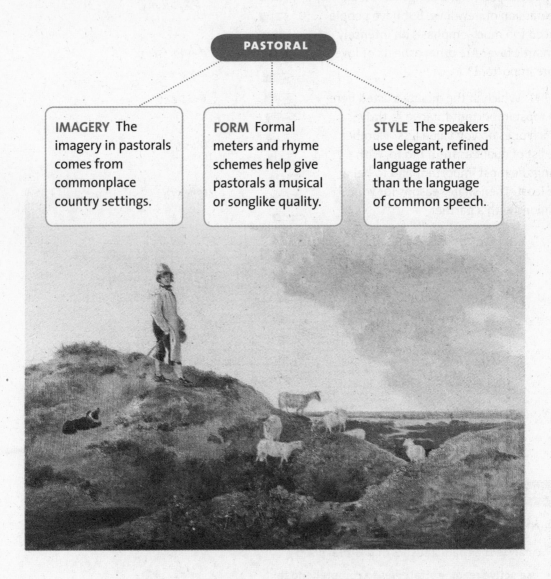

PASTORAL

IMAGERY The imagery in pastorals comes from commonplace country settings.

FORM Formal meters and rhyme schemes help give pastorals a musical or songlike quality.

STYLE The speakers use elegant, refined language rather than the language of common speech.

The Passionate Shepherd to His Love

Christopher Marlowe

MARK IT UP

Use these marks to monitor your reading:

* This is important.

? I don't understand.

! This is a surprise.

When you see this pencil ✐, you'll be asked to mark up the text. You can also write in this book in any way you find useful.

BACKGROUND Christopher Marlowe is best known as a playwright, but he also distinguished himself as a poet. His poem "The Passionate Shepherd to His Love" was so popular that it inspired responses in verse, including Sir Walter Raleigh's "The Nymph's Reply to the Shepherd." The two poems present sharply contrasting views on love.

Come live with me and be my love,
And we will all the pleasures prove[1]
That valleys, groves, hills, and fields,
Woods, or steepy mountain yields.

5 And we will sit upon the rocks,
Seeing the shepherds feed their flocks,
By shallow rivers to whose falls
Melodious birds sing madrigals.[2] ▶

And I will make thee beds of roses
10 And a thousand fragrant posies,
A cap of flowers, and a kirtle[3]
Embroidered all with leaves of myrtle;

VISUALIZE

Underline words and phrases in the boxed text that help you picture the rural setting of the poem. ✐

---

1. **prove:** experience.
2. **madrigals:** songs of a type popular during the Renaissance.
3. **kirtle:** skirt or dress.

The shepherd's vision of the future with his love can *best* be described as

Ⓐ pragmatic

Ⓑ idealized

Ⓒ materialistic

Ⓓ deceptive

TIP When you are asked to select the *best* option from a number of choices, you need to use clues from the text and your own knowledge to **make inferences** or **draw conclusions.** In this case, underline promises that the speaker makes and look for a pattern among them. Then decide which of the answers best characterizes this pattern.

A gown made of the finest wool
Which from our pretty lambs we pull;
15 Fair lined slippers for the cold,
With buckles of the purest gold;

A belt of straw and ivy buds,
With coral clasps and amber studs:
And if these pleasures may thee move,
20 Come live with me, and be my love.

The shepherds' swains⁴ shall dance and sing
For thy delight each May morning:
If these delights thy mind may move,
Then live with me and be my love. ◀

4. **swains:** country youths.

The Nymph's Reply to the Shepherd

Sir Walter Raleigh

If all the world and love were young,
And truth in every shepherd's tongue,
These pretty pleasures might me move
To live with thee and be thy love. ▶

5   Time drives the flocks from field to fold[1]
When rivers rage and rocks grow cold,
And Philomel[2] becometh dumb;[3]
The rest complains of cares to come.

The flowers do fade, and wanton[4] fields
10 To wayward winter reckoning yields;
A honey tongue, a heart of gall,
Is fancy's spring, but sorrow's fall. ▶

Thy gowns, thy shoes, thy beds of roses,
Thy cap, thy kirtle, and thy posies
15 Soon break, soon wither, soon forgotten—
In folly ripe, in reason rotten.

Thy belt of straw and ivy buds,
Thy coral clasps and amber studs,
All these in me no means can move
20 To come to thee and be thy love.

---

1. **fold:** a pen for animals, especially sheep.
2. **Philomel:** the nightingale.
3. **dumb:** silent.
4. **wanton:** here, producing abundant crops; luxuriant.

CLARIFY

Reread the boxed text. In your own words, restate what the nymph is saying to the shepherd.

_____

_____

_____

_____

MAKE INFERENCES

What concern does the nymph express in lines 11–12 about how she would eventually feel if she accepted the shepherd's proposal?

_____

_____

_____

_____

But could youth last and love still breed,
Had joys no date[5] nor age no need,
Then these delights my mind might move
To live with thee and be thy love. PAUSE & REFLECT

PAUSE & REFLECT

Underline the references
in Raleigh's poem to the
promises that the speaker
makes in Marlowe's poem.

What message does Raleigh
convey through these
references? CLARIFY

_____

_____

_____

_____

_____

5. **date:** ending.

Reading Comprehension

DIRECTIONS *Answer these questions about the poems by filling in the correct ovals.*

1. What will the speaker of "The Passionate Shepherd to His Love" seek in the different places he describes in lines 2–4?

   Ⓐ a woman who loves him

   Ⓑ a location to build a home

   Ⓒ grazing areas for his sheep

   Ⓓ different types of pleasure

2. The clothes that the shepherd describes in lines 11–14 of "The Passionate Shepherd to His Love" are

   Ⓐ made from materials found in the country

   Ⓑ expensive and fashionable

   Ⓒ practical clothes for herding

   Ⓓ made to last a lifetime

3. Which detail in "The Passionate Shepherd to His Love" is the *best* example of how nature is idealized in the pastoral form?

   Ⓐ beds made from roses

   Ⓑ a belt of straw and ivy buds

   Ⓒ melodious birds singing madrigals

   Ⓓ swains dancing and singing

4. What does the speaker of "The Passionate Shepherd to His Love" suggest will happen if his love comes to live with him?

   Ⓐ They will have great wealth.

   Ⓑ All of their needs will be taken care of.

   Ⓒ They will need to work hard.

   Ⓓ He will always be faithful to her.

5. In lines 5–10 of "The Nymph's Reply to the Shepherd," the speaker is concerned about

   Ⓐ drowning in a river

   Ⓑ people complaining too much

   Ⓒ the change of seasons

   Ⓓ losing sheep over time

6. In "The Nymph's Reply to the Shepherd," the speaker says that the gifts the shepherd has promised are

   Ⓐ likely to break or wither

   Ⓑ too fancy for a country girl

   Ⓒ things she already owns

   Ⓓ not fashionable enough for her

7. The speaker of "The Nymph's Reply to the Shepherd" hints that the shepherd

   Ⓐ is simple-minded

   Ⓑ needs to work harder

   Ⓒ might try to deceive her

   Ⓓ has grown too old

8. At the end of "The Nymph's Reply to the Shepherd," the speaker

   Ⓐ decides that she loves the shepherd after all

   Ⓑ renounces all hope of love and happiness

   Ⓒ finds another man to move in with

   Ⓓ explains what it would take to change her mind

GO ON ➡

Responding in Writing

9. Short Response Write a paragraph **comparing and contrasting** the views of love and life expressed in "The Passionate Shepherd to His Love" and "The Nymph's Reply to the Shepherd." Make sure to discuss Marlowe's and Raleigh's use of pastoral imagery.

_____

_____

_____

_____

_____

_____

For help, use the **Test-Taker's Toolkit** below.

TEST-TAKER'S TOOLKIT

GRAPHIC ORGANIZER Use the chart below to help you plan your response. Reread the poems to help you remember the details.

Pastoral Imagery Used to Convey Ideas	
Shepherd	**Nymph**
"Melodious birds sing madrigals" (line 8)	

What's the Connection?

Christopher Marlowe's "The Passionate Shepherd to His Love," a love poem in the form of a proposal, was so popular that it inspired responses from other poets, including Sir Walter Raleigh's "The Nymph's Reply to the Shepherd." In the *Smithsonian* magazine article "She Said Yes! She Said Yes! She Said Yes!," the author describes some contemporary marriage proposals that have also gotten a lot of attention.

WEB IT What's your idea of a romantic proposal? Use the word web below to describe where the proposal took place, how it was delivered, and why you consider it so romantic. You can describe a proposal you've heard about or imagine how you might propose to someone.

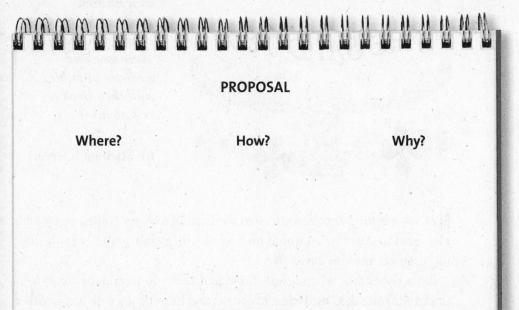

PROPOSAL

Where? How? Why?

Related Nonfiction

She Said Yes! She Said Yes! She Said Yes!
MAGAZINE ARTICLE

Use with "The Passionate Shepherd to His Love" and "The Nymph's Reply to the Shepherd," p. 66

LEARN THE SKILL: DETERMINE AUTHOR'S PURPOSE

An **author's purpose** is the reason why an author writes a particular piece. You can often figure out an author's purpose from clues such as the work's title and subject, its tone, and the author's choice of details and words. The most common purposes for writing are

- to explain or inform
- to persuade
- to entertain
- to express emotion and ideas

For more on author's purpose, see the Nonfiction Skills Handbook beginning on page R2.

SET A PURPOSE

_____

_____

_____

AUTHOR'S PURPOSE

Preview the title, the italicized introductory text, and the opening paragraph. What do these elements suggest about the purpose of the article? Give a reason for your answer.

_____

_____

_____

_____

_____

SPECIALIZED
Vocabulary

If the word _insouciance_ in line 13 is new to you, look for familiar word parts. Circle the prefix _in-_ and the suffix _–ance._ The root is from an Old French word that means "to trouble." ✏

Using these word parts as clues, what can you guess is the meaning of _insouciance_?

_____

_____

How a few brave and smitten souls got up the courage to declare their love and propose in public, and then lived to tell about it

by Michael Kernan

Not so very long ago, according to the cartoons of my youth, a guy who wanted to get married would hit his girl with a club, grab her by the hair and drag her into his cave. ◀

But a time came when it was discovered that you should _ask_ for a woman's hand. You asked her father, of course, and he put a price on her, whether in cattle, gold or debentures. Eventually what passes for enlightenment set in. Nowadays you can ask the girl herself. Or she can ask you.

Today, many amorous couples jump the gun, so to speak, draining a certain significance from a proposal. Perhaps as a result, an odd thing has
10 happened: the proposal has gone public.

This may be the influence of our advertising-besotted age and the possibility that we have to see something on TV in order to believe it. Or it may be that, beneath our hard insouciance, we are still romantics. In any case, Americans are popping the question on talk shows, on billboards and even on the concert stage. Love-struck males hire planes to fly banners over stadiums with messages like "Ethel, Will You Marry Me?" We broadcast our marital message at supermarkets, in airports and almost anywhere where there is a public to be impressed. ◀

Things have gotten to such a pass that one interested party down in
20 Texas has proposed the establishment of an official Proposal Day to occur twice a year at the equinoxes, thus symbolizing the equality of men and

women. It is aimed at the people who keep putting it off and putting it off. And there are a lot of them: baby boom women now in their 30s and 40s are roughly three times less likely to marry than were women that age a generation ago. ▶

Inevitably, a lot of ingenuity goes into proposals nowadays, even by those who don't make a public spectacle of themselves. Consider Neil Nathanson and Leslie Hamilton. They met in Palo Alto, California, where they had separate apartments in one of those wonderful old shin-
30 gled houses. Neil was studying law at Stanford. Leslie had just got her degree in city planning.

They soon discovered that they loved doing crosswords. On Sunday mornings they would hang out together working on the *San Francisco Examiner* puzzle. One Sunday Leslie noticed that many of the puzzle answers struck close to home. "State or quarterback" turned out to be MONTANA, which is where she came from. "Instrument" was CELLO, which she plays. There were references to weddings and marriage, and when she came to "Astronaut Armstrong," which could only be NEIL, she did a double take.

40 "I was about halfway through the puzzle," she remembers, "when I figured out that a string of letters running across the middle of the puzzle said 'DEAR—WILLYOU MARRYME NEIL.' The missing clue was 'Actress Caron.' I didn't know who that was, it could have been Lauren for all I knew, so I began on the Down clues. Sure enough, it was LESLIE."

She was stunned. She looked up, found him staring at her, and said, "Yes." What else?

It seems Neil had talked to Merl Reagle, the *Examiner* puzzle maker and a genius of sorts, and they had worked on the project for four months. Neil and Leslie have been married four years and now have a daughter.
50 What did the other puzzle solvers think? For them it was just a neat crossword on the theme of weddings.

Oh, and they invited Reagle to the wedding, in Great Falls, Montana. "I never did finish the puzzle," she says.

That proposal was relatively private, though attended by millions of readers. Sportscaster Ahmad Rashad proposed to *The Cosby Show* star Phylicia Ayers-Allen live on a pregame TV show. And not too long ago singer Anita Baker, during a Radio City Music Hall concert, handed the mike to a young man who had come up from the audience by prearrangement. In ringing, amplified tones he asked, "Mitzi, will you marry me?"
60 The audience gave the couple a standing ovation.

AUTHOR'S PURPOSE

Reread lines 19–25. The word *equinox* refers to the two times of the year when day and night are almost exactly the same length. What do you think was the author's main purpose in describing the plan for an official Proposal Day at the equinoxes? Explain your response.

_____

_____

_____

_____

But what if the girl says no?

Tony Ferrante of Richmond, Virginia, had this great idea: he would lure his friend, Kathryn Webber, to a mall at Christmastime and get her to sit on Santa's lap for a gag photograph. Then Santa would hand her the usual little gift, only the gift would turn out to be an engagement ring.

Unfortunately, Kathryn had just finished her college finals and was tired, hungry and cross. Tony finally persuaded her to see Santa, but the ring hadn't arrived yet. So Tony had to drag her around the mall 70 for another half-hour while a friend fetched the ring. At last Kathryn was sweet-talked into sitting on Santa's lap a second time. Santa gave her a tiny box.

Tony had to tell her to open it. She was so shaken that she couldn't give him an answer; they had never discussed marriage before. He thought he was a goner. But finally, seven hours later at dinner, she took pity on him. "I don't think I ever answered your question," she said. "Yes, I will." ◄

For Cal Ripken Jr., the great Orioles shortstop (soon-to-be third baseman), it began with an autograph.

80 One night in 1983 Joan Geer spotted the ballplayer with outfielder Al Bumbry at a restaurant. She asked him to autograph a napkin for her daughter Kelly. The gallant Ripken wrote, "If you look anything like your mother, I'm sorry I missed you."

Back home, presented with the trophy, Kelly Geer, a six-foot-tall blonde at the University of Maryland, said, "That's nice, Mom. But who is he?"

About two months later, Kelly and a friend happened to be in a restaurant where Cal was appearing for a promotion. The friend said, "Oh look, there's Cal Ripken."

90 Retorted Kelly, "You mean that guy there with 150 women around him?"

When Kelly finally got through to him, she said, "Thanks for being so nice to my mom."

"Ah," he said. "You must be Kelly."

Cal insists he is not good at names, but this one stuck. The ex-nonstop shortstop, who happens to be 6 feet 4, is a basketball fan, and remembered asking Mrs. Geer how tall her daughter was. As Kelly quipped later, "He wanted to be sure I was good material for producing basketball players."

100   Up to then she had always told people she was 5 feet 11 1/2.

They went out for lunch, and dated some more, and one thing led to another. On New Year's Eve he invited her to his house for dinner and afterward brought her out to the balcony.

"You have to see what's in my backyard," he told her.

There, spelled out in Christmas lights stuck through holes in a wooden plaque that he had made himself, she read the words, "Will you marry me?"

She said yes, and several months later, on a Friday the 13th, they were married at the United Methodist Church of Towson, Maryland. They
110 now have two children.

"He can be very romantic," Kelly says. . . .

We take you now to the Steel Valley School District in western Pennsylvania. Michael Bujdos, then a first-grade teacher at Barrett Elementary, called Jean Kabo, his high school sweetheart from Serra Catholic High in McKeesport. "Jean," he said, "I'm having some volunteers come in to read stories to the class. Would you like to help me out?"

Sure, she replied. When she got to the school, Michael said the kids had an art project they wanted to show her before she read the story. In
120 the classroom, first-graders were lined up at the blackboard with their hands behind them. She thought something was going on, because the kids were awfully serious. But giggling. While she stood there, more than somewhat bemused, Michael told the children, "All right, boys and girls. Show the lady what we made in art class."

At that, the children proudly held up sheets of paper that spelled the words, "Will You Marry Mr. B?"

"I sort of looked at it," she said recently from their home in Munhall, Pennsylvania. "I was in shock. It was really funny. I didn't notice a colleague of his videotaping the whole thing from the back of the room."
130 For a long moment everyone stood there, the kids watching her, mouths open, Michael holding his breath.

"And I said yes. And the kids loved it. And they were laughing and jumping up and down and shouting, 'She said yes! She said yes! She said yes!'" ▶

AUTHOR'S PURPOSE

Why might the author have chosen to end his article with the story of Michael Bujdos's proposal?

_____

_____

_____

_____

_____

_____

Reading Comprehension

DIRECTIONS *Answer these questions about the article and the poems in this lesson by filling in the correct ovals.*

1. What possible cause does the author give for the trend of public proposals?

   (A) Men no longer ask a father's permission to marry his daughter.

   (B) Many couples now live together before they get married.

   (C) Talk shows have become very popular with Americans.

   (D) There is now an official Proposal Day in Texas.

2. What led Leslie Hamilton to suspect that there might be a message for her in a crossword puzzle?

   (A) Many of the puzzle answers had something to do with her life.

   (B) She and her boyfriend often worked on puzzles together.

   (C) Her boyfriend was friends with the crossword-puzzle editor.

   (D) She had a degree in city planning.

3. Which detail helped Cal Ripkin remember Kelly Geer's name after her mother asked him to autograph a napkin for Kelly?

   (A) She has blond hair.

   (B) She went to the University of Maryland.

   (C) She is a tall woman.

   (D) She played basketball in college.

4. What is the main purpose of "She Said Yes! She Said Yes! She Said Yes!"?

   (A) to explain or inform

   (B) to persuade

   (C) to entertain

   (D) to express emotion and ideas

5. The marriage proposals in the article are similar to the proposal in "The Passionate Shepherd to His Love" because they are all

   (A) spontaneous

   (B) made in public

   (C) reckless

   (D) romantic

6. What does the speaker of "The Nymph's Reply to the Shepherd" have in common with the women described in the article?

   (A) She is worried about her future.

   (B) She seems intrigued by the proposal.

   (C) She fears that her suitor isn't trustworthy.

   (D) She rejects the proposal.

7. In line 26 of the article, the word *ingenuity* means

   (A) passion

   (B) innocence

   (C) deceitfulness

   (D) cleverness

8. What does the word *colleague* mean in lines 128–129?

   (A) coworker

   (B) teacher

   (C) camera operator

   (D) supervisor

Timed Writing Practice

PROMPT

In their pastoral poems, Christopher Marlowe and Sir Walter Raleigh present sharply contrasting views of rural life. Which view is closer to your own? Write an essay in which you express your opinion about life in the country. You can, like Marlowe's shepherd, idealize nature, or you can offer a more realistic view in the manner of Raleigh's nymph. Provide at least three reasons and one or two examples to support each reason. Draw examples from your own experiences as well as the two poems and other works you have read.

TEST-TAKER'S TOOLKIT

1. ANALYZE THE PROMPT

A. Underline the question in the prompt and circle key words in the sentences that follow the question. One phrase has been circled for you.

B. Jot down a list of the key elements you need to include in your essay.

2. PLAN YOUR RESPONSE

A. Make notes In a chart like the one shown here, list three good reasons for your opinion and examples to support your reasons.

B. Organize your information In the introduction, identify the topic of your essay and present a thesis statement that clearly identifies your personal opinion. Then you can write a paragraph for each reason you noted in your chart. Use your examples to support each reason. Be sure to include a conclusion in which you wrap up your ideas.

Reason 1:	Example(s):
Reason 2:	Example(s):
Reason 3:	Example(s):

3. WRITE AND REVIEW

A. An attention-grabbing opener gets readers interested in your ideas. Try beginning with an anecdote or a question:

The last time I was in the countryside _____

_____

B. Be sure to leave time to revise and to check your spelling and grammar.

UNIT 2
THE ENGLISH RENAISSANCE

LESSON 2B

Selected Poetry
BY WILLIAM SHAKESPEARE

RELATED NONFICTION
Love Is Blind

Can LOVERS
see clearly?

"Love is blind," according to an old saying. To what extent is this true? The thrill of falling in love can cloud one's perceptions of a lover, but usually those clouds drift away over time. Is it possible to see a person's faults clearly and still love him or her?

CHART IT With a partner, identify three fictional couples from books, movies, or plays. For each couple, answer the question, "How clearly did they see each other?" Discuss the reasons for your answers. What conclusions can you draw about the way love is portrayed in fiction?

Couple #1:

How clearly did they see each other?

Couple #2:

How clearly did they see each other?

Couple #3:

How clearly did they see each other?

ASSESSMENT GOALS

By the end of this cluster, you will be able to . . .

- analyze the Shakespearean sonnet form
- use active reading strategies to comprehend text
- identify an author's perspective while reading a nonfiction text
- analyze a writing prompt and plan a character description

Shakespearean Sonnet

During the Renaissance, love poems often came in the form of sonnets. A SONNET is a 14-line lyric poem with a complicated rhyme scheme and a defined structure. There are several varieties of sonnets. The most common variety used in England is called the SHAKESPEAREAN SONNET, which is also known as the English sonnet.

Shakespeare used the sonnet form to explore complex ideas about love, loss, and change. Study the graphic below to help you recognize characteristics of the Shakespearean sonnet as you read his poems.

SHAKESPEAREAN SONNET

METER: iambic pentameter lines containing five metrical units, each consisting of an unstressed syllable followed by a stressed syllable

STRUCTURE: three quatrains (stanzas of 4 lines) followed by a rhyming couplet (2 lines)

RHYME SCHEME: *abab cdcd efef gg*

TURN: a shift in thought that often occurs in the third quatrain or the couplet

Sonnet 18

William Shakespeare

MARK IT UP

Use these marks to monitor your reading:

✳ This is important.

? I don't understand.

! This is a surprise.

When you see this pencil ✏, you'll be asked to mark up the text. You can also write in this book in any way you find useful.

BACKGROUND Shakespeare expressed a great variety of thoughts and feelings in his 154 sonnets. The four sonnets you will read illustrate that variety. The first two celebrate the joy that love can bring. The third offers a definition of love. The fourth makes fun of the exaggerations that poets sometimes use in describing love.

Shall I compare thee to a summer's day?
Thou art more lovely and more temperate:
Rough winds do shake the darling buds of May,
And summer's lease hath all too short a date: ▶
5 Sometime too hot the eye of heaven shines,
And often is his gold complexion dimmed;
And every fair from fair sometime declines,
By chance or nature's changing course untrimmed;[1]
But thy eternal summer shall not fade,
10 Nor lose possession of that fair thou owest;[2]
Nor shall Death brag thou wander'st in his shade,
When in eternal lines to time thou growest:[3]
    So long as men can breathe, or eyes can see,
    So long lives this, and this gives life to thee. ▶

SUMMARIZE

What does the speaker describe in lines 3–4?

_____

_____

_____

CLARIFY

Reread the boxed text. According to the speaker, how will the subject of the poem be affected by his writing?

_____

_____

_____

_____

1. **fair from . . . untrimmed:** beauty eventually fades, due to misfortune or natural aging.
2. **thou owest:** you own; you possess.
3. **When . . . growest:** when in immortal poetry you become a part of time.

Sonnet 29

William Shakespeare

CLARIFY

Reread the first two **quatrains.** Why does the speaker curse his fate?

_____

_____

_____

_____

When in disgrace with Fortune and men's eyes
I all alone beweep my outcast state,
And trouble deaf heaven with my bootless[1] cries,
And look upon myself and curse my fate,
5 Wishing me like to one more rich in hope,
Featur'd like him,[2] like him with friends possess'd,
Desiring this man's art, and that man's scope,[3]
With what I most enjoy contented least;
Yet in these thoughts myself almost despising,
10 Haply[4] I think on thee, and then my state,
Like to the lark[5] at break of day arising
From sullen earth, sings hymns at heaven's gate,
    For thy sweet love rememb'red such wealth brings,
    That then I scorn to change my state with kings.

ANALYZE

Draw a box around the section of the poem where the poem where the **turn** occurs.

What shift in thought or feeling is expressed in this section?

_____

_____

_____

_____

1. **bootless:** futile; useless.
2. **Featur'd like him:** with his handsome features.
3. **this man's art . . . scope:** this man's skill and that man's intelligence.
4. **Haply:** by chance.
5. **lark:** the English skylark, noted for its beautiful singing while soaring in flight.

Sonnet 116

William Shakespeare

Let me not to the marriage of true minds
Admit impediments;[1] love is not love
Which alters when it alteration finds,
Or bends with the remover to remove.
5 O no, it is an ever-fixéd mark[2] ▶
That looks on tempests and is never shaken;
It is the star to every wand'ring bark,
Whose worth's unknown, although his height be taken.[3]
Love's not Time's fool, though rosy lips and cheeks
10 Within his bending sickle's compass come,[4]
Love alters not with his brief hours and weeks,
But bears it out even to the edge of doom.[5]
    If this be error and upon me proved,
      I never writ, nor no man ever loved.

---

1. **impediments:** obstacles.
2. **mark:** a landmark seen from the sea and used by sailors as a guide in navigation.
3. **the star . . . taken:** the star—usually the North Star—whose altitude sailors measure in order to help guide their ships. A **bark** is a sailing ship.
4. **within . . . come:** come within range of Time's curving sickle.
5. **bears . . . doom:** endures even to Judgment Day, the time when, Christian teachings predict, the world will end and God will make his final judgment of all people.

Sonnet 130

William Shakespeare

CLARIFY

Which statement describes the speaker's attitude toward his mistress?

☐ He considers her to be unattractive.

☐ He does not want to idealize her.

✋ **PAUSE & REFLECT**

Compare the descriptions of physical appearance in "Sonnet 18" and "Sonnet 130." Which poem offers a more vivid impression of its subject? Explain. *COMPARE AND CONTRAST*

_____

_____

_____

_____

_____

Big Question ?

Do you think any of the speakers in these poems see love clearly? Explain.

_____

_____

_____

_____

My mistress' eyes are nothing like the sun;
Coral is far more red than her lips' red;
If snow be white, why then her breasts are dun;[1]
If hairs be wires, black wires grow on her head.
5 I have seen roses damask'd,[2] red and white,
But no such roses see I in her cheeks,
And in some perfumes is there more delight
Than in the breath that from my mistress reeks.[3]
I love to hear her speak, yet well I know
10 That music hath a far more pleasing sound;
I grant I never saw a goddess go,[4]
My mistress when she walks treads on the ground. ◀
    And yet, by heaven, I think my love as rare
    As any she belied with false compare.[5] **PAUSE & REFLECT**

---

1. **dun:** grayish brown.
2. **damask'd:** mottled; spotted or streaked with different colors.
3. **reeks:** is exhaled (used here without the word's present reference to offensive odors).
4. **go:** walk.
5. **As any . . . compare:** as any woman misrepresented by exaggerated comparisons.

Reading Comprehension

DIRECTIONS *Answer these questions about the poems by filling in the correct ovals.*

1. In lines 5–6 of "Sonnet 18," the speaker describes

   (A) weather

   (B) vision

   (C) beauty

   (D) wealth

2. What does the speaker of "Sonnet 18" say will "give life" to the person he addresses?

   (A) the speaker's love

   (B) this sonnet

   (C) the warmth of summer

   (D) physical beauty

3. What does the speaker of "Sonnet 29" express by comparing his state, or condition, to a lark in lines 10–12?

   (A) his musical talent

   (B) the lifting of his depression

   (C) his soaring fortune

   (D) his love of nature

4. What idea does the speaker of "Sonnet 29" express in the poem's couplet?

   (A) He is filled with jealousy.

   (B) He has grown wealthy over time.

   (C) He hates all kings.

   (D) Love allows him to accept himself.

5. What theme, or main message, is expressed in "Sonnet 116"?

   (A) Love is full of obstacles.

   (B) Love is often stormy.

   (C) Love can doom people.

   (D) Love never changes.

6. What does the phrase "Love's not Time's fool" in line 9 of "Sonnet 116" suggest?

   (A) Love lasts forever.

   (B) Fools can never love.

   (C) Love is not foolish.

   (D) Lovers should be cautious.

7. What idea does the speaker express about his mistress in lines 11–12 of "Sonnet 130"?

   (A) She is like a goddess to him.

   (B) She will be immortal.

   (C) She is merely human.

   (D) She walks too slowly.

8. What does the speaker reveal in lines 13–14 of "Sonnet 130"?

   (A) He has deep love for his mistress.

   (B) He rarely loves his mistress

   (C) His mistress has been false to him.

   (D) His mistress rarely tells lies.

For help, use the **Test-Taker's Toolkit** below.

Responding in Writing

9. Short Response Write a summary of one of Shakespeare's sonnets, breaking it down into the four parts of its structure. Identify where the turn occurs.

_____

_____

_____

_____

_____

TEST-TAKER'S TOOLKIT

⊗ **GRAPHIC ORGANIZER** Use the chart below to help you plan your response. Reread the poems to help you remember details.

SONNET: _____	
First Quatrain	**Third Quatrain**
Second Quatrain	**Couplet**

What's the Connection?

Whether portraying love idealistically, realistically, or even comically, Shakespeare insists in his sonnets that love is inspiring and enduring. Lois Smith Brady's book *Love Lessons* offers 12 inspiring stories about real people who fall in love. In "Love Is Blind," she describes how a young woman finds true love with a man who sees past her disability.

DISCUSS IT With a small group, discuss aspects of love that you feel are very important. Use the prompts below to express five of your ideas about love.

Love is _____

_____

Love is _____

_____

Love is _____

_____

Love is _____

_____

Love is _____

_____

Related Nonfiction

Love Is Blind
BOOK EXCERPT

Use with Selected Poetry by William Shakespeare, p. 82

LEARN THE SKILL: IDENTIFY AUTHOR'S PERSPECTIVE

An **author's perspective** is the unique combination of beliefs, values, and feelings that influence the way the writer looks at a subject. To determine the author's perspective in an essay, readers should examine clues such as the following:

- statements of opinion
- details the writer chooses to include
- the writer's tone, or attitude toward a subject (such as a humorous or formal tone)

For more on identifying author's perspective, see the Nonfiction Skills Handbook beginning on page R2.

LO♥E Is BLIND

Lois Smith Brady

Real love, I've learned, is a very, very strong form of forgiveness, and I think that's partly why so many people yearn for it so much. I don't think people yearn for love because they hate staying home alone on Saturday night or because they dread going into restaurants alone and saying "Just one" to the maître d' for the millionth time. People want love because they want their taped-together eyeglasses, unstylish clothes, or lack of athletic ability to be forgiven. They want someone to look right past the surface stuff like bad hair days, a laugh that's too loud, strange family members, or potato chips crunching underneath the couch pillows
10 whenever anyone sits down. ◀

When William Neumann met Richelle Sasz, he was blind to many things about her that others found glaring. He first saw her in a crowded nightclub in Cancún, Mexico. She was with a few girlfriends, and although she was leaning on a pair of crutches and wearing braces on her legs, those weren't the first things he noticed about her. "Just looking at her, I could see she was so upbeat," he said. "She had a perky look, she was very spunky and very aggressive. She wasn't somebody who felt sorry for herself. Nothing was going to stop her. She was out on the dance floor! You don't see many disabled people at clubs. But she doesn't think
20 she's disabled."

Richelle grew up near the ocean on Long Island, in an all-American, middle-class neighborhood. . . . Until she became disabled in high school, Richelle was a cheerleader—she could do perfect splits even in a pair of tight blue jeans. At home, she and her three older sisters shared one bathroom, which made her even more patient and easygoing than she was naturally. Her oldest sister, Debbie, owned the most clothes and was

known for locking them in a closet protected with multiple padlocks. But
whenever Debbie left the house, Richelle and her other sisters would pry
open the door by unscrewing the padlocks, or, if that didn't work, they'd
30 take the entire door off its hinges and steal all the clothes.

In high school, Richelle was popular—one year, she was voted Class
Flirt, Best Personality, and Most Spirited. Besides being a quintessential,
blond, athletic cheerleader, she was also known for break-dancing in
the school hallways. "She was on a break-dancing team," said Denise
MacNamara-Bandl, her best friend from high school. "Oh my God, she
used to do headspins that would last forever." . . . ▶

One October morning in 1986, . . . Richelle caught a ride with Denise
and another friend, Tommy. Richelle describes her state of mind that
morning this way: "I had just started eleventh grade and I was dating one
40 of the most popular guys in school," she said. "I couldn't believe I got
him."

On the way to school, the three friends got into a freak car accident,
catching the bumper of another car and fishtailing out of control.
Richelle was thrown out the back window and flew ten feet through the
air and into a tree. "At first they couldn't find me," she remembers. "They
were screaming, 'Where is Richelle? Where is Richelle?' I was going in
and out of consciousness. The next thing I remember is being in the
ambulance and they were cutting up my sister's winter jacket and I was
thinking, Oh my God, my sister is going to kill me. They're cutting up
50 her new jacket."

As it turned out, Richelle had injured her spine during the accident
and was paralyzed from the waist down. The doctors said she had zero
chance of walking again. Instead of going back to high school, she
stayed in the hospital for months, then went to wheelchair school. There
are certain things you never want to experience—such as what it feels
like to drown or to be homeless—and living in a wheelchair is one of
them. "I learned how to cook in a wheelchair, how to set the table, how
to get dishes out of cabinets, brush my hair, work a blow-dryer," Richelle
remembers. "I don't know if you'd call it denial or positive thinking, but
60 I kept saying, 'Why are you teaching me this stuff? I'm not going to be in
a wheelchair.'" ▶

A year after the accident, she returned to high school, driving a car
outfitted with special hand controls, with her wheelchair folded up in the
backseat like an enormous winged insect. "I went from being one of the
popular girls in school to being in a wheelchair," she said. "The people
around me were very scared. Guys definitely looked at me differently.
No one, *no one* wanted to date me. They wanted to be friends, but
they couldn't see past the disability. It was definitely too strange. They
wondered, 'Do I open doors for her or let her do it herself? What if she

SUMMARIZE

Reread the boxed text. What
qualities does the author
emphasize in her description of
Richelle?

_____

_____

_____

_____

TESTSMART

What does Richelle refer
to as "denial or positive
thinking" in line 59?

Ⓐ the diagnosis she
received from her
doctors

Ⓑ the period she spent in
the hospital

Ⓒ her attitude at the
wheelchair school

Ⓓ the new skills she
acquired

TIP When a question
includes a quotation from
the text, first find the
paragraph in which the
quotation appears. If the
answer is not directly stated
in the text, you may have to
infer the answer, using clues
in the text as well as your
own knowledge to make
a guess. Look for clues in
Richelle's quoted statements
in this paragraph.

70 falls, what do I do?' It's just a big question mark. I made up for it by proving myself—I wanted to prove I could still have a lot of fun."

She did. Friends say she never let the wheelchair slow her down. She soon resumed her car pool, picking up the same friends she drove to school before the accident. On Saturday nights, she went out dancing with friends—she would wheel out into the middle of the dance floor and shimmy from the waist up without any self-consciousness at all. She went everywhere a wheelchair could go, and whenever her wheelchair got stuck—on bumpy sidewalks or at the bottom of the bleachers at basketball games—she would just get out and crawl. Or she would ask
80 friends for piggyback rides. . . . ◀

After high school, Richelle spent two years in intense physical therapy, learning to walk again. At first, she began walking with clunky, thigh-high metal braces, which made her lurch like the Tin Man in *The Wizard of Oz*. Then, after her legs strengthened, she started walking with high-top sneakers and white plastic calf-high braces that look like lightweight ski boots. "'Walking is such a wonderful thing," she said. "It's an awesome feeling. You're upright, you're getting exercise, you're seeing eye-to-eye with people, you're able to dance on your feet, you're able to reach things in the cabinet, you're able to walk down stairs instead
90 of crawling down them. You're talking about two different worlds, a wheelchair and walking."

Even once she started walking again, Richelle's love life ranged from nonexistent to tragicomic. "I clearly remember once when I was dating a guy and I was at his house and I had to go down these stairs that didn't have any kind of railing," she said. "I actually fell down the stairs and into a bush. When I fall, I usually laugh and people who know me laugh, but strangers freak out completely. Everyone screams, 'Oh my God! Oh my God!' People just freak out when a disabled person falls. I always feel bad for the person who's picking me up." . . . ◀

100 When she was twenty-two, Richelle moved into New York City by herself, enrolled in college, and got a part-time job at Just One Break, an employment agency for disabled people. In New York, she continued going out to parties and nightclubs with friends. . . . If people stared, she ignored them. Although Richelle sometimes loses her balance—she has fallen on crowded sidewalks, tripped while walking out of elevators, tumbled onto the carpet before a roomful of men in business suits—her personality is incredibly grounded and even-keeled. "It's hard to stay positive, but it's harder to be depressed and negative," she said, summing up her overall philosophy. "You can either choose to be upset or you can
110 choose to get over it, move on." . . .

When William saw her in a bikini, he thought she looked beautiful. The son of a fireman, William grew up with three older sisters in

AUTHOR'S PERSPECTIVE

Reread the boxed text. What does this description of Richelle's experiences in a wheelchair suggest about the author's beliefs or feelings?

_____

_____

_____

_____

SPECIALIZED
Vocabulary

The word *tragicomic* in line 93 is a compound word derived from *tragedy* and *comedy*. Use this information as well as context clues to help you come up with a definition of the way this word is used here.

_____

_____

_____

Watchung, New Jersey, in an eighteenth-century house with very low ceilings, enormous fireplaces, and walls insulated with horsehair and mud. He skis, scuba dives, drives a green pickup truck, works as a construction supervisor, and looks like Tom Cruise with curly hair and wire-rimmed glasses. While he has the muscular build of a rugby player, he also has the soft-spoken, patient, sweet temperament of a poet. "As a child, I was surrounded by females," he said. "I think it made me more
120 sensitive. My sisters taught me to have patience, to bake. They even had me crocheting." . . .

In Cancún, Richelle and William ended up spending a week together by the pool, . . . talking about everything except why she wore braces on her legs. "It was like he never saw my crutches or braces," Richelle said. "For him, other qualities of mine outshone the crutches. He saw me for who I was and he didn't see the disability."

Finally, she said to him one afternoon by the pool, "So, do you want to know what happened to me?"

Unlike most other men Richelle met, William was more interested
130 in her great jokes and sparkly presence than her accident. "I knew something had happened," he said. "I saw her in the pool and I saw her scars, but I was interested in *her*. When you find the right person, you see past certain things and concentrate on the positive side. I just didn't think about her disability that much." . . .

William has been Richelle's steady boyfriend ever since they met in Cancún. Now twenty-eight and twenty-nine, they share a high-rise apartment in New York City, a place so uncluttered and neat even the wastebaskets are empty and spotless. Sometimes, if you look closely at the white walls, you can see fingerprint marks, like pale shell prints on
140 a beach. Richelle often uses the wall for support when she's walking around the apartment, and every few months William repaints the entire place. Richelle still walks in high-top sneakers and lightweight braces, and her closet is full of identical black sneakers, like shoes lined up in a bowling alley. . . . ▶

Nowadays, William sometimes carries Richelle when she needs to be carried. On a recent trip to the Caribbean, he carried her every day from their beach chairs across the bumpy, hard-to-navigate sand and into the deep water, where she would take off like a dolphin. "When you truly love somebody so much, it doesn't matter what has happened to them,"
150 Richelle said. "You live with them and work it out no matter what comes up. That's what love is—it's understanding, it's helping, it's aiding the other person, it's encouraging them to be a better person, it's believing in them and giving them the strength to believe in themselves. It's lifting them up when they can't lift themselves up."

MAKE INFERENCES

Reread lines 135–144. Why might it be important for Richelle's apartment to be kept neat?

Reading Comprehension

DIRECTIONS *Answer these questions about the book excerpt and the poems in this lesson by filling in the correct ovals.*

1. In lines 1–10 of "Love Is Blind," the author discusses beliefs about love that have influenced her perspective. What aspect of love does she emphasize in the essay?

   Ⓐ passion

   Ⓑ acceptance

   Ⓒ physical attraction

   Ⓓ conflict

2. In what sense was William "blind to many things" (lines 11–12) about Richelle when he first met her?

   Ⓐ The glaring sun was in his eyes.

   Ⓑ He failed to see her good qualities.

   Ⓒ He didn't notice her crutches and leg braces.

   Ⓓ He unintentionally made insensitive remarks.

3. How did Richelle respond when doctors told her that she would have to spend the rest of her life in a wheelchair?

   Ⓐ She was grateful for their help.

   Ⓑ She decided to accept her fate.

   Ⓒ She became depressed and stopped trying.

   Ⓓ She refused to accept their diagnosis.

4. Which experience has helped William maintain a good relationship with Richelle?

   Ⓐ growing up surrounded by females

   Ⓑ being raised in an old house

   Ⓒ working as a construction supervisor

   Ⓓ taking trips to the Caribbean

5. Which of Shakespeare's sonnets expresses Richelle's idea that love is "understanding, it's helping, it's aiding the other person, it's giving them the strength to believe in themselves"?

   Ⓐ "Sonnet 18"

   Ⓑ "Sonnet 29"

   Ⓒ "Sonnet 116"

   Ⓓ "Sonnet 130"

6. What does Richelle's boyfriend, William, have in common with the speaker of "Sonnet 130"?

   Ⓐ Both are attracted to dark-haired women.

   Ⓑ Both are energetic and athletic.

   Ⓒ Both are poets.

   Ⓓ Both look past superficial flaws in their lovers.

7. What is the meaning of the word *quintessential* in line 32 of the book excerpt?

   Ⓐ successful

   Ⓑ necessary

   Ⓒ typical

   Ⓓ conceited

8. In line 118, the word *temperament* means

   Ⓐ personality

   Ⓑ anger

   Ⓒ reputation

   Ⓓ hot-headedness

Timed Writing Practice

PROMPT

Many literary works portray love as a powerful force that can change people's lives. Describe someone you have read about, real or fictional, whose (life was transformed by love.) The love doesn't have to be romantic—it could be the love between a parent and child or between close friends. Try to make your character description so vivid that your readers will feel that they know this person. Use an appropriate quote from one of Shakespeare's sonnets or the related nonfiction to help introduce your topic.

TEST-TAKER'S TOOLKIT

1. ANALYZE THE PROMPT

A. Identify the type of writing you are asked to do.

_____

B. Circle any key words that describe the topic or indicate what you are required to include in your writing. One phrase has been circled for you.

_____

_____

_____

2. PLAN YOUR RESPONSE

A. **Make notes** Decide which person or character you will write about. Brainstorm a list of events in his or her life, and choose examples that illustrate your ideas about love. Use this chart to list examples that you plan to include.

B. **Organize your information** Your description should begin with an introduction in which you use a quote to help convey the point you wish to make about your subject. Then you can write a paragraph for each event you included in your chart. You may not be able to describe your subject's entire life; focus on key events that relate to your topic.

Event	Importance of Love

3. WRITE AND REVIEW

A. Write a conclusion that vividly summarizes the portrait you have created of your subject. You might ask a thought-provoking question that encourages readers to relate your description to their own lives.

B. Be sure to leave time to check your spelling and grammar.

A Modest Proposal
BY JONATHAN SWIFT

RELATED NONFICTION
Children Sink to the Bottom: Thousands in Haiti Subsist on Nation's Leavings

JUST-STARVE-US.
WORKHOUSE

Tell Ah! Tell us, can aught be worse?
Than hungry Maw & empty Purse!!
MERCY SHOW & PITY US,
GREAT OVERSEER.

How can we fight
INJUSTICE?

There's an old proverb that states, "The pen is mightier than the sword." Jonathan Swift wielded his pen like a rapier, using it to slash away at injustice. Though some may claim that the power of the pen is greatly diminished these days, people still fight injustice with words—in speeches, in newspapers and magazines, and on the Internet.

CHART IT With a small group, brainstorm some contemporary examples of injustice. Write three of them down in the chart. For each example, identify some tactics that people can use to fight the injustice.

Examples of Injustice	Tactics for Fighting Injustice

ASSESSMENT GOALS

By the end of this lesson, you will be able to . . .

- analyze satire
- use active reading strategies to comprehend text
- analyze descriptive details in nonfiction
- analyze a writing prompt and plan a problem-solution essay

Satire

SATIRE is a literary technique in which behaviors or institutions are ridiculed for the purpose of improving society. What sets satire apart from other forms of social and political protest is humor. For example, Swift used his savage wit to attack prominent British politicians and to protest unjust policies in Ireland.

The following chart shows three types of IRONY that Swift used in his satires. Look for examples of these techniques as you read "A Modest Proposal."

TECHNIQUE	EXAMPLE
SITUATIONAL IRONY a contrast between what is expected and what actually occurs	After safely completing a dangerous mountain climb, a climber slips in the shower and hurts herself.
VERBAL IRONY when a writer or character says one thing but means the opposite	A football player fumbles the ball and loses the game. When he reaches the sideline, his coach tells him, "Nice play!"
UNDERSTATEMENT a form of irony that creates emphasis by saying less than what is true or appropriate	Reporting from a town that was hit by a hurricane, a reporter describes the place as "a bit messy."

A Modest Proposal

FOR PREVENTING THE CHILDREN OF POOR PEOPLE IN IRELAND
FROM BEING A BURDEN TO THEIR PARENTS OR COUNTRY,
AND FOR MAKING THEM BENEFICIAL TO THE PUBLIC

JONATHAN SWIFT

BACKGROUND By 1700, Ireland was completely dominated by England. The Catholic majority could not vote, hold public office, buy land, or receive an education—policies that reduced most Irish people to poverty. When crops failed, many faced starvation. Jonathan Swift, outraged by England's treatment of Ireland, wrote a satirical attack on this injustice in "A Modest Proposal."

It is a melancholy object to those who walk through this great town[1] or travel in the country, when they see the streets, the roads, and cabin doors, crowded with beggars of the female sex, followed by three, four, or six children, all in rags and importuning every passenger for an alms.[2] These mothers, instead of being able to work for their honest livelihood, are forced to employ all their time in strolling to beg <u>sustenance</u> for their helpless infants, who, as they grow up, either turn thieves for want[3] of work, or leave their dear native country to fight for the Pretender[4] in Spain, or sell themselves to the Barbadoes.[5]

10 I think it is agreed by all parties that this prodigious number of children in the arms, or on the backs, or at the heels of their mothers, and

---

MARK IT UP
Use these marks to monitor your reading:

✱ This is important.

? I don't understand.

! This is a surprise.

When you see this pencil ✐, you'll be asked to mark up the text. You can also write in this book in any way you find useful.

F OCUS
In this section, the speaker describes the terrible poverty that afflicts Ireland, and he proposes a solution to this problem.

sustenance (sŭs'tə-nəns) *n.* a means of support or nourishment

---

1. **this great town:** Dublin, Ireland.
2. **importuning** (ĭm'pôr-tōōn'ĭng) . . . **alms** (ämz): begging from every passerby for a charitable handout.
3. **want:** lack; need.
4. **Pretender:** James Edward Stuart, who claimed the English throne, from which his now deceased father, James II, had been removed in 1688. Because James II and his son were Roman Catholic, the common people of Ireland were loyal to them.
5. **sell . . . Barbadoes:** To escape poverty, some Irish migrated to the West Indies, obtaining money for their passage by agreeing to work as slaves on plantations there for a set period.

CLARIFY

Reread lines 10–21. What problem does the speaker hope to solve with his proposal?

_____

_____

_____

TestSmart

VOCABULARY

What does the word *raiment* mean in line 31?

Ⓐ clothing

Ⓑ weather

Ⓒ indignation

Ⓓ optimism

TIP Use **context clues** to figure out the best meaning of an unfamiliar word. Reread lines 28–32, and underline any words or phrases that provide clues to the meaning of the word *raiment.*

frequently of their fathers, is in the present deplorable state of the kingdom a very great additional grievance; and therefore whoever could find out a fair, cheap, and easy method of making these children sound, useful members of the commonwealth would deserve so well of the public as to have his statue set up for a preserver of the nation.

But my intention is very far from being confined to provide only for the children of professed beggars; it is of a much greater extent, and shall take in the whole number of infants at a certain age who are born of
20 parents in effect as little able to support them as those who demand our charity in the streets. ◀

As to my own part, having turned my thoughts for many years upon this important subject, and maturely weighed the several schemes of other projectors,[6] I have always found them grossly mistaken in their computation. It is true, a child just dropped from its dam[7] may be supported by her milk for a solar year, with little other nourishment; at most not above the value of two shillings, which the mother may certainly get, or the value in scraps, by her lawful occupation of begging; and it is exactly at one year old that I propose to provide for them in such a manner
30 as instead of being a charge upon their parents or the parish, or wanting food and raiment for the rest of their lives, they shall on the contrary contribute to the feeding, and partly to the clothing, of many thousands. ◀

There is likewise another great advantage in my scheme, that it will prevent those voluntary abortions, and that horrid practice of women murdering their bastard children, alas, too frequent among us, sacrificing the poor innocent babes, I doubt,[8] more to avoid the expense than the shame, which would move tears and pity in the most savage and inhuman breast.

The number of souls in this kingdom being usually reckoned one
40 million and a half, of these I calculate there may be about two hundred thousand couple whose wives are breeders; from which number I subtract thirty thousand couples who are able to maintain their own children, although I apprehend there cannot be so many under the present distresses of the kingdom; but this being granted, there will remain an hundred and seventy thousand breeders. I again subtract fifty thousand for those women who miscarry, or whose children die by accident or disease within the year. There only remain an hundred and twenty thousand children of poor parents annually born. The question therefore is, how this number

---

6. **projectors:** persons who propose public projects or plans.
7. **dam** (dăm): female parent. The term is used mostly for farm animals.
8. **doubt:** suspect.

shall be reared and provided for, which, as I have already said, under the present situation of affairs, is utterly impossible by all the methods hitherto proposed. For we can neither employ them in handicraft or agriculture; we neither build houses (I mean in the country) nor cultivate land. They can very seldom pick up a livelihood by stealing till they arrive at six years old, except where they are of towardly parts;[9] although I confess they learn the **rudiments** much earlier, during which time they can however be looked upon only as probationers, as I have been informed by a principal gentleman in the county of Cavan, who protested to me that he never knew above one or two instances under the age of six, even in a part of the kingdom so renowned for the quickest proficiency in that art. ▶

I am assured by our merchants that a boy or girl before twelve years old is no salable commodity; and even when they come to this age they will not yield above three pounds, or three pounds and half a crown at most on the Exchange; which cannot turn to account[10] either to the parents or the kingdom, the charge of nutriment and rags having been at least four times that value.

I shall now therefore humbly propose my own thoughts, which I hope will not be liable to the least objection.

I have been assured by a very knowing American of my acquaintance in London, that a young healthy child well nursed is at a year old a most delicious, nourishing, and wholesome food, whether stewed, roasted, baked, or boiled; and I make no doubt that it will equally serve in a fricassee or a ragout.[11]

I do therefore humbly offer it to public consideration that of the hundred and twenty thousand children, already computed, twenty thousand may be reserved for breed,[12] whereof only one fourth part to be males, which is more than we allow to sheep, black cattle, or swine; and my reason is that these children are seldom the fruits of marriage, a circumstance not much regarded by our savages, therefore one male will be sufficient to serve four females. That the remaining hundred thousand may at a year old be offered in sale to the persons of quality and fortune through the kingdom, always advising the mother to let them suck plentifully in the last month, so as to render them plump and fat for a good table. A child will make two dishes at an entertainment for friends; and when the family dines alone, the fore or hind quarter will make a

rudiment (roo′də-mənt) *n.* a basic principle or element

ANALYZE

Reread the boxed text. What is **ironic** about the speaker's discussion of stealing?

_____

_____

_____

---

9. **are of towardly** (tôrd′lē) **parts:** have a promising talent.
10. **turn to account:** earn a profit; benefit; prove useful.
11. **fricassee** (frĭk′ə-sē′) **. . . ragout** (ră-goo′): types of meat stews.
12. **reserved for breed:** kept for breeding (instead of being slaughtered).

◀

reasonable dish, and seasoned with a little pepper or salt will be very good boiled on the fourth day, especially in winter. ◀

I have reckoned upon a medium that a child just born will weigh twelve pounds, and in a solar year if tolerably nursed increaseth to twenty-eight pounds.

90   I grant this food will be somewhat dear, and therefore very proper for landlords, who, as they have already devoured most of the parents, seem to have the best title to the children.

Infant's flesh will be in season throughout the year, but more plentiful in March, and a little before and after. For we are told by a grave author, an eminent French physician,[13] that fish being a prolific[14] diet, there are more children born in Roman Catholic countries about nine months after Lent[15] than at any other season; therefore, reckoning a year after Lent, the markets will be more glutted than usual, because the number of popish infants is at least three to one in this kingdom; and therefore it will have 100 one other **collateral** advantage, by lessening the number of Papists[16] among us.

I have already computed the charge of nursing a beggar's child (in which list I reckon all cottagers, laborers, and four fifths of the farmers), to be about two shillings per annum, rags included; and I believe no gentleman would repine to give ten shillings for the carcass of a good fat child, which, as I have said, will make four dishes of excellent nutritive meat, when he hath only some particular friend or his own family to dine with him. Thus the squire will learn to be a good landlord, and grow popular among the tenants; the mother will have eight shillings net profit, 110 and be fit for work till she produces another child.

Those who are more thrifty (as I must confess the times require) may flay the carcass; the skin of which artificially dressed will make admirable gloves for ladies, and summer boots for fine gentlemen.

As to our city of Dublin, shambles[17] may be appointed for this purpose in the most convenient parts of it, and butchers we may be assured will not be wanting; although I rather recommend buying the children alive, and dressing them hot from the knife as we do roasting pigs.

PAUSE & REFLECT

---

13. **grave . . . physician:** François Rabelais (răb'ə-lā'), a 16th-century French satirist.
14. **prolific:** promoting fertility.
15. **Lent:** Catholics traditionally do not eat meat during Lent, the 40 days leading up to Easter, and instead eat a lot of fish.
16. **popish** (pō'pĭsh) **. . . Papists:** hostile or contemptuous terms referring to Roman Catholics.
17. **shambles:** slaughterhouses.

SUMMARIZE

What plan does the speaker propose for Ireland's children?

_____

_____

_____

collateral (kə-lăt'ər-əl) *adj.* accompanying as a parallel or subordinate factor; related

✋ **PAUSE & REFLECT**

1. What was your reaction to the speaker's proposal? Underline phrases that helped create this reaction. *MAKE JUDGMENTS*

_____

_____

_____

2. What attitude does the speaker have toward the poor of Ireland? *DRAW CONCLUSIONS*

_____

_____

_____

A very worthy person, a true lover of his country, and whose virtues
I highly esteem, was lately pleased in discoursing on this matter to offer
120 a refinement upon my scheme. He said that many gentlemen of this
kingdom, having of late destroyed their deer, he conceived that the want of
venison might be well supplied by the bodies of young lads and maidens,
not exceeding fourteen years of age nor under twelve, so great a number of
both sexes in every county being now ready to starve for want of work and
service; and these to be disposed of by their parents, if alive, or otherwise
by their nearest relations. But with due **deference** to so excellent a friend
and so deserving a patriot, I cannot be altogether in his sentiments; for
as to the males, my American acquaintance assured me from frequent
experience that their flesh was generally tough and lean, like that of our
130 schoolboys, by continual exercise, and their taste disagreeable; and to
fatten them would not answer the charge. Then as to the females, it would,
I think with humble submission, be a loss to the public, because they soon
would become breeders themselves; and besides, it is not improbable that
some scrupulous people might be apt to censure such a practice (although
indeed very unjustly) as a little bordering upon cruelty; which, I confess,
hath always been with me the strongest objection against any project, how
well soever intended.

But in order to justify my friend, he confessed that this **expedient**
was put into his head by the famous Psalmanazar, a native of the island
140 Formosa,[18] who came from thence to London above twenty years ago, and
in conversation told my friend that in his country when any young person
happened to be put to death, the executioner sold the carcass to persons of
quality as a prime dainty; and that in his time the body of a plump girl of
fifteen, who was crucified for an attempt to poison the emperor, was sold
to his Imperial Majesty's prime minister of state, and other great mandarins
of the court, in joints from the gibbet,[19] at four hundred crowns. Neither
indeed can I deny that if the same use were made of several plump young
girls in this town, who without one single groat[20] to their fortunes cannot
stir abroad without a chair,[21] and appear at the playhouse and assemblies in
150 foreign fineries which they never will pay for, the kingdom would not be
the worse.

FOCUS
In the next section, the
speaker responds to an
alternative proposal and
lays out the advantages of
his own.

---

18. **Psalmanazar** (săl′mə-năz′ər) **. . . Formosa** (fôr-mō′sə): a French imposter in
London who called himself George Psalmanazar and pretended to be from
Formosa (now Taiwan), where, he said, cannibalism was practiced.
19. **gibbet** (jĭb′ĭt): gallows.
20. **groat:** an old British coin worth four pennies.
21. **cannot stir . . . chair:** cannot go outside without using an enclosed chair carried
on poles by two men.

encumbrance (ĕn-kŭm′brəns)
n. a burden

famine (făm′ĭn) n. a period
in which there is a severe
shortage of food

Some persons of a desponding spirit are in great concern about that vast number of poor people who are aged, diseased, or maimed, and I have been desired to employ my thoughts what course may be taken to ease the nation of so grievous an **encumbrance**. But I am not in the least pain upon that matter, because it is very well known that they are every day dying and rotting by cold and **famine**, and filth and vermin, as fast as can be reasonably expected. And as to the younger laborers, they are now in almost as hopeful a condition. They cannot get work, and consequently

160 pine away for want of nourishment to a degree that if at any time they are accidentally hired to common labor, they have not strength to perform it; and thus the country and themselves are happily delivered from the evils to come. ◄

I have too long digressed, and therefore shall return to my subject. I think the advantages by the proposal which I have made are obvious and many, as well as of the highest importance.

For first, as I have already observed, it would greatly lessen the number of Papists, with whom we are yearly overrun, being the principal breeders of the nation as well as our most dangerous enemies; and who stay at

170 home on purpose to deliver the kingdom to the Pretender, hoping to take their advantage by the absence of so many good Protestants, who have chosen rather to leave their country than stay at home and pay tithes against their conscience to an Episcopal curate.[22]

Secondly, the poorer tenants will have something valuable of their own, which by law may be made liable to distress,[23] and help to pay their landlord's rent, their corn and cattle being already seized and money a thing unknown.

Thirdly, whereas the maintenance of an hundred thousand children, from two years old and upwards, cannot be computed at less than ten

180 shillings a piece per annum, the nation's stock will be thereby increased fifty thousand pounds per annum, besides the profit of a new dish introduced to the tables of all gentlemen of fortune in the kingdom who have any refinement in taste. And the money will circulate among ourselves, the goods being entirely of our own growth and manufacture. ◄

Fourthly, the constant breeders, besides the gain of eight shillings sterling per annum by the sale of their children, will be rid of the charge of maintaining them after the first year.

MAKE INFERENCES

Why might Swift have chosen
to have the speaker express
his lack of concern for Ireland's
poor people?

_____

_____

_____

_____

MONITOR

What questions do you have
after reading the boxed text?

_____

_____

_____

_____

22. **Protestants . . . curate** (kyŏor′ĭt): Swift is criticizing absentee Anglo-Irish landowners who lived—and spent their income from their property—in England.
23. **distress:** seizure of a person's property for the payment of debts.

Fifthly, this food would likewise bring great custom to taverns, where the vintners will certainly be so prudent as to procure the best receipts[24] for dressing it to perfection, and consequently have their houses frequented by all the fine gentlemen, who justly value themselves upon their knowledge in good eating; and a skillful cook, who understands how to oblige his guests, will contrive to make it as expensive as they please.

Sixthly, this would be a great inducement to marriage, which all wise nations have either encouraged by rewards or enforced by laws and penalties. It would increase the care and tenderness of mothers toward their children, when they were sure of a settlement for life to the poor babes, provided in some sort by the public, to their annual profit instead of expense. We should see an honest emulation among the married women, which of them could bring the fattest child to the market. Men would become as fond of their wives during the time of their pregnancy as they are now of their mares in foal, their cows in calf, or sows when they are ready to farrow; nor offer to beat or kick them (as is too frequent a practice) for fear of a miscarriage.

Many other advantages might be enumerated. For instance, the addition of some thousand carcasses in our exportation of barreled beef, the **propagation** of swine's flesh, and improvement in the art of making good bacon, so much wanted among us by the great destruction of pigs, too frequent at our tables, which are no way comparable in taste or magnificence to a well-grown, fat, yearling child, which roasted whole will make a considerable figure at a lord mayor's feast or any other public entertainment. But this and many others I omit, being studious of brevity.

Supposing that one thousand families in this city would be constant customers for infants' flesh, besides others who might have it at merry meetings, particularly weddings and christenings, I compute that Dublin would take off annually about twenty thousand carcasses, and the rest of the kingdom (where probably they will be sold somewhat cheaper) the remaining eighty thousand. ✋ **PAUSE & REFLECT**

I can think of no one objection that will possibly be raised against this proposal, unless it should be urged that the number of people will be thereby much lessened in the kingdom. This I freely own, and it was indeed one principal design in offering it to the world. I desire the reader will observe, that I calculate my remedy for this one individual kingdom of Ireland and for no other that ever was, is, or I think ever can be upon

---

24. **receipts:** recipes.

propagation (prŏp′ə-gā′shən) *n.* the act of reproducing, multiplying, or increasing

✋ **PAUSE & REFLECT**

1. What is **ironic** about the speaker's argument that his plan will make mothers behave more tenderly toward their children? *ANALYZE*

2. What does the speaker seem to assume about the people who will participate in his plan? *MAKE INFERENCES*

FOCUS
Read to find out why the speaker believes that his plan is the best.

earth. Therefore let no man talk to me of other expedients: of taxing our absentees at five shillings a pound: of using neither clothes nor household furniture except what is of our own growth and manufacture: of utterly rejecting the materials and instruments that promote foreign luxury: of curing the expensiveness of pride, vanity, idleness, and gaming in our
230 women: of introducing a vein of parsimony,[25] prudence, and temperance: of learning to love our country, in the want of which we differ even from Laplanders and the inhabitants of Topinamboo:[26] of quitting our animosities and factions, nor acting any longer like the Jews, who were murdering one another at the very moment their city was taken:[27] of being a little cautious not to sell our country and conscience for nothing: of teaching landlords to have at least one degree of mercy toward their tenants: lastly, of putting a spirit of honesty, industry, and skill into our shopkeepers; who, if a resolution could now be taken to buy only our native goods, would immediately unite to cheat and exact upon us in the
240 price, the measure, and the goodness, nor could ever yet be brought to make one fair proposal of just dealing, though often and earnestly invited to it. ◀

Therefore I repeat, let no man talk to me of these and the like expedients,[28] till he hath at least some glimpse of hope that there will ever be some hearty and sincere attempt to put them in practice.

But as to myself, having been wearied out for many years with offering vain, idle, visionary thoughts, and at length utterly despairing of success, I fortunately fell upon this proposal, which, as it is wholly new, so it hath something solid and real, of no expense and little trouble, full in our own
250 power, and whereby we can incur no danger in disobliging England. For this kind of commodity will not bear exportation, the flesh being of too tender a consistence to admit a long continuance in salt, although perhaps I could name a country which would be glad to eat up our whole nation without it.

After all, I am not so violently bent upon my own opinion as to reject any offer proposed by wise men, which shall be found equally innocent, cheap, easy, and effectual. But before something of that kind shall be

---

25. **parsimony** (pär′sə-mō′nē): frugality; thrift.
26. **Topinamboo** (tŏp′ĭ-năm′boō): an area in Brazil supposedly inhabited by wild savages.
27. **Jews . . . taken:** In A.D. 70, during a Jewish revolt against Roman rule, the inhabitants of Jerusalem, by fighting among themselves, made it easier for the Romans to capture the city.
28. **let no man . . . expedients:** In his writings, Swift had suggested "other expedients" without success.

TestSmart

Which of the following words *best* characterizes the "other expedients" that the speaker rejects as solutions to Ireland's poverty?

(A) optimistic
(B) reasonable
(C) illogical
(D) passionate

TIP Notice that the question asks which is the **best answer.** This tells you that more than one answer may be possible, so you need to look for the one that is strongest or most accurate. Reread lines 225–242 and read all of the answer choices to decide which one best describes the other expedients.

advanced in contradiction to my scheme, and offering a better, I desire the
author or authors will be pleased maturely to consider two points. First, as
260 things now stand, how they will be able to find food and raiment for an
hundred thousand useless mouths and backs. And secondly, there being
a round million of creatures in human figure throughout this kingdom,
whose sole subsistence put into a common stock[29] would leave them in
debt two millions of pounds sterling, adding those who are beggars by
profession to the bulk of farmers, cottagers, and laborers, with their wives
and children who are beggars in effect; I desire those politicians who
dislike my overture, and may perhaps be so bold to attempt an answer,
that they will first ask the parents of these mortals whether they would not
at this day think it a great happiness to have been sold for food at a year
270 old in the manner I prescribe, and thereby have avoided such a perpetual
scene of misfortunes as they have since gone through by the oppression
of landlords, the impossibility of paying rent without money or trade, the
want of common sustenance, with neither house nor clothes to cover them
from the inclemencies of the weather, and the most inevitable prospect of
entailing the like or greater miseries upon their breed forever.

I profess, in the sincerity of my heart, that I have not the least personal
interest in endeavoring to promote this necessary work, having no other
motive than the public good of my country, by advancing our trade,
providing for infants, relieving the poor, and giving some pleasure to the
280 rich. I have no children by which I can propose to get a single penny; the
youngest being nine years old, and my wife past childbearing.

✋ **PAUSE & REFLECT**

✋ **PAUSE & REFLECT**

What idea does Swift suggest
with the speaker's challenge
to "politicians who dislike my
overture" in lines 266–275?
MAKE INFERENCES

_____

_____

_____

Big Question ❓

Think about the
contemporary examples
of injustice that you listed
on page 99. How effective
would a **satire** similar to
"A Modest Proposal" be in
fighting these injustices?
Explain your answer.

_____

_____

_____

29. **common stock:** ordinary stock in a company or business venture.

Reading Comprehension

DIRECTIONS *Answer these questions about "A Modest Proposal" by filling in the correct ovals.*

1. Which of the following benefits will *not* result from the speaker's proposal?

    (A) Ireland's poor will have more money.

    (B) More Irish people will get married.

    (C) The Catholic population will decrease.

    (D) Absentee landlords will return to Ireland.

2. According to the speaker, his proposal will benefit the wealthier people of Ireland by

    (A) making them fonder of their spouses

    (B) lowering their taxes

    (C) adding variety to their diet

    (D) making money from the sale of babies

3. Which of the following is an example of verbal irony?

    (A) the title of the essay

    (B) the speaker's description of mothers begging for food

    (C) the estimate of 200,000 "breeders" in Ireland

    (D) the argument that the proposal will encourage marriage

4. What technique does Swift use to create satire in lines 133–137, where the speaker suggests that some people might consider slaughtering and eating girls 12 to 14 years old "a little bordering upon cruelty"?

    (A) situational irony

    (B) verbal irony

    (C) understatement

    (D) hyperbole

5. Why does the speaker lack faith in the alternative solutions listed near the end of the essay?

    (A) Similar proposals have been ignored in the past.

    (B) These solutions have been tried and they didn't work.

    (C) He is jealous of the people who have proposed these solutions.

    (D) He thinks his own proposal is the most humane.

6. Which word *best* describes the effect that Swift wanted to have on his readers?

    (A) exciting

    (B) persuasive

    (C) convincing

    (D) horrifying

7. The word *prodigious* in line 10 means

    (A) impoverished

    (B) athletic

    (C) enormous

    (D) insignificant

8. What does the word *procure* mean in line 189?

    (A) heal

    (B) obtain

    (C) prohibit

    (D) cook

For help, use the **Test-Taker's Toolkit** below.

Responding in Writing

9. Short Response Does the real message of "A Modest Proposal" come across clearly, or could Swift's use of irony confuse readers into mistaking the satire for a sincere proposal? Write a brief evaluation of the essay, referring to at least two examples of irony to support your opinion.

_____

_____

_____

_____

_____

_____

TEST-TAKER'S TOOLKIT

- ⊗ **ACADEMIC VOCABULARY** Remember that **situational irony** is a contrast between what is expected and what actually occurs; **verbal irony** occurs when a writer says one thing but means the opposite; and **understatement** is saying less than what is true or appropriate.

- ⊗ **GRAPHIC ORGANIZER** Use the chart below to help you plan your response.

Example of Irony	How It Relates to Swift's Message

Children Sink to the Bottom: Thousands in Haiti Subsist on Nation's Leavings
NEWSPAPER ARTICLE

Use with "A Modest Proposal," p. 98

What's the Connection?

In his satirical essay, Swift describes children whom society does not value—a condition that remains true for millions of children today. This article describes the poverty and misery of Haiti's street children.

CHART IT In the K-W-L chart, write down what you know about children who are living on the street, either in the United States or abroad and then write down what you want to find out. After you read the article, complete the chart by writing down important information you have learned.

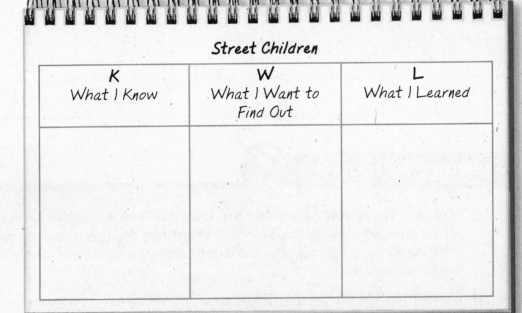

Street Children

K What I Know	W What I Want to Find Out	L What I Learned

LEARN THE SKILL: ANALYZE DESCRIPTIVE DETAILS

Although news articles are usually written in a concise manner, some journalists skillfully use **descriptive details** to create a mood or convey a tone (the writer's attitude toward a subject). As you read "Children Sink to the Bottom," pay attention to the following:

- **imagery**—words that describe sensory experiences
- **figurative language**—language that goes beyond the literal meaning
- **diction**—a writer's choice of words and word order

For more on descriptive details, see the Author's Craft entry in the Nonfiction Skills Handbook beginning on page R2.

Children Sink to the Bottom: Thousands in Haiti Subsist on Nation's Leavings

by Ian James

On the edge of town, dozens of boys congregate below a statue of Jesus. It's their home as they scratch out lives on the town's littered streets noisy with trucks and motorcycles.

Forced from their homes by poverty and broken families, the children load and sweep buses for
10 meager tips. They don't attend school, their clothes are ragged, and fellow citizens largely regard them as a nuisance.

"I don't know my age," says a barefoot Jean-Claude George, who has the body of a 10-year-old but the gaze of a man who has known years of suffering. "I've been on the street a long time." ▶

20 Like others among the children who sleep on buses or near the white statue, Jean-Claude fled an abusive home in the countryside for this town on Haiti's southern coast, 100 miles from the capital of Port-au-Prince.

He earns small change on the buses to pay for food and shoes, but the sandals often disappear in
30 the company he keeps. "The other kids keep an eye on me all night,"

A child searches through garbage for food in Port-au-Prince, Haiti.

he says. "Once I go to sleep, they steal them."

Street children struggle in cities around the globe, from São Paulo to Bombay. But in this Caribbean nation, the Western Hemisphere's poorest, the problem of homelessness among children is especially
40 severe. Some experts say the situation has worsened in recent years amid Haiti's political turmoil. Thousands of children wander the cities, looking for odd jobs, begging or stealing to eat.

DESCRIPTIVE DETAILS

Why might the author have included the metaphor that Jean-Claude has "the gaze of a man who has known years of suffering" (lines 17–18)?

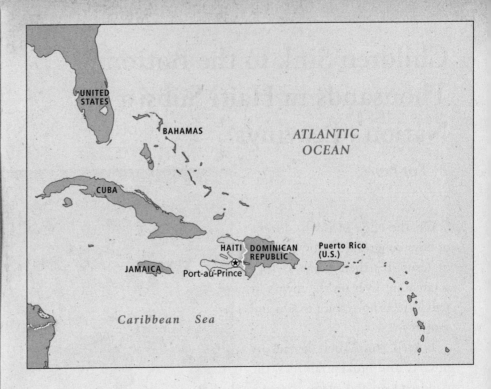

CHILDREN REMAIN ON STREET

President Jean-Bertrand Aristide, a former Roman Catholic priest, 50 tried to make children's issues a cornerstone of his presidency, but government efforts have failed to bring the children off the streets.

In 1986, before he was president, Aristide founded the Family Is Life orphanage. His political involvement eventually made it a target for opponents. In 1991, the same year he was ousted in a coup, five 60 children died in a suspicious fire at the facility. In 1992, some children were wounded when Aristide opponents stormed the building and began shooting. The orphanage eventually closed in 1999 amid protests by orphans who said promises of jobs weren't kept.

Dominique Esperant, the former regional head of the social 70 affairs ministry in Les Cayes, hopes to put street children back on the political agenda. "Everyone seems to think the best way to deal with this is to kick these kids out of town," Esperant says. "I believe they can become good citizens like anyone else if someone is there to help them out." ◄

CENTER WOULD 80 HOUSE CHILDREN

Frustrated by a lack of government funds, Esperant is trying to raise money independently to start a center to house street children.

He meets with the children below the statue of Jesus, drawing a crowd as he writes their names on a list. At last count, the list had 57 names.

"There is no work back home," says Lesene Souverain, 17, who says he left home when he was 9 because his parents couldn't pay for school. "At least on the streets, there are people who can help me."

In the nearby hills, deforested land is turning into desert. Curls of smoke rise as farmers use remaining trees to make charcoal for cooking. Esperant says most of Les Cayes' street children come from this wasteland.

"They don't have any arable land to plant anymore," he says. "So they came to the city to look for life, to look for a way to survive." ▶

CHILD LABOR IS COMMON

Child labor is common even for those who stay at home. Boys in Les Cayes sell crackers and muffins from trays on their heads. In Port-au-Prince, some young girls work as prostitutes to augment family earnings.

Sometimes, poor parents give away children to be servants for better-off families. It's widely accepted in Haiti to keep a child servant, or *restavek*, a Creole term that means "staying with." The children often are mistreated, and human rights groups criticize the practice as child slavery.

This boy carrying a heavy container of water is a *restavek*, a poor Haitian child handed over to a family to be a servant.

DESCRIPTIVE DETAILS

Which detail in lines 96–106 helps readers visualize the destruction of land in Haiti?

_____

_____

_____

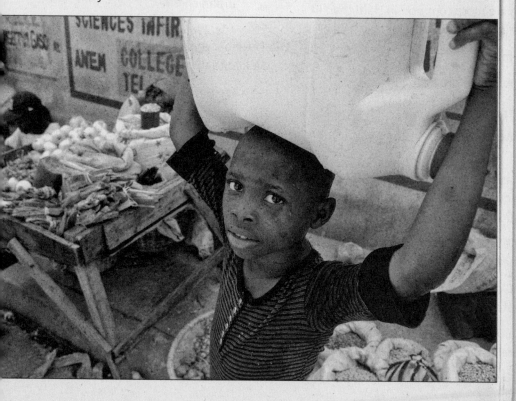

Reading Comprehension

DIRECTIONS *Answer these questions about the two selections in this lesson by filling in the correct ovals.*

1. Which word *best* describes the way Haitians generally react to the street children?

    Ⓐ alarmed

    Ⓑ sympathetic

    Ⓒ annoyed

    Ⓓ desperate

2. Why did Jean-Claude leave the countryside?

    Ⓐ He wanted a better education.

    Ⓑ His family was abusing him.

    Ⓒ He needed to support his family.

    Ⓓ He got into trouble with the police.

3. What factor explains why homeless children are more common in Haiti than in most neighboring countries?

    Ⓐ climate

    Ⓑ population growth

    Ⓒ illegal immigration

    Ⓓ poverty

4. What has been the effect of farmers cutting down trees to make charcoal for cooking?

    Ⓐ The loss of farmland has increased unemployment.

    Ⓑ Children are finding jobs in restaurants.

    Ⓒ Haiti has become less dependent on foreign oil.

    Ⓓ Farmers have more income to care for children.

5. What does Dominique Esperant have in common with Jonathan Swift?

    Ⓐ running an orphanage

    Ⓑ writing satirical essays about poverty

    Ⓒ concern about deforestation

    Ⓓ drawing attention to neglected children

6. Which statement is supported by both selections?

    Ⓐ The needs of poor children are often overlooked.

    Ⓑ Children should be made to work hard.

    Ⓒ Poor people should not have children.

    Ⓓ Rural children are worse off than urban children.

7. The word *arable* in line 103 of "Children Sink to the Bottom" refers to land that is

    Ⓐ well-irrigated

    Ⓑ fit for growing crops

    Ⓒ ready to be plowed

    Ⓓ hardened from drought

8. The word *augment* in line 114 means

    Ⓐ implement

    Ⓑ replace

    Ⓒ supplement

    Ⓓ expend

Timed Writing Practice

PROMPT

Swift wasn't serious about the plan he outlined in "A Modest Proposal," but he took the problem of Irish poverty very seriously. Write a problem-solution essay in which you propose one step that should be taken to help the poor. Narrow the focus of your essay to (address a specific example of poverty). You can focus on the conditions described in one of the selections you have read, or you can choose another example of poverty that you are familiar with. Provide at least three reasons for your solution, and one or two details to support each reason.

BUDGET YOUR TIME

You have **45 minutes** to respond. Decide how much time to spend on each step.

Analyze _____

Plan _____

Write _____ 45

Review _____

TEST-TAKER'S TOOLKIT

1. ANALYZE THE PROMPT

A. Underline the type of writing you are being asked to do.

B. Circle any key words that describe what should be included in your writing. One example has been circled for you.

2. PLAN YOUR RESPONSE

A. **Make notes** Decide which example of poverty you will focus on, and brainstorm a list of possible solutions. Choose the solution you will propose in your essay. In the chart here, list three reasons why your solution will help the poor, and list details to support your reasons.

B. **Organize your information** In the introductory paragraph, describe the specific problem of poverty that you will address in the essay, and clearly state a solution. Then you can write a paragraph for each reason you noted in your chart. Use your details to support each reason. End the essay with a conclusion in which you sum up your ideas.

Reason 1	Detail(s)
Reason 2	Detail(s)
Reason 3	Detail(s)

3. WRITE AND REVIEW

A. Capture your readers' attention by including a vivid description or a striking question in your introduction.

B. Be sure to leave time to check your spelling and grammar.

UNIT 3

THE RESTORATION AND THE 18TH CENTURY

LESSON 3B

from *A Vindication of the Rights of Woman*

BY MARY WOLLSTONECRAFT

RELATED NONFICTION
Fight Like a Girl

What makes
EQUALITY *elusive?*

Thomas Jefferson wrote that "all men are created equal," but he and the other Founding Fathers left out many men and all women when they first considered rights in the new United States. Writing 16 years after the Declaration of Independence, Mary Wollstonecraft was one of the first to confront the issue of equality for women, although even she confined her arguments to education.

DISCUSS With a partner, consider why the issue of equal rights has historically been so difficult to achieve. Respond to the questions in the notebook, and then share your thoughts with a classmate.

Issues of Equality

1. What policies and actions can help promote equal rights among all citizens in a nation?

_____

_____

_____

_____

2. Why are groups of people sometimes opposed to these measures?

_____

_____

_____

_____

ASSESSMENT GOALS

By the end of this lesson, you will be able to . . .

- recognize the elements of an argument
- use active reading strategies to comprehend text
- analyze an author's style in a work of nonfiction
- analyze a writing prompt and plan a position paper

Argument

Mary Wollstonecraft has been called everything from a "hyena in petticoats" to "the mother of feminism." Both of these titles came in reaction to her arguments concerning women's rights. An **ARGUMENT** is speech or writing that expresses a position on an issue and then supports it with reasons and evidence.

Sound arguments include the elements listed in the chart below. You can practice answering questions about argument as you read the excerpt from *A Vindication of the Rights of Woman*.

ELEMENTS OF AN ARGUMENT	STRATEGIES FOR EVALUATION
CLAIM: the writer's position on an issue or problem	The claim is often stated directly in the introduction or conclusion of an argument. Make sure to look for clues in the title as well.
REASONS: statements that explain or justify the claim	Watch for errors in logic, such as overgeneralizations—conclusions that are too broad to be valid.
EVIDENCE: facts, statistics, examples, or the views of experts	Does the information come from trustworthy sources? Is there enough to support the claim?

A VINDICATION
of the RIGHTS of WOMAN

MARY WOLLSTONECRAFT

BACKGROUND In the late 18th century, daughters of English gentlemen were educated at home before being sent away to school for a few years. In addition to reading and studying foreign languages, girls learned how to play the piano, sing, draw, and do needlework. Young women were expected to marry. Barred from any profession, an unmarried woman could only support herself as a servant, a nurse, a governess, or some similar occupation.

FROM THE INTRODUCTION

After considering the historic page, and viewing the living world with anxious solicitude, the most melancholy emotions of sorrowful indignation have depressed my spirits, and I have sighed when obliged to confess, that either nature has made a great difference between man and man, or that the civilization which has hitherto taken place in the world has been very partial. I have turned over various books written on the subject of education, and patiently observed the conduct of parents and the management of schools; but what has been the result?—a profound conviction that the neglected education of my fellow-creatures is the grand
10 source of the misery I deplore; and that women, in particular, are rendered weak and wretched by a variety of concurring causes, originating from one hasty conclusion. The conduct and manners of women, in fact, evidently prove that their minds are not in a healthy state; for, like the flowers which are planted in too rich a soil, strength and usefulness are sacrificed to beauty; and the flaunting leaves, after having pleased a fastidious eye, fade, disregarded on the stalk, long before the season when they ought to have arrived at maturity. One cause of this barren blooming I attribute to a false system of education, gathered from the books written on this subject by men who, considering females rather as women than human

MARK IT UP

Use these marks to monitor your reading:

* This is important.

? I don't understand.

! This is a surprise.

When you see this pencil ✏, you'll be asked to mark up the text. Don't forget, you can always write in this book in any way you find useful.

vindication (vĭn′dĭ-kā′shən) *n.* clearing from criticism, blame, guilt, or suspicion; justification

Focus
Before you begin reading, review the background information to help you understand the conditions women lived under during Wollstonecraft's time. Then read the first part of the essay to find out what Wollstonecraft wanted to change.

20 creatures, have been more anxious to make them alluring mistresses than affectionate wives and rational mothers; and the understanding of the sex has been so bubbled by this specious homage,[1] that the civilized women of the present century, with a few exceptions, are only anxious to inspire love, when they ought to cherish a nobler ambition, and by their abilities and virtues exact respect. ◀

In a treatise,[2] therefore, on female rights and manners, the works which have been particularly written for their improvement must not be overlooked; especially when it is asserted, in direct terms, that the minds of women are enfeebled by false refinement; that the books of instruction, 30 written by men of genius, have had the same tendency as more frivolous productions; and that . . . they are treated as a kind of subordinate beings, and not as a part of the human species, when improvable reason is allowed to be the dignified distinction which raises men above the brute creation, and puts a natural scepter in a feeble hand.

Yet, because I am a woman, I would not lead my readers to suppose that I mean violently to agitate the contested question respecting the quality or inferiority of the sex; but as the subject lies in my way, and I cannot pass it over without subjecting the main tendency of my reasoning to misconstruction, I shall stop a moment to deliver, in a few words, my 40 opinion. In the government of the physical world it is observable that the female in point of strength is, in general, inferior to the male. This is the law of nature; and it does not appear to be suspended or abrogated in favor of woman. A degree of physical superiority cannot, therefore, be denied—and it is a noble **prerogative**! But not content with this natural pre-eminence, men endeavor to sink us still lower merely to render us alluring objects for a moment; and women, intoxicated by the adoration which men, under the influence of their senses, pay them, do not seek to obtain a durable interest in their hearts, or to become the friends of the fellow creatures who find amusement in their society.

50 I am aware of an obvious inference: from every quarter have I heard exclamations against masculine women; but where are they to be found? If by this appellation men mean to inveigh against their ardor[3] in hunting, shooting, and gaming, I shall most cordially join in the cry; but if it be against the imitation of manly virtues, or, more properly speaking, the attainment of those talents and virtues, the exercise of which ennobles the

ANALYZE

What is Wollstonecraft's **claim?**
Complete the sentences below.

Society educates women

to be _____

_____

not _____

_____

This causes _____

_____

because _____

_____

_____

prerogative (prĭ-rŏg′ə-tĭv)
n. a privilege or distinctive advantage

1. **bubbled by this specious homage** (spē′shəs hŏm′ĭj): deceived by this false honor.
2. **treatise:** a formal, detailed article or book on a particular subject.
3. **If by . . . inveigh** (ĭn-vā′) **against their ardor:** if by this term ("masculine women") men mean to condemn some women's enthusiasm.

human character, and which raise females in the scale of animal being, when they are comprehensively termed mankind; all those who view them with a philosophic eye must, I should think, wish with me, that they may every day grow more and more masculine. . . .

My own sex, I hope, will excuse me, if I treat them like rational creatures, instead of flattering their *fascinating* graces, and viewing them as if they were in a state of perpetual childhood, unable to stand alone. I earnestly wish to point out in what true dignity and human happiness consists—I wish to persuade women to endeavor to acquire strength, both of mind and body, and to convince them that the soft phrases, susceptibility of heart, delicacy of sentiment, and refinement of taste, are almost synonymous with epithets[4] of weakness, and that those beings who are only the objects of pity and that kind of love, which has been termed its sister, will soon become objects of contempt. . . . ▶

The education of women has, of late, been more attended to than formerly; yet they are still reckoned a frivolous sex, and ridiculed or pitied by the writers who endeavor by satire or instruction to improve them. It is acknowledged that they spend many of the first years of their lives in acquiring a smattering of accomplishments;[5] meanwhile strength of body and mind are sacrificed to libertine[6] notions of beauty, to the desire of establishing themselves—the only way women can rise in the world—by marriage. And this desire making mere animals of them, when they marry they act as such children may be expected to act: they dress; they paint, and nickname God's creatures. Surely these weak beings are only fit for a seraglio![7] Can they be expected to govern a family with judgment, or take care of the poor babes whom they bring into the world? ▶

If then it can be fairly deduced from the present conduct of the sex, from the prevalent fondness for pleasure which takes place of ambition and those nobler passions that open and enlarge the soul; that the instruction which women have hitherto received has only tended, with the constitution of civil society, to render them insignificant objects of desire—mere propagators of fools!—if it can be proved that in aiming to accomplish them, without cultivating their understandings, they are taken out of their sphere of duties, and made ridiculous and useless when the short-lived bloom of beauty is over, I presume that *rational* men will

ANALYZE

Reread the boxed text. What **evidence** does Wollstonecraft offer to support her **claim** that women's education has made them weak?

_____

_____

_____

_____

_____

CLARIFY

Why does Wollstonecraft think it is wrong for young women to focus only on acquiring the skills that will attract a husband?

_____

_____

_____

_____

---

4. **epithets** (ĕp′ə-thĕts′): descriptive terms.
5. **accomplishments:** This term, when applied to women, designated only those achievements then considered suitable for middle- and upper-class women, such as painting, singing, playing a musical instrument, and embroidery.
6. **libertine** (lĭb′ər-tēn′): indecent or unseemly.
7. **seraglio** (sə-răl′yō): harem.

PAUSE & REFLECT

Does Wollstonecraft give convincing **reasons** for men to support better education for women? Why or why not? *EVALUATE*

_____

_____

_____

FOCUS

As you read the second part of the essay, note the opposing viewpoints—those of Rousseau and Dr. Gregory—that Wollstonecraft introduces. Pay attention to how Wollstonecraft refutes these **arguments**.

inculcate (ĭn-kŭl′kāt′) *v.* to impress on the mind by frequent repetition; to teach; to instill

evanescent (ĕv′ə-nĕs′ənt) *adj.* quick to disappear

excuse me for endeavoring to persuade them to become more masculine and respectable.

Indeed the word masculine is only a bugbear:[8] there is little reason to fear that women will acquire too much courage or fortitude; for their apparent inferiority with respect to bodily strength, must render them, in some degree, dependent on men in the various relations of life; but why should it be increased by prejudices that give a sex to virtue, and confound simple truths with sensual reveries?[9]   **PAUSE & REFLECT**

FROM CHAPTER 2

Youth is the season for love in both sexes; but in those days of thoughtless
100 enjoyment provision should be made for the more important years of life, when reflection takes place of sensation. But Rousseau,[10] and most of the male writers who have followed his steps, have warmly **inculcated** that the whole tendency of female education ought to be directed to one point: to render them[11] pleasing.

Let me reason with the supporters of this opinion who have any knowledge of human nature, do they imagine that marriage can eradicate the habitude of life? The woman who has only been taught to please will soon find that her charms are oblique sunbeams, and that they cannot have much effect on her husband's heart when they are seen every day,
110 when the summer is passed and gone. Will she then have sufficient native energy to look into herself for comfort, and cultivate her dormant faculties? or, is it not more rational to expect that she will try to please other men; and, in the emotions raised by the expectation of new conquests, endeavor to forget the mortification her love or pride has received? When the husband ceases to be a lover—and the time will inevitably come, her desire of pleasing will then grow languid, or become a spring of bitterness; and love, perhaps, the most **evanescent** of all passions, gives place to jealousy or vanity.

I now speak of women who are restrained by principle or prejudice;
120 such women, though they would shrink from an intrigue with real abhorrence, yet, nevertheless, wish to be convinced by the homage of gallantry that they are cruelly neglected by their husbands; or, days and

---

8. **bugbear:** an object of exaggerated fear.
9. **confound . . . reveries** (rĕv′ə-rēz): confuse simple truths with men's sexual daydreams.
10. **Rousseau** (rōō-sō′): The Swiss-born French philosopher Jean-Jacques Rousseau (1712–1778) presented a plan for female education in his famous 1762 novel *Émile.*
11. **them:** that is, females.

weeks are spent in dreaming of the happiness enjoyed by congenial souls till their health is undermined and their spirits broken by discontent. How then can the great art of pleasing be such a necessary study? it is only useful to a mistress; the chaste wife, and serious mother, should only consider her power to please as the polish of her virtues, and the affection of her husband as one of the comforts that render her talk less difficult and her life happier. But, whether she be loved or neglected, her first wish
130　should be to make herself respectable, and not to rely for all her happiness on a being subject to like infirmities with herself. ▶

　　The worthy Dr. Gregory fell into a similar error. I respect his heart; but entirely disapprove of his celebrated Legacy to his Daughters.[12] . . .

　　He actually recommends dissimulation, and advises an innocent girl to give the lie to her feelings, and not dance with spirit, when gaiety of heart would make her feet eloquent without making her gestures immodest. In the name of truth and common sense, why should not one woman acknowledge that she can take more exercise than another? or, in other words, that she has a sound constitution; and why, to damp innocent
140　vivacity, is she darkly to be told that men will draw conclusions which she little thinks of? Let the libertine draw what inference he pleases; but, I hope, that no sensible mother will restrain the natural frankness of youth by instilling such indecent cautions. Out of the abundance of the heart the mouth speaketh; and a wiser than Solomon[13] hath said, that the heart should be made clean, and not trivial ceremonies observed, which it is not very difficult to fulfil with scrupulous exactness when vice reigns in the heart.

　　Women ought to endeavor to purify their heart; but can they do so ▶ when their uncultivated understandings make them entirely dependent
150　on their senses for employment and amusement, when no noble pursuit sets them above the little vanities of the day, or enables them to curb the wild emotions that agitate a reed over which every passing breeze has power? To gain the affections of a virtuous man, is affectation necessary? Nature has given woman a weaker frame than man; but, to ensure her husband's affections, must a wife, who by the exercise of her mind and body whilst she was discharging the duties of a daughter, wife, and mother,

---

12. **Dr. Gregory . . . Daughters:** In his 1774 work *A Father's Legacy for His Daughters*, John Gregory (1724–1773) offered a plan for female education that remained popular for decades.

13. **a wiser than Solomon:** King David, reputed author of many psalms in the Bible and the father of King Solomon, who was known for his wisdom. The words that follow draw on ideas in Psalm 24, which states that only those with "clean hands, and a pure heart" shall ascend into Heaven.

ANALYZE

Rousseau argued that women's education should make them "pleasing" to men. What, in Wollstonecraft's opinion, is the problem with this view?

_____

_____

_____

_____

_____

TestSmart

VOCABULARY

From its context in line 148, you can tell that *endeavor* means

Ⓐ pay

Ⓑ strive

Ⓒ effort

Ⓓ purity

TIP When a test item asks you to define a word in context, it can help to **replace the word with each possible answer choice.** Think about what Wollstonecraft wants women to achieve. Then replace the word *endeavor* in line 148 with each answer choice above. Which substitution makes the most sense?

has allowed her constitution to retain its natural strength, and her nerves
a healthy tone, is she, I say, to condescend to use art and **feign** a sickly
delicacy in order to secure her husband's affection? Weakness may excite
160 tenderness, and gratify the arrogant pride of man; but the lordly caresses of
a protector will not gratify a noble mind that pants for, and deserves to be
respected. Fondness is a poor substitute for friendship! . . . ◄

Besides, the woman who strengthens her body and exercises her mind
will, by managing her family and practicing various virtues, become the
friend, and not the humble dependent of her husband; and if she, by
possessing such substantial qualities, merit his regard, she will not find it
necessary to conceal her affection, nor to pretend to an unnatural coldness
of constitution to excite her husband's passions. . . . ◄

If all the faculties of woman's mind are only to be cultivated as they
170 respect her dependence on man; if, when a husband be obtained, she have
arrived at her goal, and meanly proud rests satisfied with such a paltry
crown, let her grovel contentedly, scarcely raised by her employments
above the animal kingdom; but, if, struggling for the prize of her
high calling, she look beyond the present scene, let her cultivate her
understanding without stopping to consider what character the husband
may have whom she is destined to marry. Let her only determine, without
being too anxious about present happiness, to acquire the qualities that
ennoble a rational being, and a rough inelegant husband may shock her
taste without destroying her peace of mind. She will not model her soul
180 to suit the frailties of her companion, but to bear with them: his character
may be a trial, but not an impediment to virtue. . . .

These may be termed Utopian dreams. Thanks to that Being who
impressed them on my soul, and gave me sufficient strength of mind to
dare to exert my own reason, till, becoming dependent only on him for the
support of my virtue, I view, with indignation, the mistaken notions that
enslave my sex.

I love man as my fellow; but his scepter, real, or usurped, extends not
to me, unless the reason of an individual demands my homage; and even
then the submission is to reason, and not to man. In fact, the conduct
190 of an accountable being must be regulated by the operations of its own
reason; or on what foundation rests the throne of God?

It appears to me necessary to dwell on these obvious truths, because
females have been insulated, as it were; and, while they have been stripped
of the virtues that should clothe humanity, they have been decked with
artificial graces that enable them to exercise a short-lived tyranny. Love, in
their bosoms, taking place of every nobler passion, their sole ambition is
to be fair, to raise emotion instead of inspiring respect; and this ignoble

desire, like the servility in absolute monarchies, destroys all strength of character. Liberty is the mother of virtue, and if women be, by their very

200 constitution, slaves, and not allowed to breathe the sharp invigorating air of freedom, they must ever languish like exotics,[14] and be reckoned beautiful flaws in nature. 🖐 **PAUSE & REFLECT**

🖐 **PAUSE & REFLECT**

In line 182, Wollstonecraft says that some people will consider her ideas "Utopian dreams." What does this remark suggest about how the status of women in Western society has changed since her time? *COMPARE AND CONTRAST*

_____

_____

_____

_____

_____

Big Question ⭐

In Wollstonecraft's eyes, education is crucial to gaining equality. Do you agree, or do you think that poorly educated people can play an equal role in society? Explain your answer.

_____

_____

_____

_____

_____

14. **languish** (lăng′gwĭsh) **like exotics:** wilt like plants grown away from their natural environment.

Reading Comprehension

DIRECTIONS *Answer these questions about the excerpt from* A Vindication
of the Rights of Woman *by filling in the correct ovals.*

1. In which way does Wollstonecraft concede that men are superior to women?

   (A) morally

   (B) mentally

   (C) physically

   (D) rationally

2. According to Wollstonecraft, why do most women go along with the "false system of education" that fails to develop their mental and physical abilities?

   (A) They are anxious to get married.

   (B) They don't know any better.

   (C) They prefer to be weak and ignorant.

   (D) They would rather be alluring mistresses than dutiful wives.

3. Wollstonecraft believes that women need strong minds and bodies so that

   (A) they can compete with men

   (B) they will no longer be the physically weaker sex

   (C) they can be better wives and mothers

   (D) they can attract enlightened men

4. Which statement *best* sums up Wollstonecraft's argument in this essay?

   (A) Men will never allow women to improve their status.

   (B) Women's education needs to focus more on improving their physical and mental abilities.

   (C) Intelligent women find it easier to attract good husbands.

   (D) Women should become physically and mentally equal to men.

5. Which reason does Wollstonecraft *not* use to support her claim?

   (A) Strengthening their bodies and minds makes women better mothers.

   (B) Developing character through education enables women to be better partners to their husbands.

   (C) Women raised only to be pleasing to men are at the mercy of their own senses.

   (D) Women who are allowed to participate in sports and hunting activities make better, more playful wives.

6. Wollstonecraft's comparison of women to exotic flowers in lines 12–17 emphasizes her point that

   (A) women are raised to be pleasing at the expense of their strength and intelligence

   (B) women should be beautiful and healthy, like carefully tended flowers

   (C) though beauty fades, women, like flowers, can bloom again

   (D) women who receive too much education can wither, just like flowers that receive too much water

7. In the context of line 42, *abrogated* means

   (A) praised

   (B) abolished

   (C) deceived

   (D) imposed

8. In line 153, *affectation* means

   (A) tender feeling

   (B) bias

   (C) depression

   (D) false behavior

Responding in Writing

9. Short Response In a paragraph, summarize Wollstonecraft's argument about women's rights in this excerpt from *A Vindication of the Rights of Woman*. Be sure to discuss her views on education and explain what she thought women should strive for. Use quotations from the essay to support your summary.

TEST-TAKER'S TOOLKIT

- **ACADEMIC VOCABULARY** When you **summarize** an author's ideas, you restate his or her most important points in your own words. Unlike a paraphrase, a summary is usually shorter than the original text. It also often uses simpler language.

- **GRAPHIC ORGANIZER** Use the chart below to organize your thoughts and gather evidence before you begin your response.

WOLLSTONECRAFT ON WOMEN'S RIGHTS

The Author's Ideas	Support from the Essay
Wollstonecraft believed that women's place in society was a miserable one, and that lack of female education was largely to blame.	"... the neglected education of my fellow-creatures is the grand source of the misery I deplore ..." (lines 9–10)

Use with the excerpt *from* A Vindication of the Rights of Woman, *p. 118*

What's the Connection?

Mary Wollstonecraft wrote her famous argument for women's rights over 200 years ago, but this battle is still being fought today. The book excerpt you are about to read urges readers to join the fight, offering modern ways to "Fight Like a Girl" in the battle for equality.

LIST IT With a classmate, think of a group that lacks equal standing in society. You don't have to focus on women—your example may involve discrimination due to factors such as race, ethnicity, religion, or disability. Then list things that people could do to help end discrimination against this group.

Ways to Fight Discrimination

LEARN THE SKILL: ANALYZE AUTHOR'S STYLE

An author's **style** is the individual way he or she communicates ideas—not *what* is said, but *how* it is said. The following tips can help you analyze an author's style in a work of nonfiction:

- Identify the author's **tone,** or attitude. Does the author sound forceful or hesitant, energized or resigned?

- Consider the author's **word choice.** Is the language formal or informal? Does the author use figurative language?

- Think about the type of sentences the author uses. Do you find more long, flowing sentences or short, direct ones?

- Finally, think about how the text affects you as a reader. Does the author's writing make you feel enthusiastic and ready for action or quietly reflective?

For more on author's style, see the Author's Craft entry in the Nonfiction Skills Handbook beginning on page R2.

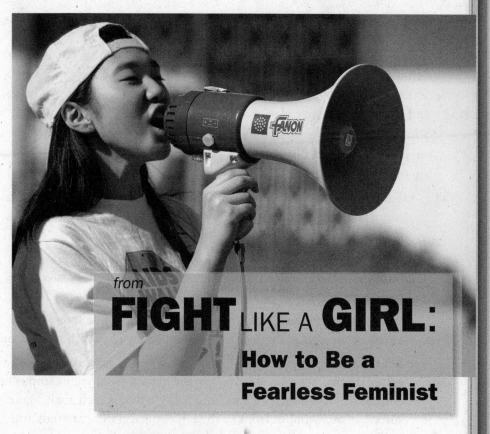

from

FIGHT LIKE A GIRL:

How to Be a Fearless Feminist

by Megan Seely

Feminism is not dead. Indeed, we have achieved many rights and made many gains, but we are not there yet. The fight for true political, social, and economic justice continues. And, while we often enjoy the benefits of a fight for equality that we were not required to undertake, we must realize that this equality is not universal and that it is this generation that must take up the fight. This movement belongs to us all. We each have a stake; we all can contribute. All voices, experiences, perspectives, and visions can be incorporated and represented, for we all benefit from shared
10 and practiced equality. We can raise our voices to speak against injustice at every level—individually and institutionally. . . . We can join together, work together, protect and support one another. We can be individuals who also find a common ground from which to speak collectively. We can share our stories, lead by example, and be activists in our daily lives. This is what it means to fight like a girl. ▶

AUTHOR'S STYLE

The author uses the first-person plural pronouns *we, us,* and *our.* Reread lines 1–16, circling each of these pronouns where they appear in the text. ✏

What effect does this stylistic choice have on you as a reader? How does it make you feel?

HOW TO FIGHT LIKE A GIRL

No act is too small; you may never know the full extent of your impact.
Activism is contagious. While you may be one person, your voice and
20 actions can touch others, whose voices and actions can touch still others,
and so forth until we experience change. This is how activism works. . . .
Social change begins on a small level with a small group of people who
envision a new way. But before we get too far, let's get right to it. Here
are some actions you can take: ◄

- **Talk to friends,** family, students, and/or co-workers about political
  or social issues that concern you. Gather information to share with
  them from organizations, Web sites, books, or classes.

- **Make a phone call** to an elected official, advertising sponsor,
  business, or school to let them know how you feel about their
30 policies, practices, or products.

- **Write a letter** to the editor of your local newspaper in response to an
  article about women, health care, politics, or any issue that interests you.

- **Set up a table** to give out information in your community or on
  your campus. You may need to get permission from your campus or
  community business, or check into using a free-speech area. Make
  sure that you stand in front of the table to hand out materials and
  answer questions—don't hide behind the table; be accessible. . . .

- **Host a consciousness-raising group**—bring together friends,
  family, or colleagues to discuss an important issue.

40 - **Organize a house party** to educate and mobilize your friends to
  vote or to support a feminist candidate running for office. Invite
  people to come over to discuss an upcoming election—have each
  participant research a different issue and bring the information to
  the group. Make it a potluck, or meet over coffee.

- **Work on a voter registration campaign;** register people in your
  community to vote in the next election. ◄

- **Offer to watch the children** of someone you know so that the
  person can go to the polls and vote.

- **Give testimony** at your local city hall or before the state legislature
50 or Congress.

- **Organize a human billboard action**—gather some friends to line
  a main street in your town with signs that have a message, each sign
  carrying a portion of the message: for example, "Honk . . . if you . . .
  support . . . equality."

- **Organize a candlelight vigil** to raise awareness about an issue or to
  commemorate an important event/date. . . .

AUTHOR'S STYLE

Reread lines 18–24. Would
you describe the language
the author uses as formal or
informal?

☐ formal
☐ informal

Explain your answer, citing
one or two examples from the
text.

_____

_____

_____

_____

SPECIALIZED
Vocabulary

If the term *voter registration
campaign* in line 45 is new
to you, be sure to note the
definition included in the
same bullet point. Authors
often include a definition
of specialized terms to aid
readers. Find and underline
another example of a
specialized term the author
defines in this bulleted list. ✏

WORD ANALYSIS

- **Organize a speakout,** like the Take Back the Night rallies, where women have the opportunity to speak about their experiences with violence in a safe and supportive environment. This can be done with any issue.

- **Organize an informational picket**—make signs, bring together a bunch of people, and walk back and forth in front of a business, courthouse, or legislature, sharing information with people passing by.

- **Boycott**—a boycott is the withholding of financial support (e.g., by refusing to buy a particular product) as a form of protest against the policies or practices of a business, institution, or organization. There are many legal guidelines for a boycott, so make sure to get legal advice before calling for one.

- **Plan a girlcott** or a "boycott" related to a specifically woman-centered cause. Sometimes, a "girlcott" is defined as bringing resources into an organization, business, or institution to support their efforts—in other words, the opposite of a boycott.

- **Organize street theater.** Dress up and act out your concerns in a public venue. During the 2000 elections, I was one of nine people who dressed up as the Supreme Court justices and then held a press conference about what we saw as a threat to the Court.

- **Organize a benefit**—for example, a walk-a-thon, a concert, a comedy night, an art show.

- **Organize a rally**—small, medium, or large. Have people come together in a central location to hear speakers and receive information about a given event.

- **Organize a march**—small, medium, or large. Have people gather in one place, hear speakers, and then walk in an organized fashion to another location. People carry signs with political messages and sign and shout chants to raise awareness about an important issue. . . . ▶

The possibilities for action are endless; I've provided just a few ideas that I've taught. Talk to organizations, talk to friends, and come up with your own ideas. Don't let taking action overwhelm you; start at the level you are comfortable. ▶

EVALUATE

Which bulleted action on this page would be most effective in your community? Which, do you think, would be least effective? Explain your choices.

Most:

Least:

AUTHOR'S STYLE

What words would you use to describe the author's **tone** in this article? List three adjectives below.

Circle specific words and phrases from the text that influenced your answer. ✎

Reading Comprehension

DIRECTIONS *Answer these questions about the two selections in this lesson by filling in the correct ovals.*

1. In the excerpt from *Fight Like a Girl*, Megan Seely's style can *best* be described as

   (A) witty and whimsical

   (B) formal and argumentative

   (C) resigned and brisk

   (D) impassioned and informal

2. The author's inclusion of the bulleted list of actions mainly supports the idea that

   (A) feminism is not dead

   (B) activism is difficult work

   (C) we can all take steps to make a difference

   (D) people must find common ground

3. Which of the following is *not* a feature of this author's style?

   (A) the use of informal language

   (B) an energetic, exciting tone

   (C) the use of the pronouns *we, us,* and *our*

   (D) long, flowing sentences containing figurative language

4. What does Seely mean by the statement "This movement belongs to us all"?

   (A) Everyone benefits from equality, so everyone should be involved in the feminist movement.

   (B) The public has a right to know about the discrimination women suffer.

   (C) Every feminist should share in the profits made by women's rights groups.

   (D) The founders of the movement should not take all the credit.

5. The excerpts from *A Vindication of the Rights of Woman* and *Fight Like a Girl* share the same

   (A) tone   (C) main idea

   (B) style   (D) general topic

6. How do the two selections in this lesson differ?

   (A) Wollstonecraft limits her argument to education, while Seely's focus is much broader.

   (B) Seely focuses on the discrimination minorities face as well as that endured by women.

   (C) Wollstonecraft's essay offers a wider variety of actions one can take to support women's rights.

   (D) Seely thinks discrimination has ended, but Wollstonecraft argues that women lack most rights.

7. In line 14 of the excerpt from *Fight Like a Girl*, the word *collectively* means

   (A) separately   (C) with force

   (B) as one   (D) earnestly

8. What does the word *mobilize* mean in line 40?

   (A) to travel quickly

   (B) to make comfortable

   (C) to assemble or coordinate for a purpose

   (D) to present with false information

Timed Writing Practice

PROMPT

If you were the head of a government, business, or university, what would you do to ensure that all members of your community had equal rights, regardless of gender? Imagine yourself in one of the three roles above. Write a position paper in which you (explain your policy) and tell what it does to ensure equality.

TEST-TAKER'S TOOLKIT

1. ANALYZE THE PROMPT

A. Underline the question that the prompt asks you to answer.

B. Circle key words and phrases that tell you what to include. One phrase has been circled for you.

C. Restate the prompt in your own words.

I am being asked to _____

_____

_____

_____

_____

_____

2. PLAN YOUR RESPONSE

A. **Make notes** Choose which role you will imagine yourself in. Then think about the equality issues your specific institution might face. For example, if you were the head of a university, you might have to make sure that men's and women's sports teams receive equal funding and equal publicity. Brainstorm a list of issues you might face in your chosen role, and note how you might solve each one.

B. **Organize your information** Your position paper should start with a strong introduction that explains why you think it is important to strive for equality. You should tell what position you've chosen to promote. You might also give an overview of your policy—that is, a summary of the ways you fight discrimination at your institution. Each paragraph that follows your introduction can go into more detail about one issue and how you solve it.

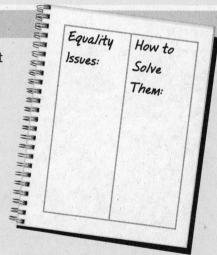

Equality Issues: | How to Solve Them:

3. WRITE AND REVIEW

A. Write your full response on a separate piece of paper.

B. Be sure to leave time to review your work and to check your spelling and grammar.

LESSON 4A

Selected Poetry
BY WILLIAM WORDSWORTH

RELATED NONFICTION
Wordsworth Enters the Hip-Hop Era

Where do we find
PEACE?

When filled with the stresses and strains of everyday life, people sometimes go to a particular place to regain a sense of peace. Like William Wordsworth, many people seek peace in a natural setting. Others find comfort in a grandparent's home or in a place of worship.

SKETCH IT What place gives you a peaceful feeling? In the notebook shown, draw a simple sketch of that place. Then complete the sentences. Share your work with a partner.

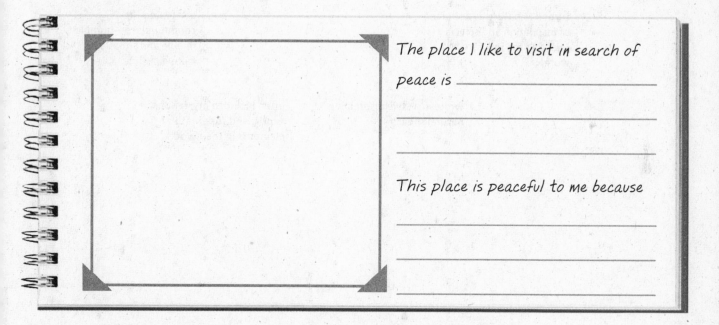

The place I like to visit in search of peace is _____

_____

_____

This place is peaceful to me because

_____

_____

_____

ASSESSMENT GOALS

By the end of this lesson, you will be able to . . .

- analyze romantic poetry
- use active reading strategies to comprehend text
- analyze a feature article
- analyze a writing prompt and plan a descriptive essay

Romantic Poetry

In England, **ROMANTICISM** was a literary and artistic movement that began in the late 18th century and lasted through the first few decades of the 19th century. Romantic poets stressed the importance of the individual's subjective experiences, paying more attention to their inner lives than to social issues. Unlike most 18th-century poets, the romantics valued emotion, spontaneity, and imagination over reason and orderliness.

William Wordsworth helped launch the romantic movement in England, and he was the most influential poet of the period. Review the methods used by romantic poets in the graphic below to help you analyze Wordsworth's poetry.

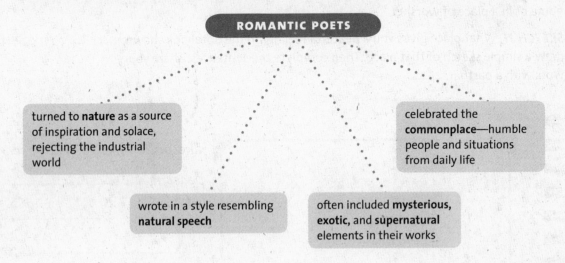

ROMANTIC POETS

turned to **nature** as a source of inspiration and solace, rejecting the industrial world

wrote in a style resembling **natural speech**

often included **mysterious, exotic,** and **supernatural** elements in their works

celebrated the **commonplace**—humble people and situations from daily life

Lines Composed a Few Miles Above
Tintern Abbey

William Wordsworth

MARK IT UP

Use these marks to monitor your reading:

* This is important.

? I don't understand.

! This is a surprise.

When you see this pencil ✐, you'll be asked to mark up the text. You can also write in this book in any way you find useful.

BACKGROUND In many of his poems, Wordsworth explores his thoughts and feelings about a particular setting. He wrote "Tintern Abbey" five years after his first visit to a ruined medieval abbey in the Wye River valley in Wales. In the poem, he describes returning to the site accompanied by his beloved sister, Dorothy. Another of his poems, "I Wandered Lonely As a Cloud," was inspired by a walk he took with Dorothy near their home in the picturesque Lake District.

FOCUS

In this section, the speaker describes his feelings as he returns to Tintern Abbey after a five-year absence. Read to find out how his experiences in **nature** have affected him.

 Five years have passed; five summers, with the length
Of five long winters! and again I hear
These waters, rolling from their mountain-springs
With a soft inland murmur. Once again
5 Do I behold these steep and lofty cliffs,
That on a wild secluded scene impress
Thoughts of more deep seclusion; and connect
The landscape with the quiet of the sky.
The day is come when I again repose[1]
10 Here, under this dark sycamore, and view
These plots of cottage ground, these orchard tufts,
Which at this season, with their unripe fruits,
Are clad in one green hue, and lose themselves
'Mid groves and copses.[2] Once again I see
15 These hedgerows, hardly hedgerows, little lines
Of sportive wood run wild; these pastoral[3] farms,

---

1. **repose:** lie at rest.
2. **copses** (kŏp'sĭz): thickets of small trees.
3. **pastoral** (păs'tər-əl): rural and serene.

VISUALIZE

Reread lines 1–22. Underline words and phrases that help you picture the landscape near Tintern Abbey.

TESTSMART

Reread lines 22–49. Which word describes the effect that city life has on the speaker?

(A) rejuvenation

(B) uneasiness

(C) tranquility

(D) forgetfulness

TIP On some test questions, the answer is not stated directly in the text. You will have to **infer the answer** by combining clues from the text with your own knowledge. In this case, underline the words and phrases that describe the speaker's feelings in the city or explain why the landscape near Tintern Abbey has meant so much to him. Use these clues to figure out how he is affected by city life.

Green to the very door; and wreaths of smoke
Sent up, in silence, from among the trees!
With some uncertain notice, as might seem
20 Of vagrant[4] dwellers in the houseless woods,
Or of some Hermit's cave, where by his fire
The Hermit sits alone. ◀

            These beauteous forms,
Through a long absence, have not been to me
As is a landscape to a blind man's eye;
25 But oft, in lonely rooms, and 'mid the din
Of towns and cities, I have owed to them,
In hours of weariness, sensations sweet,
Felt in the blood, and felt along the heart;
And passing even into my purer mind,
30 With tranquil restoration—feelings too
Of unremembered pleasure; such, perhaps,
As have no slight or trivial influence
On that best portion of a good man's life,
His little, nameless, unremembered, acts
35 Of kindness and of love. Nor less, I trust,
To them I may have owed another gift,
Of aspect more sublime; that blessed mood,
In which the burthen[5] of the mystery,
In which the heavy and the weary weight
40 Of all this unintelligible world,
Is lightened—that serene and blessed mood,
In which the affections gently lead us on—
Until, the breath of this corporeal[6] frame
And even the motion of our human blood
45 Almost suspended, we are laid asleep
In body, and become a living soul;
While with an eye made quiet by the power
Of harmony, and the deep power of joy,
We see into the life of things. ◀

                    If this
50 Be but a vain belief, yet, oh! how oft—

---

4. **vagrant:** wandering.

5. **burthen:** burden.

6. **corporeal** (kôr-pôr′ē-əl): bodily.

In darkness and amid the many shapes
Of joyless daylight; when the fretful stir
Unprofitable, and the fever of the world,
Have hung upon the beatings of my heart—
55 How oft, in spirit, have I turned to thee,
O sylvan⁷ Wye!⁸ thou wanderer through the woods,
How often has my spirit turned to thee!

And now, with gleams of half-extinguished thought
With many recognitions dim and faint,
60 And somewhat of a sad perplexity,
The picture of the mind revives again;
While here I stand, not only with the sense
Of present pleasure, but with pleasing thoughts
That in this moment there is life and food
65 For future years. And so I dare to hope,
Though changed, no doubt, from what I was when first
I came among these hills; when like a roe⁹
I bounded o'er the mountains, by the sides
Of the deep rivers, and the lonely streams,
70 Wherever nature led—more like a man
Flying from something that he dreads than one
Who sought the thing he loved. For nature then
(The coarser pleasures of my boyish days,
And their glad animal movements all gone by)
75 To me was all in all.—I cannot paint ▶
What then I was. The sounding cataract¹⁰
Haunted me like a passion; the tall rock,
The mountain, and the deep and gloomy wood,
Their colors and their forms, were then to me
80 An appetite; a feeling and a love,
That had no need of a remoter charm,
By thought supplied, nor any interest
Unborrowed from the eye.—That time is past,
And all its aching joys are now no more,
85 And all its dizzy raptures. Not for this

CLARIFY

What does the speaker mean
when he says **nature** used to
be "all in all" to him?

_____

_____

_____

_____

_____

---

7. **sylvan:** located in a wood or forest.
8. **Wye:** a river near Tintern Abbey.
9. **roe:** deer.
10. **cataract** (kăt′ə-răkt′): waterfall.

PAUSE & REFLECT

1. How has the speaker's response to **nature** changed since he last visited Tintern Abbey? *COMPARE AND CONTRAST*

_____

_____

_____

_____

2. Do you think the speaker regrets the loss of his youth? Explain why or why not. *DRAW CONCLUSIONS*

_____

_____

_____

_____

FOCUS
The speaker now turns to his sister, who stands beside him on the riverbank. Read to learn about his hopes for her future.

Faint I,[11] nor mourn nor murmur; other gifts
Have followed; for such loss, I would believe,
Abundant recompense.[12] For I have learned
To look on nature, not as in the hour
90 Of thoughtless youth; but hearing oftentimes
The still, sad music of humanity,
Nor harsh nor grating, though of ample power
To chasten[13] and subdue. And I have felt
A presence that disturbs me with the joy
95 Of elevated thoughts; a sense sublime
Of something far more deeply interfused,
Whose dwelling is the light of setting suns,
And the round ocean and the living air,
And the blue sky, and in the mind of man:
100 A motion and a spirit, that impels
All thinking things, all objects of all thought,
And rolls through all things. Therefore am I still
A lover of the meadows and the woods,
And mountains; and of all that we behold
105 From this green earth; of all the mighty world
Of eye, and ear—both what they half create,
And what perceive; well pleased to recognize
In nature and the language of the sense
The anchor of my purest thoughts, the nurse,
110 The guide, the guardian of my heart, and soul
Of all my moral being. **PAUSE & REFLECT**

                                    Nor perchance,[14]
If I were not thus taught, should I the more
Suffer my genial[15] spirits to decay:
For thou art with me here upon the banks
115 Of this fair river; thou my dearest Friend,[16]
My dear, dear Friend; and in thy voice I catch

---

11. **Faint I:** I lose heart.
12. **recompense** (rĕk′əm-pĕns′): compensation.
13. **chasten** (chā′sən): scold; make modest.
14. **perchance:** by chance; perhaps.
15. **genial** (jēn′yəl): relating to genius; creative.
16. **thou my dearest Friend:** Wordsworth's sister, Dorothy.

The language of my former heart, and read
My former pleasures in the shooting lights
Of thy wild eyes. Oh! yet a little while
120 May I behold in thee what I was once,
My dear, dear Sister! and this prayer I make,
Knowing that Nature never did betray
The heart that loved her; 'tis her privilege,
Through all the years of this our life, to lead
125 From joy to joy: for she can so inform
The mind that is within us, so impress
With quietness and beauty, and so feed
With lofty thoughts, that neither evil tongues,
Rash judgments, nor the sneers of selfish men,
130 Nor greetings where no kindness is, nor all
The dreary intercourse of daily life,
Shall e'er prevail against us, or disturb
Our cheerful faith, that all which we behold
Is full of blessings. Therefore let the moon ▶

CLARIFY

What faith does the speaker have in **nature**?

_____

_____

_____

_____

135 Shine on thee in thy solitary walk;
And let the misty mountain winds be free
To blow against thee: and, in after years,
When these wild ecstasies shall be matured
Into a sober pleasure; when thy mind
140 Shall be a mansion for all lovely forms,
Thy memory be as a dwelling place
For all sweet sounds and harmonies; oh! then,
If solitude, or fear, or pain, or grief
Should be thy portion, with what healing thoughts
145 Of tender joy wilt thou remember me,
And these my exhortations![17] Nor, perchance—
If I should be where I no more can hear
Thy voice, nor catch from thy wild eyes these gleams
Of past existence[18]—wilt thou then forget
150 That on the banks of this delightful stream
We stood together; and that I, so long
A worshiper of Nature, hither came
Unwearied in that service; rather say

---

17. **exhortations:** words of encouraging advice.
18. **past existence:** the speaker's own past experience five years before (see lines 116–119).

With warmer love—oh! with far deeper zeal

155 Of holier love. Nor wilt thou then forget,
That after many wanderings, many years
Of absence, these steep woods and lofty cliffs,
And this green pastoral landscape, were to me
More dear, both for themselves and for thy sake!

PAUSE & REFLECT

PAUSE & REFLECT

Underline images that describe the speaker's sister.

Do you get a vivid impression of her from the poem? Explain why or why not. *EVALUATE*

_____

_____

_____

_____

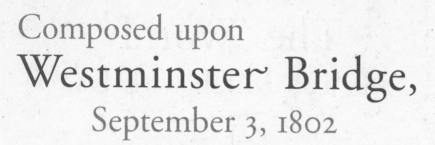

Composed upon Westminster Bridge, September 3, 1802

William Wordsworth

Earth has not anything to show more fair:
Dull would he be of soul who could pass by
A sight so touching in its majesty;
This City now doth, like a garment, wear
5 The beauty of the morning; silent, bare,
Ships, towers, domes, theaters, and temples lie
Open unto the fields, and to the sky;
All bright and glittering in the smokeless air.
Never did sun more beautifully steep[1]
10 In his first splendor, valley, rock, or hill;
Ne'er saw I, never felt, a calm so deep!
The river[2] glideth at his own sweet will:
Dear God! the very houses[3] seem asleep;
And all that mighty heart is lying still! ▶

CLARIFY

Underline words and phrases that indicate time of day in the poem. ✎

How does the time influence the speaker's impression of the city?

_____

_____

_____

_____

---

1. **steep:** soak; saturate.
2. **the river:** the Thames (tĕmz)—the principal river in London.
3. **houses:** possibly a pun on the Houses of Parliament, near Westminster Bridge.

The World
Is Too Much with Us

William Wordsworth

CLARIFY

Reread lines 1–4. What do you think the speaker means by the phrase "The world is too much with us"?

The world is too much with us; late and soon,
Getting and spending, we lay waste our powers;
Little we see in Nature that is ours;
We have given our hearts away, a sordid boon![1]
5　This Sea that bares her bosom to the moon,
The winds that will be howling at all hours,
And are up-gathered now like sleeping flowers,
For this, for everything, we are out of tune;
It moves us not.—Great God! I'd rather be
10　A Pagan[2] suckled in a creed outworn;[3]
So might I, standing on this pleasant lea,[4]
Have glimpses that would make me less forlorn;
Have sight of Proteus rising from the sea;
Or hear old Triton[5] blow his wreathèd horn. ◀

---

1. **sordid boon:** tarnished or selfish gift.
2. **Pagan** (pā′gən): someone who is not Christian, Jewish, or Muslim.
3. **suckled in a creed outworn:** raised in an outdated faith or belief system.
4. **lea:** meadow.
5. **Proteus** (prō′tē-əs) . . . **Triton** (trīt′n): sea gods of Greek mythology.

I Wandered
Lonely As a Cloud

William Wordsworth

I wandered lonely as a cloud
That floats on high o'er vales[1] and hills,
When all at once I saw a crowd,
A host, of golden daffodils;
5 Beside the lake, beneath the trees,
Fluttering and dancing in the breeze.

Continuous as the stars that shine
And twinkle on the milky way,
They stretched in never-ending line
10 Along the margin of a bay:
Ten thousand saw I at a glance,
Tossing their heads in sprightly dance. ▶

The waves beside them danced; but they
Outdid the sparkling waves in glee;
15 A poet could not but be gay,
In such a jocund[2] company;
I gazed—and gazed—but little thought
What wealth the show to me had brought:

For oft, when on my couch I lie
20 In vacant or in pensive mood,
They flash upon that inward eye
Which is the bliss of solitude;
And then my heart with pleasure fills,
And dances with the daffodils. ✋ **PAUSE & REFLECT**

---

1. **vales:** valleys.
2. **jocund** (jŏk'ənd): merry.

VISUALIZE

Underline words and phrases that help you picture the movement of the daffodils. ✏

✋ **PAUSE & REFLECT**

In what way has the speaker's understanding of this incident changed over time? *CLARIFY*

_____

_____

_____

_____

Big Question ❓

Think about the peaceful place you sketched on page 137. How have you been affected by memories of that place?

_____

_____

_____

_____

Reading Comprehension

DIRECTIONS *Answer these questions about the selected poetry by filling in the correct ovals.*

1. Which of the following does Wordsworth *not* describe in "Lines Composed a Few Miles Above Tintern Abbey"?

   (A) the Wye River

   (B) farms

   (C) mountains

   (D) Tintern Abbey

2. The speaker of "Tintern Abbey" values his memories from five years earlier because they have

   (A) inspired some of his poems

   (B) comforted him when he was lonely

   (C) made him feel close to his sister

   (D) taught him to appreciate nature

3. Which statement *best* describes how the speaker of "Tintern Abbey" currently responds to nature?

   (A) He no longer takes pleasure in nature's beauty.

   (B) His response has remained the same over time.

   (C) He senses the spiritual power of nature.

   (D) He wishes he felt at home in nature.

4. Which characteristic of romantic poetry does the speaker of "Tintern Abbey" emphasize to his sister in lines 119–134?

   (A) turning to nature for inspiration and solace

   (B) celebrating the commonplace

   (C) style resembling natural speech

   (D) exotic and supernatural elements

5. In "Composed upon Westminster Bridge," Wordsworth describes a

   (A) sunrise

   (B) sunset

   (C) crowded street

   (D) garment factory

6. What does the speaker complain about in "The World Is Too Much with Us"?

   (A) Too many people are powerless.

   (B) The weather has become harsh.

   (C) People have lost touch with nature.

   (D) Pagan gods are no longer worshipped.

7. When the speaker of "I Wandered Lonely As a Cloud" says that the daffodils "flash upon that inward eye / Which is the bliss of solitude" in lines 21–22, he means that they

   (A) bring tears to his eyes

   (B) become very bright

   (C) make him feel alone

   (D) form a picture in his mind

8. Which phrase from "I Wandered Lonely As a Cloud" is the *best* example of Wordsworth's use of a style resembling natural speech?

   (A) "That floats on high o'er vales and hills"

   (B) "Beside the lake, beneath the trees"

   (C) "Tossing their heads in sprightly dance"

   (D) "For oft, when on my couch I lie"

Responding in Writing

9. Short Response The romantic poets stressed the importance of the individual's subjective experiences. How is this emphasis reflected in the poems of William Wordsworth? Provide at least three examples in your response.

_____

_____

_____

_____

_____

_____

_____

*For help, use the **Test-Taker's Toolkit** below.*

TEST-TAKER'S TOOLKIT

GRAPHIC ORGANIZER Use the chart below to help you plan your response.

Experience Described in Poem	How It Affects Speaker

Wordsworth Enters the Hip-Hop Era
NEWSPAPER ARTICLE

Use with Selected Poetry by William Wordsworth, p. 136

What's the Connection?

For two centuries, "I Wandered Lonely As a Cloud" has been one of Wordsworth's best-known poems. Some British officials hope to sustain its popularity by promoting a new hip-hop version. You can find out more about this update of a classic in the feature article "Wordsworth Enters the Hip-Hop Era."

LIST IT With a partner, think of examples of a classic getting adapted into a popular art form. For example, you might recall a cartoon version of an opera or a Shakespeare play performed with puppets. Offer a brief description of each example.

1. _____

_____

2. _____

_____

3. _____

_____

4. _____

_____

5. _____

_____

LEARN THE SKILL: ANALYZE A FEATURE ARTICLE

A **feature article** is a newspaper or magazine article that is lighter or more general than a news article. Although they may provide a great deal of information, feature articles usually focus on human-interest or lifestyle stories rather than important events. When you read a feature article, pay attention to the following:

- What tone does the writer use? The tone of a feature article may be neutral or humorous, for example.

- Decide who might be interested in the topic. Those readers are the intended audience.

For more on feature articles, see the Narrative Nonfiction entry in the Nonfiction Skills Handbook beginning on page R2.

WORDSWORTH ENTERS THE HIP-HOP ERA

by Cindy Bayard

When people talk about "old-school rap," they're usually referring to music of the 1970s and 1980s. That term might take on a different meaning now that one of William Wordsworth's most famous poems has been adapted into a hip-hop song. The new ver-
10 sion of "I Wandered Lonely As a Cloud" was commissioned by tourism officials who want to attract younger readers to Wordsworth's poetry. They also hope it will draw more visitors to England's picturesque Lake District, where the poem is set. ▶

On April 15, 1802, Wordsworth and his sister Dorothy took a walk on the banks of Lake Ullswater,
20 near their home in Grasmere village. Dorothy wrote in her diary that they had seen a huge cluster of daffodils that "tossed and reeled and danced and seemed as if they verily laughed at the wind that blew upon them over the lake." Two years later, Wordsworth wrote "I Wandered Lonely As a Cloud," which is also known as "Daffodils."
30 The poem was first published in 1807, though Wordsworth's 1815 revision is the most familiar version. David Wilson, the Robert Woof Director of the Wordsworth Trust, said that it "always achieves very high ratings in any survey of famous English poems. It is a poem about the mind's growing awareness over time of the deepening value of
40 an experience, in this case observing the dancing daffodils."

The hip-hop adaptation stays close to the original poem, but the language has been updated. For example, Wordsworth describes daffodils "tossing their heads in a

SET A PURPOSE

_____

_____

_____

FEATURE ARTICLE

Read lines 1–16, and circle words and phrases that indicate that the article is a human-interest story rather than a hard-news story. ✏

SPECIALIZED
Vocabulary

Knowing a word's etymology, or history, can help you figure out its meaning. For example, the adverb _verily_ in line 25 derives from the Latin _verus_, which means "true." Use context clues and your knowledge of the word's origin to write a definition of _verily_.

_____

_____

sprightly dance." In the new version, the flowers are "tossing up their heads like a pogo dance." Not

50 surprisingly, the hip-hop speaker has a casual tone, using "so check it" and other slangy expressions. The powerful rhythm of the song helps carry off amusing rhymes such as "retina" and "etcetera."

Why change a classic that has been popular for so long? According to David Wilson, "Two hundred years after it was pub-

60 lished, the poem is still reaching new audiences and inspiring people. Part of our work here at Grasmere is demonstrating how Wordsworth's poetry is relevant today and encouraging young people to enrich their lives by exploring his poetry in their own ways." ◀

The most novel result of this effort to promote Wordsworth is

70 the music video that accompanies the hip-hop song. It features MC Nuts, who raps out the lyrics dressed in a red squirrel costume as he dances around the Lake District. Although no squirrels appear in "I Wandered Lonely As a Cloud," the red squirrel is native to the region. Wordsworth, who once wrote about a girl as "light

80 and beauteous as a squirrel," might have appreciated this humorous touch.

NEW HIP-HOP VERSION

I wandered lonely along as if I was
   a cloud
That floats on high over vales and
   hills
90 When all at once I looked down
   and saw a crowd
And in my path there was a host of
   golden daffodils so check it

The kind of sight that puts your
   mind at ease
I saw beside the lake and beneath
   the trees
And they moved me

Like they were based on the keys
100 They were fluttering and dancing
inside the breeze and seemed
infinite
Just like the stars that shine up
in the belt of Orion across to
the Milky Way
They stretched along the coast in
a never-ending line
All across the water marching
up the golden silky bay

110 Must have been 10,000 I saw in
my retina
No more than a glance then
I register they're beautiful
etcetera
I never knew in advance but they
were tossing up their heads
like a pogo dance

In a contrast to the plants, there
were waves beside them
120 The way they crashed and
sparkled added to the marvel
And the writer couldn't help but

feeling bright like a sunbeam
'cause the flowers and the waves
they were quite something yeah
Across the spot . . . just lost the plot
. . . just watched and watched all
the yellow and green
And at the time I didn't really have
130 to pay them no mind but when I
think back to the day it was a hell
of a scene

So often when I'm on my couch just
sitting
In a vacant mood or idle position
With nothing to do, my face screwed
—time ticking
I gotta rewind to my vision
I get a flashback in my mind's eye
140 Feel the bliss of solitude from the
hindsight
My heart fills up until the pleasure
has spilled yeah
I'm taking back to dancing with
the daffodils . . . daffodils . . .
daffodils . . .

Reading Comprehension

DIRECTIONS *Answer these questions about the article and the poems in this lesson by filling in the correct ovals.*

1. According to the article, "I Wandered Lonely As a Cloud" is

   (A) Wordsworth's greatest poem

   (B) one of the most popular English poems

   (C) the first English poem turned into a rap song

   (D) a very controversial poem

2. In the quotation from her journal, Dorothy Wordsworth describes

   (A) the movement of the daffodils

   (B) William Wordsworth's laughter

   (C) picking flowers by the lake

   (D) the daffodils' bright color

3. Which version of "I Wandered Lonely As a Cloud" is most famous?

   (A) the 1802 version

   (B) the 1807 version

   (C) the 1815 version

   (D) the new hip-hop version

4. What is the intended audience for the article?

   (A) young people

   (B) Wordsworth scholars

   (C) tourists

   (D) the general public

5. What can be found in the hip-hop version of the poem that is not in Wordsworth's original version?

   (A) rhyme

   (B) rhythm

   (C) imagery

   (D) slang

6. What does the speaker of the hip-hop version describe in lines 133–146?

   (A) dancing on his couch

   (B) reading Wordsworth's poetry

   (C) remembering daffodils

   (D) celebrating with friends

7. The word *reeled* in line 24 means

   (A) swayed

   (B) grew dizzy

   (C) wound on

   (D) fell off

8. In line 68, the word *novel* means

   (A) literary

   (B) unusual

   (C) amusing

   (D) offensive

Timed Writing Practice

PROMPT

Whether describing a natural landscape or a view of London, Wordsworth creates vivid word pictures in his poems. Write a descriptive essay about a place that has made a strong impression on you. (Use different types of sensory details), and explain how the place you are describing makes you feel. In your essay, refer to at least one idea from the selections you have read.

TEST-TAKER'S TOOLKIT

1. ANALYZE THE PROMPT

A. Identify the type of writing you are asked to do.

B. Circle any key words that describe the topic or indicate what you are required to include in your writing. One example has been circled for you.

2. PLAN YOUR RESPONSE

A. **Make notes** Decide which place you will write about. In the chart, list sensory details about that place.

B. **Organize your information** Choose a logical pattern for your description. You may present details in spatial order—the order in which they appear, such as near to far or inside to outside. Or you may present details in the order in which you experience them, starting out with the one that you first notice.

3. WRITE AND REVIEW

A. Begin your essay with a strong introductory paragraph that catches your readers' attention. You might start off with a humorous observation or a question.

B. Write out your response. Leave enough time to read through it and make sure you have met all the requirements of the prompt.

UNIT 4

THE FLOWERING OF ROMANTICISM

LESSON 4B

Selected Poetry
BY PERCY BYSSHE SHELLEY

RELATED NONFICTION
Collecting Leaves

What can NATURE teach us?

Romantic poets thought that profound lessons could be learned from observing nature. They believed that there was no greater beauty than that found in nature, and they saw higher truths reflected in natural scenes.

VISUALIZE IT Visualize one of the following elements of nature—a sand dune, the wind, or a bird. Think deeply about it. What lessons about life could it suggest to you? Contemplating the wind, for example, might make you realize that any life circumstance can suddenly change, as the wind does. Note which element you chose to visualize in the notebook. Jot down one possible lesson about life that it suggests to you.

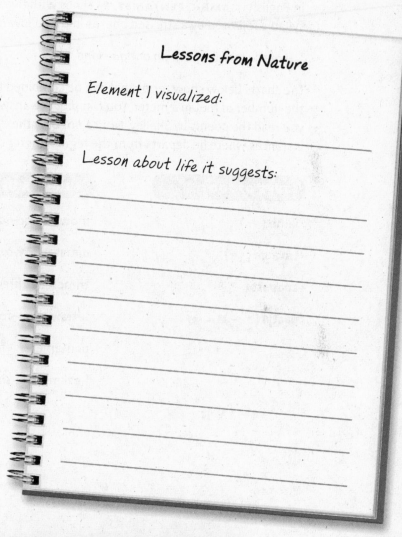

Lessons from Nature

Element I visualized:

_____

Lesson about life it suggests:

_____

ASSESSMENT GOALS

By the end of this lesson, you will be able to . . .

- recognize rhythmic patterns in poetry
- use active reading strategies to comprehend text
- follow directions in a work of nonfiction
- analyze a writing prompt and plan an analysis of poetry

Rhythmic Patterns

A poem's **RHYTHM**, or pattern of stressed and unstressed syllables, can help give it a musical quality. In most English poetry prior to the 20th century, the rhythm follows a regular pattern called a **METER**. Each unit of meter, known as a **FOOT**, consists of one stressed syllable (´) and one or more unstressed syllables (˘). The most common meter in English is **IAMBIC PENTAMETER**—lines with five feet that consist of an unstressed syllable followed by a stressed one, as in the following line from Shelley's "Ozymandias":

˘ ´ | ˘ ´ ˘ | ˘ ´ | ˘ ´ ˘ | ˘ ´
I mét | a tráve ler from | an án | tique lánd

The charts below show terms that can be combined to indicate the types of feet and the number of feet in a meter. You can practice answering questions about meter as you read the poems by Shelley. Notice not only the type of meter Shelley uses but also instances where he departs from the regular meter of a poem.

TYPE OF FOOT
iamb (˘ ´)
trochee (´ ˘)
anapest (˘ ˘ ´)
dactyl (´ ˘ ˘)

NUMBER OF FEET
monometer—one
dimeter—two
trimeter—three
tetrameter—four
pentameter—five
hexameter—six

Ozymandias

Percy Bysshe Shelley

BACKGROUND Percy Bysshe Shelley was part of a generation of English poets known as the late romantics. An idealist and a political radical, he passionately opposed all injustice and dreamed of changing the world through poetry. He wrote with the fervent conviction that poetry nourishes the imagination, and that the imagination—by enabling empathy for others—brings about social change.

I met a traveler from an antique land
Who said: Two vast and trunkless legs[1] of stone
Stand in the desert . . . Near them, on the sand,
Half sunk, a shattered visage[2] lies, whose frown,
5 And wrinkled lip, and sneer of cold command,
Tell that its sculptor well those passions read
Which yet survive, stamped on these lifeless things,
The hand that mocked them, and the heart that fed:[3]
And on the pedestal these words appear:
10 "My name is Ozymandias,[4] king of kings:
Look on my works, ye Mighty, and despair!" ▶
Nothing beside remains. Round the decay
Of that colossal wreck, boundless and bare
The lone and level sands stretch far away. ▶

---

1. **trunkless legs:** legs separated from the rest of the body.
2. **visage** (vĭz′ĭj): face.
3. **The hand . . . that fed:** the sculptor's hand that imitated the passions of the king and the heart that fed them.
4. **Ozymandias** (ŏz′ĭ-măn′dē-əs): a Greek name for the Egyptian pharaoh Rameses II, who reigned from 1279 to 1213 B.C.

MAKE INFERENCES

Underline details about the statue's facial expression. Circle Ozymandias's words as they appear on the statue's inscription. ✏

What kind of man was Ozymandias?

_____

_____

_____

_____

CLARIFY

What has happened to Ozymandias's statue?

_____

_____

_____

ODE TO THE
West Wind

Percy Bysshe Shelley

I

O wild West Wind, thou breath of Autumn's being,
Thou, from whose unseen presence the leaves dead
Are driven, like ghosts from an enchanter fleeing,

Yellow, and black, and pale, and hectic[1] red,
5 Pestilence-stricken multitudes: O thou,
Who chariotest to their dark wintry bed

The wingéd seeds, where they lie cold and low,
Each like a corpse within its grave, until
Thine azure sister of the Spring[2] shall blow

10 Her clarion[3] o'er the dreaming earth, and fill
(Driving sweet buds like flocks to feed in air)
With living hues and odors plain and hill:

Wild Spirit, which art moving everywhere;
Destroyer and preserver; hear, oh, hear! ◀

---

1. **hectic:** feverish.
2. **sister . . . Spring:** the reviving south wind of spring.
3. **clarion:** a trumpet with a clear, ringing tone.

CLARIFY

In his poetry, Shelley often uses personification, or figurative language that attributes human qualities to an object, animal, or idea. What object does the speaker address in this poem?

_____

What effect does the object have on the leaves in lines 2–5?

_____

_____

_____

What does it do to the seeds in lines 6–8?

_____

_____

II

15 Thou on whose stream, mid the steep sky's commotion,
Loose clouds like earth's decaying leaves are shed,
Shook from the tangled bough of Heaven and Ocean,

Angels[4] of rain and lightning: there are spread
On the blue surface of thine aëry[5] surge,
20 Like the bright hair uplifted from the head

Of some fierce Maenad, even from the dim verge
Of the horizon to the zenith's height,[6]
The locks of the approaching storm. Thou dirge[7]

Of the dying year, to which this closing night
25 Will be the dome of a vast sepulcher,[8]
Vaulted with all thy congregated might

Of vapors, from whose solid atmosphere
Black rain, and fire, and hail will burst: oh, hear! ▶

III

Thou who didst waken from his summer dreams
30 The blue Mediterranean, where he lay,
Lulled by the coil of his crystálline[9] streams,

Beside a pumice isle in Baiae's bay,[10]
And saw in sleep old palaces and towers
Quivering within the wave's intenser day,

---

4. **angels:** messengers.

5. **aëry:** airy.

6. **Like the bright . . . height:** The clouds lie in streaks from the horizon upward, looking like the streaming hair of a maenad (mē′năd′)—a wildly dancing female worshiper of Dionysus, the Greek god of wine.

7. **dirge:** funeral song.

8. **sepulcher** (sĕp′əl-kər): tomb.

9. **crystálline** (krĭs-tăl′ĭn) **streams:** the different-colored currents of the Mediterranean Sea.

10. **pumice** (pŭm′ĭs): a light volcanic rock; **Baiae's** (bī′ēz′) **bay:** the Bay of Naples, site of the ancient Roman resort of Baiae.

ANALYZE

Reread lines 27–28 aloud, tapping your desk with each stressed syllable to hear the **rhythm.** Then scan the lines again, this time marking the stressed and unstressed syllables.

How many **feet** are in each line? What type of feet are they? The charts on page 158 can help you answer these questions.

35 All overgrown with azure moss and flowers
   So sweet, the sense faints picturing them! Thou
   For whose path the Atlantic's level powers[11]

   Cleave themselves into chasms, while far below
   The sea-blooms and the oozy woods which wear
40 The sapless foliage of the ocean, know

   Thy voice, and suddenly grow gray with fear,
   And tremble and despoil themselves: oh, hear! ◄

                    IV

   If I were a dead leaf thou mightest bear;
   If I were a swift cloud to fly with thee;
45 A wave to pant beneath thy power, and share

   The impulse of thy strength, only less free
   Than thou, O uncontrollable! If even
   I were as in my boyhood, and could be

   The comrade of thy wanderings over Heaven,
50 As then, when to outstrip thy skyey speed[12]
   Scarce seemed a vision;[13] I would ne'er have striven

   As thus with thee in prayer in my sore need.
   Oh, lift me as a wave, a leaf, a cloud!
   I fall upon the thorns of life! I bleed!

55 A heavy weight of hours has chained and bowed
   One too like thee: tameless, and swift, and proud. ◄

11. **level powers:** surface.
12. **skyey** (skī′ē) **speed:** the swiftness of clouds moving across the sky.
13. **vision:** something impossible to achieve.

TestSmart

What does Shelley describe in lines 38–42?

(A) leaves falling from trees in a forest

(B) underwater plants waving in the churned-up ocean

(C) sailors frightened by a powerful storm

(D) colorful petals blowing off of flowers

TIP Some test questions may ask you to interpret imagery and figurative language. To answer this question, carefully reread lines 38–42 and **paraphrase** the lines, or restate them in your own words. Which answer choice matches what Shelley is describing in these lines?

INTERPRET

What does the speaker complain about in lines 54–56?

_____

_____

_____

_____

V

Make me thy lyre,[14] even as the forest is:
What if my leaves are falling like its own!
The tumult of thy mighty harmonies

60　Will take from both a deep, autumnal tone,
Sweet though in sadness. Be thou, Spirit fierce,
My spirit! Be thou me, impetuous[15] one!

Drive my dead thoughts over the universe
Like withered leaves to quicken a new birth!
65　And, by the incantation[16] of this verse,

Scatter, as from an unextinguished hearth
Ashes and sparks, my words among mankind!
Be through my lips to unawakened earth

The trumpet of a prophecy! O Wind,
70　If Winter comes, can Spring be far behind?  **PAUSE & REFLECT**

PAUSE & REFLECT

Underline words on this page that describe the qualities and effects of the west wind.

What does the west wind represent for the speaker? *DRAW CONCLUSIONS*

_____

_____

_____

_____

---

14. **lyre:** a reference to the Aeolian harp, an instrument whose strings make musical sounds when the wind blows over them.

15. **impetuous** (ĭm-pĕch′o͞o-əs): violently forceful; impulsive.

16. **incantation:** recitation, as of a magic spell.

TO A
Skylark

Percy Bysshe Shelley

CLARIFY

How does the speaker characterize the skylark in lines 1–15?

_____

_____

_____

_____

Circle words and phrases that support your answer.

Hail to thee, blithe[1] Spirit!
    Bird thou never wert,
That from Heaven, or near it,
    Pourest thy full heart
5 In profuse strains of unpremeditated[2] art.

    Higher still and higher
      From the earth thou springest
Like a cloud of fire;
      The blue deep thou wingest,
10 And singing still dost soar, and soaring ever singest.

    In the golden lightning
      Of the sunken sun,
O'er which clouds are bright'ning,
      Thou dost float and run;
15 Like an unbodied joy whose race is just begun. ◀

---

1. **blithe** (blīth): carefree.
2. **unpremeditated** (ŭn′prĭ-mĕd′ĭ-tā′tĭd): natural; not planned out ahead of time.

The pale purple even[3]
    Melts around thy flight;
Like a star of Heaven,
    In the broad daylight
20 Thou art unseen, but yet I hear thy shrill delight,

Keen as are the arrows
    Of that silver sphere,[4]
Whose intense lamp narrows
    In the white dawn clear
25 Until we hardly see—we feel that it is there.

All the earth and air
    With thy voice is loud,
As, when night is bare,
    From one lonely cloud
30 The moon rains out her beams, and Heaven is overflowed.

What thou are we know not;
    What is most like thee?
From rainbow clouds there flow not
    Drops so bright to see
35 As from thy presence showers a rain of melody. ▶

Like a Poet hidden
    In the light of thought,
Singing hymns unbidden,
    Till the world is wrought
40 To sympathy with hopes and fears it heeded not:

Like a high-born maiden
    In a palace tower
Soothing her love-laden
    Soul in secret hour
45 With music sweet as love, which overflows her bower:[5] ▶

---

3. **even:** evening.
4. **silver sphere:** the planet Venus, called the morning star because it is visible in the east just before daybreak.
5. **bower:** private room; boudoir or bedroom.

ANALYZE

Mark the pattern of stressed and unstressed syllables in lines 21 and 31. What **meter** did Shelley use in these lines?

_____

_____

CLARIFY

Reread the boxed text. In what ways are the poet and maiden similar to the skylark?

_____

_____

_____

PARAPHRASE

Complete the following
sentence, restating lines 51–55
in your own words.

The skylark is like

_____

_____

_____

_____

_____

_____

CLARIFY

Reread lines 61–65. What does
the speaker request of the
skylark, and why?

_____

_____

_____

_____

Like a glowworm[6] golden
      In a dell of dew,
Scattering unbeholden
      Its aërial[7] hue
50 Among the flowers and grass, which screen it from the view!

Like a rose embowered
      In its own green leaves,
By warm winds deflowered,[8]
      Till the scent it gives
55 Makes faint with too much sweet those heavy-wingéd thieves:[9] ◀

Sound of vernal[10] showers
      On the twinkling grass,
Rain-awakened flowers,
      All that ever was
60 Joyous, and clear, and fresh, thy music doth surpass:

Teach us, Sprite or Bird,
      What sweet thoughts are thine:
I have never heard
      Praise of love or wine
65 That panted forth a flood of rapture so divine. ◀

Chorus Hymeneal,[11]
      Or triumphal chant,
Matched with thine would be all
      But an empty vaunt,[12]
70 A thing wherein we feel there is some hidden want.

---

6. **glowworm:** wingless female firefly or firefly larva.
7. **aërial** (âr′ē-əl) **hue:** insubstantial glow.
8. **deflowered:** fully opened.
9. **thieves:** the warm winds.
10. **vernal:** spring.
11. **Chorus Hymeneal** (hī′mə-nē′əl): a wedding song.
12. **vaunt:** boast.

What objects are the fountains[13]
    Of thy happy strain?
What fields, or waves, or mountains?
    What shapes of sky or plain?
75 What love of thine own kind? what ignorance of pain?

    With thy clear keen joyance
        Languor[14] cannot be:
    Shadow of annoyance
        Never came near thee:
80 Thou lovest—but ne'er knew love's sad satiety.[15]

    Waking or asleep,
        Thou of death must deem[16]
    Things more true and deep
        Than we mortals dream,
85 Or how could thy notes flow in such a crystal stream? ▶

    We look before and after,
        And pine for what is not:
    Our sincerest laughter
        With some pain is fraught;
90 Our sweetest songs are those that tell of saddest thought. ▶

    Yet if[17] we could scorn
        Hate, and pride, and fear;
    If we were things born
        Not to shed a tear,
95 I know not how thy joy we ever should come near.

    Better than all measures
        Of delightful sound,
    Better than all treasures
        That in books are found,
100 Thy skill to poet were, thou scorner of the ground!

---

13. **fountains:** sources.
14. **languor** (lăng'gər): lack of energy; listlessness.
15. **satiety** (sə-tī'ĭ-tē): fulfillment to excess.
16. **deem:** know.
17. **if:** even if.

ANALYZE

Compare the number of stressed syllables in the fourth and fifth lines of each stanza in the boxed text. What effect does this **rhythmic pattern** create?

_____

_____

_____

_____

CLARIFY

Reread lines 86–90. According to the speaker, what are humans incapable of?

_____

_____

_____

_____

PAUSE & REFLECT

What conclusion can you draw based on the speaker's comments about poetry in "To a Skylark"? *DRAW CONCLUSIONS*

_____

_____

_____

_____

_____

Big Question ?

Review the visualization activity you completed on page 157. How do your thoughts about the element of nature compare with Shelley's thoughts on the same topic?

_____

_____

_____

_____

_____

Teach me half the gladness
   That thy brain must know,
Such harmonious madness
   From my lips would flow
105 The world should listen then—as I am listening now.

PAUSE & REFLECT

Reading Comprehension

DIRECTIONS *Answer these questions about the poems in this lesson by
filling in the correct ovals.*

1. The "passions" referred to in line 6 of
   "Ozymandias" are those of

   (A) Ozymandias

   (B) the traveler

   (C) the sculptor

   (D) the speaker

2. In "Ozymandias," what is ironic about the
   words inscribed on the statue's pedestal?

   (A) The writing has been worn down over
   time.

   (B) Ozymandias has been dead for so
   long.

   (C) Ozymandias's "works" are now ruins.

   (D) The sculpture of Ozymandias was
   poorly made.

3. What are the "pestilence-stricken
   multitudes" referred to in line 5 of "Ode to
   the West Wind"?

   (A) seeds blown from trees

   (B) colorful leaves

   (C) dark rain clouds

   (D) autumn winds

4. In the last section of "Ode to the West
   Wind," the speaker prays that the wind will

   (A) carry him back to his childhood

   (B) churn up waves in the ocean

   (C) bring mild winter weather

   (D) spread his thoughts everywhere

5. What is the "unpremeditated art" referred
   to in line 5 of "To a Skylark"?

   (A) the speaker's verse

   (B) heavenly music

   (C) the skylark's singing

   (D) clouds in the sky

6. In lines 36–40 of "To a Skylark," Shelley
   suggests that poets are

   (A) better singers than skylarks

   (B) often ignored by the world

   (C) more mysterious than skylarks

   (D) invisible to nature

7. Which of the following does the speaker of
   "To a Skylark" want to learn?

   (A) how the skylark remains invisible

   (B) why roses give off a sweet scent

   (C) why humans can't be joyful

   (D) what inspires the skylark's singing

8. In which of the following lines is the meter
   correctly marked?

   (A) The hand that mocked them, and the
   heart that fed:

   (B) Yellow, and black, and pale, and
   hectic red,

   (C) If Winter comes, can Spring be far
   behind?

   (D) Hail to thee, blithe Spirit!

GO ON ➡

For help, use the **Test-Taker's Toolkit** below.

Responding in Writing

9. Short Response Choose one poem from this lesson, and record and scan three to five of its lines. In a paragraph, identify the meter of the poem, indicating the type of foot and the number of feet per line. Point out two or three examples of how the stressed syllables in the lines emphasize words that are important to the poem's meaning.

_____

_____

_____

_____

_____

_____

TEST-TAKER'S TOOLKIT

- ⊗ **ACADEMIC VOCABULARY** When you **scan** a line of poetry, you analyze its **rhythm** by marking the stressed (´) and unstressed (˘) syllables. If you are unsure about any of the terms related to rhythmic patterns, review the instruction and the charts on page 158.

- ⊗ **GRAPHIC ORGANIZER** In the chart below, record the lines you have chosen to analyze. Then scan the lines, marking the stressed and unstressed syllables. Note how many and what kind of feet the lines contain. Then you can start to consider how the rhythm helps convey the lines' meaning.

Poem:	
Lines from the poem:	
Meter:	**How the rhythm helps convey meaning:**

What's the Connection?

In "Ode to the West Wind," Shelley describes autumn leaves blowing in the air, "Yellow, and black, and pale, and hectic red." The article "Collecting Leaves" explains how you can create a collection of colorful autumn leaves.

CLASSIFY OBJECTS Classification is the arrangement of organisms, objects, or information into groups according to shared characteristics. For example, animal fur can be classified according to its color, texture, and length. Use the chart below to classify objects that you encounter in your daily life. Group them according to three characteristics.

Related Nonfiction

Collecting Leaves
MAGAZINE ARTICLE

Use with Selected Poetry by Percy Bysshe Shelley, p. 156

CLASSIFICATION OF _____

CHARACTERISTICS	EXAMPLES

LEARN THE SKILLS: FOLLOW DIRECTIONS

In articles and consumer documents, you will often find directions for carrying out a task, such as assembling a piece of furniture or operating a household appliance. The following tips can help you follow directions correctly:

- Read the directions all the way through at least once. Note down any **materials** or **tools** that you will need.

- Look for **numbers** or **letters** that indicate the order in which steps should be followed, or look for **signal words** such as *first* and *next*. Make sure not to skip any steps.

- Note **verbs** that describe actions you should take, such as *insert* and *fasten*.

For more on following directions, see the Text Features, Transitions, and Other Text Clues entry in the Nonfiction Skills Handbook beginning on page R2.

_____

_____

_____

Collecting
LEAVES

by Cathy Johnson

ANALYZE

Circle words and phrases in lines 1–6 that refer to classical music. Why might the author have chosen to use such language in a description of the autumn landscape? ✎

_____

_____

_____

_____

I f you don't count the scarlet leaves of poison ivy and the sumac vine, the first color to appear in the autumn landscape is a subtle maroon. In the few weeks that follow, that first note of contrasting color becomes a symphony of hues with an intricate score. As densely woven as a passage from Vivaldi, the individual shapes and hues can be invaluable when attempting to identify certain trees. ◀

Unlike most evergreens, deciduous trees shed their leaves in a last, glorious conflagration of color each fall, then stand as stark as etchings all winter long. From towering walnuts, locusts, and oaks to the
10 delicate redbuds, dogwoods, and pawpaws of the forest understory, every type of deciduous tree has a distinct leaf. There are swamp-loving trees and desert trees, trees that grow in a dense fringe right up to the bald pate of a mountaintop, and trees that prefer more civilized, backyard climes. There are even trees that thrive beautifully in the cracks in city sidewalks—you can hardly discourage a fast-growing, oddly scented ailanthus (or tree of heaven) that has decided on making its home there.

In autumn, the leaves of the ash tree are among the first to lose their brilliant green color, turning a royal purple maroon. Elms
20 become a glowing yellow almost overnight. Maples and sweet gums

are the show-offs, possessing shades ranging from red to orange to scarlet to gold.

Oaks, with their gnarled limbs and beret-capped acorns, are only slightly more sedate. Their colors tend to be darker and richer. Stubbornly, they hang onto their crisp, brown leaves until winter's winds snatch them away or spring's buds elbow them aside.

In the fall, a corky layer forms between leaf stem and twig on most trees, and liquid nutrients no longer pass between them. Leaves lose their hold on the mother tree and blanket the earth with nature's own mulch, 30 protecting the young plants of the coming spring—and providing safe haven for insects and small mammals. Squirrels use dry leaves to line their winter nests; they're fine insulation against the cold. Even the Virginia opossum finds them to be satisfactory nesting materials, carrying loads of them wrapped tight in its prehensile tail. I once found a possum's leaf cache in my basement; the marsupial didn't know that the heat radiated by the furnace would soon make his leafy comforter superfluous, except as padding.

I can't stalk through the autumn woods as silently as I do the rest of the year. It's not as easy to sneak a look at a deer or a wild turkey; the rattle 40 of dry leaves gives me away, almost as if I have blared through the forest with a boom box. But by spring, the long autumn rains and the snows that follow will have gentled the crackle of leaves. They will by then be well on their way to becoming humus, new soil to feed the next generation of trees and wildflowers. ▶

Identifying Fall Leaves

When leaves are freshly fallen and still full of color, you may notice them as you did not while they wore an anonymous green. There are simple leaves and hand-shaped leaves, single leaves that grow from a single stem and leaves that grow in bunches from a long central stem, looking 50 more like a fern; these may appear opposite one another on the stem or alternately. Leaf edges vary from smooth to toothed to lobed—and the lobes may be rounded or spiky or bearing hairlike extensions. Some may not look like stereotypical leaves at all, but more like fans (palm leaves) or mittens (sassafras and mulberry). This dizzying array of autumn leaves can provide a wonderful opportunity for planning an outdoor adventure and broadening your understanding of nature. In fact, starting a leaf collection can be an enriching means by which to explore your region of the country as well as to learn about the variety of shapes and colors leaves exhibit. Beginning such a collection is easy, inexpensive, and legal—once 60 leaves turn color in the fall and drop to the earth, they are fair game. ▶

SPECIALIZED Vocabulary

Although this article is intended for the general public, the author includes some scientific terms in her discussion of animals and plant material. Use context clues to help you figure out the meaning of the following terms. Then consult a dictionary and revise your definitions as needed. WORD ANALYSIS

mulch (line 29)

_____

_____

prehensile (line 34)

_____

_____

marsupial (line 35)

_____

_____

humus (line 43)

_____

_____

ANALYZE

Look ahead to the chart on page 174. Then uderline sentences in lines 46–60 that refer to characteristics shown in the chart.

When I was a child, my mother helped me start a leaf collection. We pressed and dried leaves at the height of their color. Although they faded somewhat as they dried, when sleet whispered at our windows, the leaves remained lovely reminders of our long rambles together through the fall woods. I daydreamed over them as though they were pages in a romance novel, remembering warmer weather, the excitement of discovery, and the scent of damp leaves and woodsmoke.

A good field guide will help nature sleuths of all ages identify the leaves they find; if you can't figure out a tree's identity by leaf alone, these books
70 will show the overall shape and size of the tree, the pattern of the bark, the flowers, and the fruits or nuts it might produce. Among the best of these books are the *Audubon Society Field Guide to North American Trees* and Roger Phillips's *A Photographic Guide to More Than 500 Trees of North America and Europe*, an oversize paperback with wonderful color photographs. The *Golden Guide to Trees* is a winner, too, and like the Audubon guide, it is small enough to carry with you.

Once home with your colorful treasures, tuck them between sheets of clean paper (blotting paper is best, but typing paper will do), then layer them once again between several sheets of newspaper. If you have a wild-
80 flower press, so much the better. If not, weigh down the leaves with heavy books or tuck them into a phone book until they are as dry and as flat as paper themselves. Then if you like, you can carefully fasten the dry leaves

Leaf Characteristics

Certain leaf characteristics—such as the leaf type, the vein pattern, and the shape of the leaf margin—can be used to identify plants.

LEAF TYPE
Compound leaf
Simple leaf
Double compound leaf

LEAF VEINS
Parallel veins
Pinnate veins

LEAF MARGIN
Toothed margin   Entire margin
Lobed margin

to fresh paper with white glue or transparent tape. Then, as you identify them, write the common name of the tree beside the leaf. Add the scientific Latin name, if you like, and what shape the leaf is. Label each example with the date and the location (county, state, and type of habitat) from which it was collected. You might even want to note what condition the leaf is in, or speculate as to what creature has chewed on it, if applicable. ▶

90   You may wonder why you should bother with such details—and you needn't if you don't want to. But collections well noted and correctly labeled can tell us a great deal about what grows in a specific area and what trees flourish in which habitats. In later years, such a book can be a botanist's treasure. I was recently given an old botany book that has leaves so labeled taped into it, giving me a fascinating peek at what the environs of one part of the Midwest was like in the year 1918.

FOLLOW DIRECTIONS

Circle any **verbs** in lines 77–88 that describe steps you should take. ✎

Build a Simple Plant Press

You may want to fashion a plant press for preparing your leaf collection.

1   Obtain two 12-by-12-inch pieces of plywood, then trim a stack of blotting paper to about 11-by-11 inches. Supplement expensive blotting paper with newspaper, if you like.

2   Press the leaves between two sheets of blotting paper, then sandwich several sheets of newspaper between the stack and another layer of leaves between sheets of blotting paper. Continue until all of your leaves are sandwiched between sheets of paper.

3   Make a leaf-and-paper sandwich with the plywood serving as the "bread," one piece on either side of the paper stack, then tie the bundle tight with twine or with an old leather belt. Let the leaves dry in this contraption; if it's a particularly wet year, you might want to check them every few days to make sure nothing is getting moldy. If the leaves seem too damp or mold is beginning to form, turn the blotting paper so the back side is in contact with the leaves and replace the newspaper sheets to help absorb moisture. Discard any mildewed sheets.

    A more elaborate press can be made by inserting long, threaded bolts and wing nuts at each corner of the plywood. Drill a hole at least 3/4 of an inch from the corners of both plywood sheets, then pass the bolt through each corner, from the bottom up. Add your leaves and paper stack, put on the top piece of plywood, and tighten each wing nut slowly—but not too tight. You don't want to break the press. ▶

FOLLOW DIRECTIONS

What **materials** are needed to build the simple plant press?

_____

_____

_____

_____

_____

Reading Comprehension

DIRECTIONS *Answer these questions about the article and the poems in this lesson by filling in the correct ovals.*

1. In what way do evergreens differ from deciduous trees?

   (A) They are green in the summer.

   (B) They keep their leaves in the winter.

   (C) They can grow in dry climates.

   (D) They change color in autumn.

2. What happens when a corky layer forms between a twig and leaf stem?

   (A) The leaf turns green.

   (B) The tree's bark thickens.

   (C) The leaf stops receiving nutrients.

   (D) The twig changes color.

3. The loss of leaves helps tree growth in the spring by

   (A) creating new soil

   (B) saving green pigment

   (C) providing safe haven for insects

   (D) keeping small mammals warm

4. In the directions in "Build a Simple Plant Press," what suggestion is offered that would save money?

   (A) tying the bundle with twine

   (B) trimming the plywood

   (C) adding bolts and wing nuts

   (D) substituting newspaper for blotting paper

5. What is the function of the blotting paper in the plant press?

   (A) to hold the press together

   (B) to absorb water from the leaves

   (C) to help identify the leaves

   (D) to weigh the leaves down

6. What step needs to be followed carefully to avoid breaking the press?

   (A) trimming the blotting paper

   (B) pressing leaves between blotting paper

   (C) tying the bundle with twine or a belt

   (D) tightening each wing nut

7. In line 28 of "Collecting Leaves," *nutrients* means

   (A) nourishment

   (B) pigments

   (C) pollen

   (D) roots

8. The word *habitat* in line 86 of "Collecting Leaves" refers to

   (A) appearance

   (B) routine

   (C) environment

   (D) season

Timed Writing Practice

PROMPT

In his essay "A Defense of Poetry," Shelley writes that poetry "strips the veil of familiarity from the world, and lays bare the naked and sleeping beauty which is the spirit of its forms." Write an analysis of one of Shelley's poems in which you discuss his insight into the beauty or power of nature. In your analysis, (refer to specific examples of imagery and figurative) (language) that Shelley uses to convey his idea.

BUDGET YOUR TIME

You have **45 minutes** to respond. Decide how much time to spend on each step.

Analyze _____

Plan _____

Write _____

Review _____

TEST-TAKER'S TOOLKIT

1. ANALYZE THE PROMPT

A. Identify the type of writing you are asked to do.

B. Circle any key words that describe the topic or indicate what you are required to include in your writing. One example has been circled for you.

C. Note that you are asked to focus on one poem. Write the name of the poem you will analyze. _____

2. PLAN YOUR RESPONSE

A. **Make notes** Create a chart like the one shown to gather specific examples for your essay.

B. **Organize your information** Use your notes to help structure your essay. Begin with an introduction in which you state your thesis. Then you can write a paragraph for each example of imagery or figurative language that you will analyze. Finish with a conclusion in which you summarize your analysis.

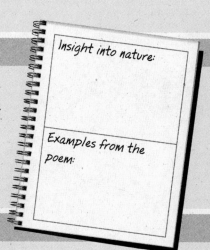

Insight into nature:

Examples from the poem:

3. WRITE AND REVIEW

A. In your introduction, make sure to identify which poem you have chosen and clearly state the insight into nature that you will discuss. Give readers a sense of what is new or exciting about this insight; for example, you might explain how Shelley "strips the veil of familiarity" from the subject of the poem.

B. Write your full response on a separate sheet of paper. Leave time to review your writing.

LESSON 5A

Selected Poetry
BY ALFRED, LORD TENNYSON

RELATED NONFICTION

Alfred, Lord Tennyson's Journey Through Grief

How do you live LIFE to the FULLEST?

People who constantly seek out new experiences are said to be "living life to the fullest." Often, this phrase is used to describe adventurers, athletes, connoisseurs, or others who aim for extraordinary goals or seek to enjoy the very best of what life has to offer. In your opinion, what constitutes a full life?

LIST IT List five experiences that you think are essential to living life to the fullest. Discuss your list with a partner or a small group of classmates.

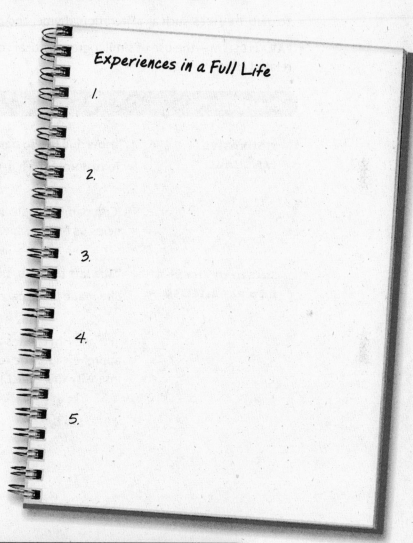

Experiences in a Full Life

1.

2.

3.

4.

5.

ASSESSMENT GOALS

By the end of this lesson, you will be able to . . .

- identify mood in poetry
- use active reading strategies to comprehend text
- analyze a literary essay
- analyze a writing prompt and plan a compare-and-contrast essay

Mood

MOOD is the feeling or atmosphere a writer creates for the reader. For example, a poem may be described as mysterious, somber, joyful, or suspenseful. Elements that can help convey the mood of a poem include

- **IMAGERY** and **FIGURATIVE LANGUAGE**

- **SOUND DEVICES** such as alliteration, rhyme, and rhythm

- **PARALLELISM**—the use of similar grammatical constructions to express related ideas

EXAMPLES	
FIGURATIVE LANGUAGE	**"How dull it is to pause, to make an end,** **To rust unburnish'd, not to shine in use!"** *—"Ulysses," lines 22–23* (Comparing an idle life to a dull, unused sword helps us feel the speaker's dissatisfaction.)
SOUND DEVICES AND PARALLELISM	**"She left the web, she left the loom,** **She made three paces through the room,"** *—"The Lady of Shalott," lines 109–110* (Parallelism creates a mood of tense apprehension. The regular rhythm and the rhyme intensify this effect.)

THE *Lady* OF SHALOTT

ALFRED, LORD TENNYSON

BACKGROUND Alfred, Lord Tennyson, was the most prominent poet of the Victorian era. His poem "The Lady of Shalott" reflects his fascination with the Arthurian legends. In the excerpts from the long poem *In Memoriam,* that you read, Tennyson expresses his grief over the loss of his closest friend, Arthur Henry Hallam, who died suddenly at age 22. The two other poems in this selection, "Ulysses" and "Crossing the Bar," both have speakers who face old age with courage and determination.

FOCUS

As you read the first part of the poem, find out why the Lady of Shalott never leaves her island.

Part I

On either side the river lie
Long fields of barley and of rye,
That clothe the wold[1] and meet the sky;
And through the field the road runs by
5   To many-towered Camelot;
And up and down the people go,
Gazing where the lilies blow[2]
Round an island there below,
    The island of Shalott.

10 Willows whiten, aspens quiver,
Little breezes dusk and shiver
Through the wave that runs forever
By the island in the river
    Flowing down to Camelot.

---

1. **wold:** rolling plain.
2. **blow:** bloom.

What **mood** is created by the description of the island in lines 10–18?

_____

_____

Underline words that contribute to the mood. 🖉

15 Four gray walls, and four gray towers,
    Overlook a space of flowers,
    And the silent isle imbowers³
        The Lady of Shalott. ◀

    By the margin, willow-veiled,
20 Slide the heavy barges trailed
    By slow horses; and unhailed
    The shallop⁴ flitteth silken-sailed
        Skimming down to Camelot:
    But who hath seen her wave her hand?
25 Or at the casement⁵ seen her stand?
    Or is she known in all the land,
        The Lady of Shalott?

    Only reapers, reaping early
    In among the bearded barley,
30 Hear a song that echoes cheerly
    From the river winding clearly,
        Down to towered Camelot;
    And by the moon the reaper weary,
    Piling sheaves in uplands airy,
35 Listening, whispers "'Tis the fairy
        Lady of Shalott."

    Part II
    There she weaves by night and day
    A magic web with colors gay.
    She has heard a whisper say,
40 A curse is on her if she stay
        To look down to Camelot.
    She knows not what the curse may be,
    And so she weaveth steadily,
    And little other care hath she,
45   The Lady of Shalott. ◀

What will happen if the Lady of Shalott looks at Camelot?

_____

_____

_____

3. **imbowers:** encloses; surrounds.
4. **shallop** (shăl'əp): a small open boat.
5. **casement:** a hinged window that opens outward.

And moving through a mirror clear
That hangs before her all the year,
Shadows of the world appear.[6]
There she sees the highway near
50   Winding down to Camelot;
There the river eddy whirls,
And there the surly village churls,[7]
And the red cloaks of market girls,
     Pass onward from Shalott. ▶

55 Sometimes a troop of damsels[8] glad,
An abbot on an ambling pad,[9]
Sometimes a curly shepherd lad,
Or long-haired page[10] in crimson clad,
     Goes by to towered Camelot;
60 And sometimes through the mirror blue
The knights come riding two and two:
She hath no loyal knight and true,
     The Lady of Shalott.

But in her web she still delights
65 To weave the mirror's magic sights,
For often through the silent nights
A funeral, with plumes and lights
     And music, went to Camelot;
Or when the moon was overhead,
70 Came two young lovers lately wed:
"I am half sick of shadows," said
     The Lady of Shalott. ✋ PAUSE & REFLECT

CLARIFY

Reread lines 46–54. What knowledge does the Lady of Shalott have of the outside world?

_____

_____

_____

_____

✋ **PAUSE & REFLECT**

How does the Lady of Shalott feel about the life she leads? *MAKE INFERENCES*

_____

_____

_____

_____

Underline details that support your opinion. ✏

---

6. Weavers often used mirrors while working from the back of a tapestry to view the tapestry's appearance, but this one is used to view the outside world.

7. **surly village churls:** rude members of the lower class in a village.

8. **damsels:** young, unmarried women.

9. **abbot . . . pad:** the head monk in a monastery on a slow-moving horse.

10. **page:** a boy in training to be a knight.

FOCUS

In this section, Camelot's greatest knight passes beneath the lady's window. Read to find out how she responds to his presence.

Part III

A bowshot[11] from her bower eaves,[12]
He rode between the barley sheaves,
75 The sun came dazzling through the leaves,
And flamed upon the brazen greaves[13]
    Of bold Sir Lancelot.
A red-cross knight forever kneeled
To a lady in his shield,[14]
80 That sparkled on the yellow field,
    Beside remote Shalott.

The gemmy[15] bridle glittered free,
Like to some branch of stars we see
Hung in the golden Galaxy.
85 The bridle bells rang merrily
    As he rode down to Camelot;
And from his blazoned baldric[16] slung
A mighty silver bugle hung,
And as he rode his armor rung,
90   Beside remote Shalott.

All in the blue unclouded weather
Thick-jeweled shone the saddle leather,
The helmet and the helmet-feather
Burned like one burning flame together,
95   As he rode down to Camelot;
As often through the purple night,
Below the starry clusters bright,
Some bearded meteor, trailing light,
    Moves over still Shalott.

VISUALIZE

Reread the boxed text. Write an *S* next to **images** that appeal to sight. Write an *H* next to images that appeal to hearing.

What impression do you have of Sir Lancelot?

_____

_____

_____

ANALYZE

Reread lines 73–99. What examples of repetition can you find in this passage?

_____

_____

_____

_____

---

11. **bowshot:** the distance an arrow can be shot.
12. **bower** (bou′ər) **eaves:** the part of the roof that extends above the lady's private room.
13. **brazen greaves:** metal armor protecting the legs below the knees.
14. **A red-cross . . . shield:** His shield showed a knight wearing a red cross and kneeling to honor a lady. The red cross was a symbol worn by knights who had fought in the Crusades.
15. **gemmy:** studded with gems.
16. **blazoned** (blā′zənd) **baldric:** a decorated leather belt, worn across the chest to support a sword or, as in this case, a bugle.

100 His broad clear brow in sunlight glowed;
On burnished hooves his war horse trode;
From underneath his helmet flowed
His coal-black curls as on he rode,
   As he rode down to Camelot.
105 From the bank and from the river
He flashed into the crystal mirror,
"Tirra lirra," by the river
   Sang Sir Lancelot.

She left the web, she left the loom,
110 She made three paces through the room,
She saw the water lily bloom,
She saw the helmet and the plume,
   She looked down to Camelot.
Out flew the web and floated wide;
115 The mirror cracked from side to side;
"The curse is come upon me," cried
   The Lady of Shalott. ▶

Part IV

In the stormy east wind straining,
The pale yellow woods were waning,
120 The broad stream in his banks complaining,
Heavily the low sky raining
   Over towered Camelot;
Down she came and found a boat
Beneath a willow left afloat,
125 And round about the prow she wrote
   The Lady of Shalott. ▶

And down the river's dim expanse
Like some bold seër[17] in a trance,
Seeing all his own mischance[18]—
130 With a glassy countenance
   Did she look to Camelot.

CLARIFY

Reread lines 113–117. Why does the mirror crack?

_____

_____

_____

_____

ANALYZE

What change of **mood** has occurred in the poem?

_____

_____

_____

How does the poet's use of **parallelism** help convey this change?

_____

_____

_____

17. **seër** (sē′ər): someone who can see into the future; a prophet.
18. **mischance**: misfortune; bad luck.

And at the closing of the day
She loosed the chain, and down she lay;
The broad stream bore her far away,
135   The Lady of Shalott.

Lying, robed in snowy white
That loosely flew to left and right—
The leaves upon her falling light—
Through the noises of the night
140   She floated down to Camelot;
And as the boat-head wound along
The willowy hills and fields among,
They heard her singing her last song,
        The Lady of Shalott.

145   Heard a carol, mournful, holy,
Chanted loudly, chanted lowly,
Till her blood was frozen slowly,
And her eyes were darkened wholly,
        Turned to towered Camelot.
150   For ere[19] she reached upon the tide
The first house by the waterside,
Singing in her song she died,
        The Lady of Shalott. ◀

Under tower and balcony,
155   By garden wall and gallery,
A gleaming shape she floated by,
Dead-pale between the houses high,
        Silent into Camelot.
Out upon the wharfs they came,
160   Knight and burgher,[20] lord and dame,
And round the prow they read her name,
        The Lady of Shalott.

TESTSMART

Which word *best* describes the mood of the poem in lines 136–153?

(A) suspenseful

(B) mysterious

(C) tragic

(D) calm

TIP If a test question asks you to identify the **mood** of a poem, think about the **images** the poet uses. This passage includes images of falling leaves, a boat drifting down a river at night, and the sound of a dying woman's last song. What feeling do these images evoke?

---

19. **ere** (âr): before.
20. **burgher:** a middle-class citizen of a town.

Who is this? and what is here?
And in the lighted palace near
165 Died the sound of royal cheer;
And they crossed themselves for fear,
    All the knights at Camelot:
But Lancelot mused a little space;
He said, "She has a lovely face;
170 God in his mercy lend her grace,
    The Lady of Shalott." ✋ PAUSE & REFLECT

✋ **PAUSE & REFLECT**

1. Why does the Lady of Shalott leave her room? *MAKE INFERENCES*

_____

_____

_____

2. In what way does Lancelot's reaction to the arrival of the Lady of Shalott differ from the reaction of others at Camelot? *CONTRAST*

_____

_____

_____

_____

Ulysses

ALFRED, LORD TENNYSON

FOCUS

In this poem, the epic hero Ulysses, now an old man, reflects on his past and present life. Find out what he longs for.

It little profits that an idle king,
By this still hearth, among these barren crags,
Match'd with an aged wife, I mete and dole[1]
Unequal laws unto a savage race,
5   That hoard, and sleep, and feed, and know not me.
I cannot rest from travel: I will drink
Life to the lees:[2] all times I have enjoy'd
Greatly, have suffer'd greatly, both with those
That loved me, and alone; on shore, and when
10   Thro' scudding drifts[3] the rainy Hyades[4]
Vext the dim sea: I am become a name;
For always roaming with a hungry heart
Much have I seen and known; cities of men
And manners, climates, councils, governments,
15   Myself not least, but honor'd of them all;
And drunk delight of battle with my peers,
Far on the ringing plains of windy Troy.[5]
I am a part of all that I have met;
Yet all experience is an arch wherethro'
20   Gleams that untravell'd world, whose margin fades
For ever and for ever when I move.
How dull it is to pause, to make an end,
To rust unburnish'd, not to shine in use! ◀
As tho' to breathe were life. Life piled on life
25   Were all too little, and of one to me

SUMMARIZE

Note what you learn about Ulysses in lines 1–23. ✏

When Ulysses was younger, he

_____

_____

_____

_____

Now Ulysses feels

_____

_____

---

1. **mete** (mēt) **and dole:** give and distribute.
2. **to the lees:** to the dregs or bottom of the cup; completely.
3. **scudding drifts:** windblown rainclouds.
4. **Hyades:** a constellation whose rising was believed to signify the coming of rain.
5. **Troy:** the ancient city conquered by the Greeks in the Trojan War, in which Ulysses (Odysseus) was among the Greek leaders.

Little remains: but every hour is saved
From that eternal silence, something more,
A bringer of new things; and vile it were
For some three suns[6] to store and hoard myself,
30 And this gray spirit yearning in desire
To follow knowledge like a sinking star,
Beyond the utmost bound of human thought.

This is my son, mine own Telemachus,[7]
To whom I leave the sceptre[8] and the isle—
35 Well-loved of me, discerning to fulfil
This labor, by slow prudence to make mild
A rugged people, and thro' soft degrees
Subdue them to the useful and the good.
Most blameless is he, centred in the sphere
40 Of common duties, decent not to fail
In offices of tenderness, and pay
Meet[9] adoration to my household gods,
When I am gone. He works his work, I mine. ▶

There lies the port; the vessel puffs her sail:
45 There gloom the dark broad seas. My mariners,
Souls that have toil'd, and wrought, and thought with me—
That ever with a frolic[10] welcome took
The thunder and the sunshine, and opposed
Free hearts, free foreheads—you and I are old;
50 Old age hath yet his honor and his toil;
Death closes all: but something ere the end,
Some work of noble note, may yet be done,
Not unbecoming men that strove with Gods. ▶
The lights begin to twinkle from the rocks;
55 The long day wanes; the slow moon climbs; the deep
Moans round with many voices. Come, my friends,
'Tis not too late to seek a newer world.
Push off, and sitting well in order smite
The sounding furrows;[11] for my purpose holds

MAKE INFERENCES

Reread the boxed text. Does Ulysses seem to feel that his son will be a great leader or an average leader? Explain.

_____

_____

_____

_____

CLARIFY

What wish does Ulysses express in lines 44–53?

_____

_____

_____

---

6. **three suns:** three years.

7. **Telemachus** (tə-lĕm′ə-kəs).

8. **sceptre** (sĕp′tər): a staff held by a king or a queen as a symbol of royal authority.

9. **meet:** appropriate.

10. **frolic:** merry.

11. **smite . . . furrows:** strike the waves with the boat's oars.

1. How does the **mood** at
the beginning of the poem
differ from the mood at the
end? *CONTRAST*

At the beginning:

_____

_____

_____

At the end:

_____

_____

_____

2. How does the speaker
characterize himself and
his companions in lines
65–70? *DRAW CONCLUSIONS*

_____

_____

_____

60 To sail beyond the sunset, and the baths
    Of all the western stars,[12] until I die.
    It may be that the gulfs will wash us down:
    It may be we shall touch the Happy Isles,
    And see the great Achilles,[13] whom we knew.
65 Tho' much is taken, much abides; and tho'
    We are not now that strength which in old days
    Moved earth and heaven; that which we are, we are;
    One equal temper of heroic hearts,
    Made weak by time and fate, but strong in will
70 To strive, to seek, to find, and not to yield. PAUSE & REFLECT

---

12. **baths . . . stars:** The ancient Greeks believed the earth was surrounded by an
    outer ocean or river, into which the stars descended.

13. **Happy Isles . . . Achilles:** the Islands of the Blessed, where the souls of heroes, like
    Achilles, dwelt after death.

In Memoriam

ALFRED, LORD TENNYSON

27

I envy not in any moods
    The captive void of[1] noble rage,
    The linnet[2] born within the cage,
That never knew the summer woods;

5 I envy not the beast that takes
    His license[3] in the field of time,
    Unfettered[4] by the sense of crime,
To whom a conscience never wakes;

Nor, what may count itself as blest,
10   The heart that never plighted troth
    But stagnates in the weeds of sloth;
Nor any want-begotten rest.[5] ▶

I hold it true, whate'er befall;
    I feel it, when I sorrow most;
15 'Tis better to have loved and lost
Than never to have loved at all.

---

1. **void of:** lacking in.
2. **linnet:** a kind of small songbird.
3. **license:** freedom of action; liberty.
4. **unfettered:** unrestricted.
5. **nor, what . . . rest:** nor do I envy the supposed peace of mind that arises from remaining sunk in inaction, never pledging one's love, or from any deficiency.

FOCUS

Three parts of *In Memoriam* are presented here. Each part reveals a different way of responding to grief. Find out what these responses are.

MONITOR

In the first three stanzas, the speaker lists three things he does not envy. Write them below. The first one has been done for you.

Stanza 1: *The speaker doesn't envy people who are content to live without freedom.*

Stanza 2: _____

_____

_____

Stanza 3: _____

_____

_____

In part 54, the speaker expresses several beliefs that he accepts as wise and truthful. One belief has been underlined for you. Restate this belief in your own words.

_____

_____

_____

_____

Underline another belief in lines 21–32 and restate it. ✏

_____

_____

_____

_____

MAKE INFERENCES

Despite his wise beliefs, how does the speaker feel about the loss of his loved one?

_____

_____

_____

54

O, yet we trust that somehow good
   Will be the final goal of ill,
    To pangs of nature,[6] sins of will,
20 Defects of doubt, and taints of blood;[7]

That nothing walks with aimless feet;
   That not one life shall be destroyed,
    Or cast as rubbish to the void,[8]
When God hath made the pile complete;

25 That not a worm is cloven[9] in vain;
   That not a moth with vain desire
    Is shriveled in a fruitless fire,
Or but subserves[10] another's gain.

Behold, we know not anything;
30   I can but trust that good shall fall
    At last—far off—at last, to all,
And every winter change to spring. ◀

So runs my dream; but what am I?
   An infant crying in the night;
35   An infant crying for the light,
And with no language but a cry. ◀

130

Thy voice is on the rolling air;
   I hear thee where the waters run;
    Thou standest in the rising sun,
40 And in the setting thou art fair.

---

6. **pangs of nature:** physical pain.
7. **taints of blood:** inherited faults.
8. **void:** empty space.
9. **cloven:** split.
10. **subserves:** promotes or assists.

What are thou then? I cannot guess;
    But though I seem in star and flower
    To feel thee some diffusive[11] power,
I do not therefore love thee less.

45 My love involves the love before;
    My love is vaster passion now;
    Though mixed with God and Nature thou,
I seem to love thee more and more.

    Far off thou art, but ever nigh;[12]
50   I have thee still, and I rejoice;
    I prosper, circled with thy voice;
I shall not lose thee though I die. PAUSE & REFLECT

PAUSE & REFLECT

1. How does the **mood** of part 130 different from the mood of part 54? *CONTRAST*

_____

_____

_____

2. What does *In Memoriam* suggest about the nature of grief? *DRAW CONCLUSIONS*

_____

_____

_____

_____

_____

---

11. **diffusive:** scattered about.
12. **nigh:** nearby.

CROSSING THE *Bar*

ALFRED, LORD TENNYSON

FOCUS

In this poem, the speaker reflects on the end of his life.

Sunset and evening star,
    And one clear call for me!
And may there be no moaning of the bar,[1]
    When I put out to sea,

5 But such a tide as moving seems asleep,
    Too full for sound and foam,
When that which drew from out the boundless deep
    Turns again home.

Twilight and evening bell,[2]
10   And after that the dark!
And may there be no sadness of farewell,
    When I embark;

For though from out our bourne of Time and Place[3]
    The flood[4] may bear me far,
15 I hope to see my Pilot face to face
    When I have crossed the bar.   **PAUSE & REFLECT**

PAUSE & REFLECT

What experience does the speaker compare to a voyage out to sea?

_____

_____

_____

_____

Underline words and phrases that help you clarify this comparison. ✎

Big Question ?

Reread your response to the activity on page 179. What would you add to the list after having read Tennyson's poems?

_____

_____

_____

1. **moaning of the bar:** the sound of the ocean waves pounding against a sandbar at the mouth of a harbor.
2. **evening bell:** a ship's bell rung to announce the changing of the watch.
3. **from out . . . Place:** beyond the boundary of our lifetimes.
4. **flood:** ocean.

Reading Comprehension

DIRECTIONS *Answer these questions about Tennyson's poems by filling in the correct ovals.*

1. At the beginning of "The Lady of Shalott," the lady experiences the outside world by

   Ⓐ gazing at images in weavings

   Ⓑ looking at reflections in a mirror

   Ⓒ talking to travelers

   Ⓓ staring out her window

2. What prompts the Lady of Shalott to risk having a curse fall upon her?

   Ⓐ She finds a boat beneath a willow tree.

   Ⓑ The mirror in her room cracks.

   Ⓒ Sir Lancelot passes by her tower.

   Ⓓ She no longer enjoys weaving.

3. In "Ulysses," what do the "ringing plains of windy Troy" (line 17) represent?

   Ⓐ present sorrows

   Ⓑ present victories

   Ⓒ past loves

   Ⓓ past battles

4. Ulysses wants to leave his kingdom because

   Ⓐ his son Telemachus has taken over

   Ⓑ he feels restless at home

   Ⓒ he is too old to be a good ruler

   Ⓓ his enemies have declared war on him

5. Which words *best* describe the mood in lines 22–32 of "Ulysses"?

   Ⓐ weary and bored

   Ⓑ optimistic and exciting

   Ⓒ mysterious and frightening

   Ⓓ solemn and reverent

6. In part 27 of *In Memoriam*, the speaker suggests that

   Ⓐ we are often deceived by our feelings

   Ⓑ when love goes wrong it is like a cage

   Ⓒ true love never causes suffering

   Ⓓ one should love even if it leads to sorrow

7. In part 130 of *In Memoriam*, the speaker suggests that his loved one has

   Ⓐ become part of nature

   Ⓑ vanished from his life

   Ⓒ undertaken a long journey

   Ⓓ returned to his home

8. The mood in the last stanza of "Crossing the Bar" can *best* be described as

   Ⓐ mysterious

   Ⓑ tragic

   Ⓒ peaceful

   Ⓓ tense

GO ON ➡

For help, use the **Test-Taker's Toolkit** below.

Responding in Writing

9. Short Response Tennyson is often described as a spokesman for Victorian values. Which of the poems in this lesson seems most relevant to your own generation? What enduring theme does it convey? Use details from the poem to support your answer.

_____

_____

_____

_____

_____

_____

TEST-TAKER'S TOOLKIT

⊗ **GRAPHIC ORGANIZER** Use the chart below to help you plan your response. Reread the poems to help you remember the details.

Poem: _____

Enduring Theme: _____

_____

Details that Make It Relevant Today:

-
-
-

What's the Connection?

You have read three parts of Tennyson's book-length poem *In Memoriam,* which took him 17 years to complete. In the following literary essay, you will learn about the poem's background and gain insight into Tennyson's process of writing this masterpiece.

DISCUSS Life dishes out a mix of experiences that affect us in different ways. Curiously, we often learn the most from experiences that are the most difficult to endure. Think about how each experience listed below might affect someone. Write your responses in the chart. Then discuss your ideas with a partner.

Experiences	Negative Effects	Positive Effects
death of a loved one		
being rejected by a boyfriend or girlfriend		
failing at something		
falling in love		

Related Nonfiction

Alfred, Lord Tennyson's Journey Through Grief
LITERARY ESSAY

Use with the selected poetry by Alfred, Lord Tennyson, p. 178

LEARN THE SKILL: ANALYZE A LITERARY ESSAY

A **literary essay** seeks to help readers better understand and appreciate a literary work. Typically it does this by providing the following:

- information about the work's historical, biographical, or literary context
- a description of the text itself
- an evaluation of the work that is supported by reasons and evidence

For more on analyzing a literary essay, see the Critical Essays entry in the Nonfiction Skills Handbook beginning on page R2.

Alfred, Lord Tennyson's Journey Through Grief

by Randal Brown

LITERARY ESSAY

What main idea about _In Memoriam_ does the author express in lines 1–13?

_____

_____

_____

_____

LITERARY ESSAY

Reread the boxed text. What direct connection does the author make between Tennyson's life and _In Memoriam_?

_____

_____

_____

_____

Anyone who has lost a loved one knows that mourning is a long, slow process. Months or years pass by, and you continue to grieve deeply. Then one day you notice that your sorrow is lifting. You may take a step backward for every two steps forward, but you gradually learn to enjoy life again.

Alfred, Lord Tennyson captured such a journey in his masterpiece _In Memoriam A. H. H._ In this long poem he explores the intense grief he felt over the death of his best friend, Arthur Henry Hallam, at the age of 22. Both universal and highly intimate, the poem was a critical and
10 popular success after its anonymous publication in 1850. Some lines from _In Memoriam_ have become famous, including "nature red in tooth and claw" and "'Tis better to have loved and lost / Than never to have loved at all." ◀

Tennyson showed early promise as a writer. When he was 12, he completed a 6,000 line epic poem. In 1827—the same year he left home for Trinity College, Cambridge—he published a book of poetry with his brother Charles. _Poems by Two Brothers_ was not a mature work, but it drew the attention of a college literary club called the Apostles, which Tennyson joined. One of its members was Hallam, who saw in Tennyson
20 the potential for great artistic success.

The two formed a very close bond. They toured Europe together twice, and Hallam even became engaged to Tennyson's sister. Hallam's friendship seems to have changed how Tennyson thought of himself as a poet and as a person. Then Hallam died suddenly in 1833 while traveling with his father. The loss sent Tennyson into a spiral of depression. His grief seems to have been crippling at times, but it provided the inspiration for _In Memoriam_. ◀

The poem, which took 17 years to complete, is divided into 131 sections. It is written in four-line stanzas with an _abba_ rhyme scheme.

30 When Tennyson began writing, he didn't intend to create one long work—each section was composed to stand on its own. Tennyson later combined the sections and added a prologue and epilogue to form the unified poem we know today.

If you read the poem straight through from start to finish, you'll notice that the tone often changes. The transitions between sections may seem awkward at times, but this awkwardness reflects the contradictory feelings of someone struggling to overcome grief. One stanza might be full of despair:

> This year I slept and woke with pain,
40 > —I almost wish'd no more to wake,
> —And that my hold on life would break
> Before I heard those bells again:

Another might express determination to go on with life:

> I will not shut me from my kind,
> —And, lest I stiffen into stone,
> —I will not eat my heart alone,
> Nor feed with sighs a passing wind: ▶

Repeatedly in the poem, Tennyson uses the celebration of Christmas as a symbol of change. Each year when the holiday comes around, he
50 feels the loss of Hallam less intensely. As his sorrow fades, his spiritual connection to Hallam grows stronger.

At the end of *In Memoriam*, Tennyson celebrates his sister's marriage. This event is especially meaningful because the same sister had intended to marry Hallam. The great power of Tennyson's poem is that it provides an intimate view of Tennyson's journey from the deepest grief to acceptance of loss, yet it also expresses universal themes about mourning. Tennyson's personal ordeal is one we can all appreciate and learn from.

Arthur Henry Hallam

LITERARY ESSAY

In lines 34–47, how does the author help readers appreciate a quality of *In Memoriam* that might seem like a flaw? Explain.

_____

_____

_____

_____

_____

Reading Comprehension

DIRECTIONS *Answer these questions about the essay and the poems in this lesson by filling in the correct ovals.*

1. According to the essay, *In Memoriam* reflects both

   (A) maturity and immaturity

   (B) sorrow and joy

   (C) a personal and a collective injury

   (D) a personal journey and universal themes

2. Which idea supports the essay's conclusion that we can all appreciate and learn from *In Memoriam*?

   (A) *In Memoriam* took 17 years to complete.

   (B) The poem captures the process of mourning.

   (C) The poem is written in four-line stanzas.

   (D) Grief over Hallam's death inspired the poem.

3. Which idea from the essay is a generalization about the poem's style?

   (A) It has a prologue.

   (B) The ending celebrates a marriage.

   (C) Many transitions seem awkward.

   (D) The poem has 131 sections.

4. Parts 27, 54, and 130 of *In Memoriam* are similar to the stanzas that appear in the literary essay in that they express

   (A) the poet's deepest sorrow

   (B) comforting thoughts

   (C) a range of emotions

   (D) conventional wisdom

5. The word *promise* in line 14 of the essay means

   (A) agreement

   (B) potential

   (C) intention

   (D) talent

6. The word *prologue* in line 32 of the essay refers to

   (A) an introductory section

   (B) a conclusion

   (C) a thesis statement

   (D) explanatory notes

Timed Writing Practice

PROMPT

Write an essay in which you compare and contrast *In Memoriam* with one of the other poems by Tennyson in this lesson. Discuss how the two poems are similar or different in subject, theme, style, and mood. Include details from the poems to support your ideas.

TEST-TAKER'S TOOLKIT

1. ANALYZE THE PROMPT

A. Underline the type of essay you are being asked to write, and circle key words in the directions. One phrase has been circled for you.

B. Jot down a list of the key elements you need to include in your essay.

Key elements:_____

_____

_____

_____

2. PLAN YOUR RESPONSE

A. **Make notes** Use a chart like the one shown to note the points your essay will make.

B. **Organize your information** The first paragraph of your essay should state which poems you will compare and explain which elements you will examine. You can then discuss all of the elements of one poem first and then the elements of the other poem. Or you can compare and contrast both poems one point at a time. End your essay with a conclusion in which you sum up your ideas.

In Memoriam	Second poem:
Subject:	Subject:
Theme:	Theme:
Style:	Style:
Mood:	Mood:

3. WRITE AND REVIEW

A. In your introduction, include an interesting quote or observation to grab your readers' attention.

B. Be sure to leave time to check your spelling and grammar.

LESSON 5B

Malachi's Cove

BY ANTHONY TROLLOPE

RELATED NONFICTION

*One Rescuer Lives, One Drowns
Saving Sisters in Rough Palm
Beach Surf*

How do we learn to TRUST?

Babies learn to trust instinctively by responding to adults who love them. But as we get older, trust becomes a tricky proposition—especially if experience has taught us to be wary of others. What allows us to overcome suspicion and reach out to others?

LIST IT List five actions or qualities that signal that a person is trustworthy. Then list five actions or qualities that tell you to be wary. Share your response with a group of classmates. How do your lists compare?

You can trust a person who . . .

1.

2.

3.

4.

5.

You can't trust a person who . . .

1.

2.

3.

4.

5.

ASSESSMENT GOALS

By the end of this lesson, you will be able to . . .

- analyze realism in a work of fiction
- use active reading strategies to comprehend text
- analyze cause-and-effect relationships in nonfiction texts
- analyze a writing prompt and plan a literary analysis

Realism

REALISM refers to writing that portrays everyday life in accurate detail. It also refers to a literary movement that developed in mid-19th century France and later spread to England. The graphic below shows important characteristics of realism.

You can practice answering questions about realism as you analyze "Malachi's Cove," a short story by one of the masters of realist fiction.

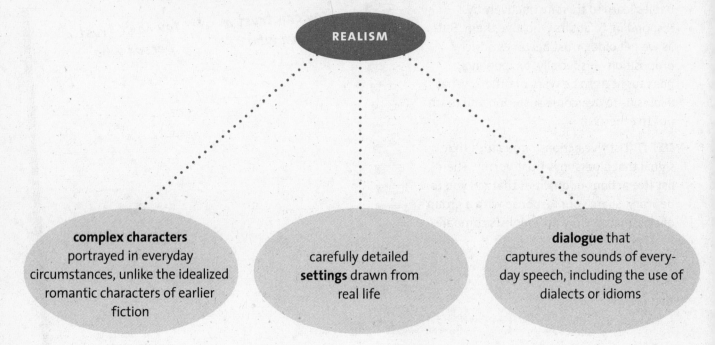

REALISM

complex characters portrayed in everyday circumstances, unlike the idealized romantic characters of earlier fiction

carefully detailed **settings** drawn from real life

dialogue that captures the sounds of every-day speech, including the use of dialects or idioms

MALACHI'S COVE

Anthony Trollope

BACKGROUND Anthony Trollope (1815–1882) was one of the most prolific writers of the Victorian era. His works are widely respected for their true-to-life characters and astute analysis of class dynamics. Many of his novels are set in England or Ireland. This story takes place on the coast of Cornwall, a rugged, rocky, and remote peninsula in southwestern England. Cornwall is one of Britain's most picturesque regions—and one of its poorest.

On the northern coast of Cornwall, between Tintagel and Bossiney,[1] down on the very margin of the sea, there lived not long since an old man who got his living by saving seaweed from the waves, and selling it for manure. The cliffs there are bold and fine, and the sea beats in upon them from the north with a grand violence. I doubt whether it be not the finest morsel of cliff scenery in England, though it is beaten by many portions of the west coast of Ireland, and perhaps also by spots in Wales and Scotland. Cliffs should be nearly **precipitous**, they should be broken in their outlines, and should barely admit here and there of an insecure passage
10 from their summit to the sand at their feet. The sea should come, if not up to them, at least very near to them, and then, above all things, the water below them should be blue, and not of that dead leaden color which is so familiar to us in England. At Tintagel all these requisites are there, except that bright blue color which is so lovely. But the cliffs themselves are bold and well broken, and the margin of sand at high water is very narrow—so narrow that at spring tides there is barely a footing there. ▶

---

1. **Cornwall . . . Tintagel** (tĭn-tăj′əl) **and Bossiney** (bôs′ĭ-nē): a remote peninsula on the southwestern tip of England that includes the picturesque village of Tintagel and an adjoining beach area called Bossiney.

FOCUS
In the first part of the story you will meet a reclusive old man and his granddaughter, Mally. Find out what makes Mally so remarkable.

precipitous (prĭ-sĭp′ĭ-təs) *adj.* nearly vertical; very steep

VISUALIZE

Underline details in lines 1–16 that help you visualize the story's **setting**. ✏

Close upon this margin was the cottage or hovel of Malachi Trenglos,[2] the old man of whom I have spoken. But Malachi, or old Glos, as he was commonly called by the people around him, had not built his house
20 absolutely upon the sand. There was a fissure in the rock so great that at the top it formed a narrow ravine, and so complete from the summit to the base that it afforded an opening for a steep and rugged track from the top of the rock to the bottom. This fissure was so wide at the bottom that it had afforded space for Trenglos to fix his habitation on a foundation of rock, and here he had lived for many years. It was told of him that in the early days of his trade he had always carried the weed in a basket on his back to the top, but latterly[3] he had been possessed of a donkey which had been trained to go up and down the steep track with a single pannier[4] over his loins, for the rocks would not admit of panniers hanging by his side;
30 and for this assistant he had built a shed adjoining his own, and almost as large as that in which he himself resided.

But, as years went on, old Glos procured other assistance than that of the donkey, or, as I should rather say, Providence[5] supplied him with other help; and, indeed, had it not been so, the old man must have given up his cabin and his independence and gone into the workhouse at Camelford.[6] For rheumatism[7] had afflicted him, old age had bowed him till he was nearly double, and by degrees he became unable to attend the donkey on its upward passage to the world above, or even to assist in rescuing the coveted weed from the waves. ◀

40 At the time to which our story refers Trenglos had not been up the cliff for twelve months, and for the last six months he had done nothing towards the furtherance of his trade, except to take the money and keep it, if any of it was kept, and occasionally to shake down a bundle of fodder[8] for the donkey. The real work of the business was done altogether by Mahala Trenglos, his granddaughter.

2. **Malachi Trenglos** (măl′ə-kī′ trĕn′glôs): Many Cornish family names begin with *Tre*, which means "dwelling" in Cornish.
3. **latterly:** more recently.
4. **pannier** (păn′yər): one of a pair of baskets usually hung on either side of a pack animal to carry loads.
5. **Providence:** the helpful guidance or aid of God, fate, or nature.
6. **workhouse at Camelford:** the poorhouse at Camelford, a larger town near Tintagel. In Victorian times, poor people whose relatives could not support them were sent to workhouses; healthy residents were put to work.
7. **rheumatism** (rōō′mə-tĭz′əm): painful inflammation and stiffness of the joints and muscles.
8. **fodder:** coarse food for cattle and other farm animals.

MAKE INFERENCES

What does the information in lines 17–39 suggest about Malachi's life?

_____

_____

_____

Underline details that support your inferences. ✎

Mally Trenglos was known to all the farmers round the coast, and to all the small tradespeople in Camelford. She was a wild-looking, almost unearthly creature, with wild-flowing, black, uncombed hair, small in stature, with small hands and bright black eyes; but people said that she was very strong, and the children around declared that she worked day and night and knew nothing of fatigue. As to her age there were many doubts. Some said she was ten, and others five-and-twenty, but the reader may be allowed to know that at this time she had in truth passed her twentieth birthday. The old people spoke well of Mally, because she was so good to her grandfather; and it was said of her that though she carried to him a little gin and tobacco almost daily, she bought nothing for herself—and as to the gin, no one who looked at her would accuse her of meddling with that. But she had no friends and but few acquaintances among people of her own age. They said that she was fierce and ill-natured, that she had not a good word for anyone, and that she was, complete at all points, a thorough little vixen.[9] The young men did not care for her; for, as regarded dress, all days were alike with her. She never made herself smart on Sundays. She was generally without stockings, and seemed to care not at all to exercise any of those feminine attractions which might have been hers had she studied to attain them. All days were the same to her in regard to dress; and, indeed, till lately, all days had, I fear, been the same to her in other respects. Old Malachi had never been seen inside a place of worship since he had taken to live under the cliff. ▶

But within the last two years Mally had submitted herself to the teaching of the clergyman at Tintagel, and had appeared at church on Sundays, if not absolutely with punctuality, at any rate so often that no one who knew the peculiarity of her residence was disposed to quarrel with her on that subject. But she made no difference in her dress on these occasions. She took her place in a low stone seat just inside the church door, clothed as usual in her thick red serge petticoat[10] and loose brown serge jacket, such being the apparel which she had found to be best adapted for her hard and perilous work among the waters. She had pleaded to the clergyman when he attacked her on the subject of church attendance with vigor that she had got no church-going clothes. He had explained to her that she would be received there without distinction to her clothing. Mally had taken him at his word, and had gone, with a courage which certainly deserved admiration, though I doubt whether there was not mingled with it an obstinacy which was less admirable. ▶

CLARIFY

How do people in town react to Mally?

Old people:

_____

_____

_____

Young people:

_____

_____

_____

MONITOR

What thoughts do you have about Mally's **character**?

_____

_____

_____

_____

9. **vixen** (vĭk'sən): a bad-tempered woman; a shrew.
10. **serge petticoat:** a skirt made of a strong twilled woolen or silken fabric.

indefatigable
(ĭn'dĭ-făt'ĭ-gə-bəl) *adj.* tireless

✋ **PAUSE & REFLECT**

In what ways is Mally unlike a typical romantic heroine? Cite details from the text to support your answer. **CONTRAST**

_____

_____

_____

_____

_____

🔍 **F**OCUS
In the next part of the story, a conflict develops between Mally and one of her neighbors. Read to find out how she reacts to this situation.

For people said that old Glos was rich, and that Mally might have proper clothes if she chose to buy them. Mr. Polwarth, the clergyman, who, as the old man could not come to him, went down the rocks to the old man, did make some hint on the matter in Mally's absence. But old Glos, who had been patient with him on other matters, turned upon him so angrily when he made an allusion to money, that Mr. Polwarth found himself obliged to give that matter up, and Mally continued to sit upon the stone bench in her short serge petticoat, with her long hair streaming down her face. She did so far sacrifice to decency as on such occasions to tie up her black hair with an old shoestring. So tied it would remain through the Monday and Tuesday, but by Wednesday afternoon Mally's hair had generally managed to escape.

As to Mally's **indefatigable** industry there could be no manner of doubt, for the quantity of seaweed which she and the donkey amassed between them was very surprising. Old Glos, it was declared, had never collected half what Mally gathered together; but then the article was becoming cheaper, and it was necessary that the exertion should be greater. So Mally and the donkey toiled and toiled, and the seaweed came up in heaps which surprised those who looked at her little hands and light form. Was there not someone who helped her at nights, some fairy, or demon, or the like? Mally was so snappish in her answers to people that she had no right to be surprised if ill-natured things were said of her.

✋ **PAUSE & REFLECT**

No one ever heard Mally Trenglos complain of her work, but about this time she was heard to make great and loud complaints of the treatment she received from some of her neighbors. It was known that she went with her plaints to Mr. Polwarth; and when he could not help her, or did not give her such instant help as she needed, she went—ah, so foolishly! to the office of a certain attorney at Camelford, who was not likely to prove himself a better friend than Mr. Polwarth.

Now the nature of her injury was as follows. The place in which she collected her seaweed was a little cove—the people had come to call it Malachi's Cove from the name of the old man who lived there—which was so formed that the margin of the sea therein could only be reached by the passage from the top down to Trenglos's hut. The breadth of the cove when the sea was out might perhaps be two hundred yards, and on each side the rocks ran out in such a way that both from north and south the domain of Trenglos was guarded from intruders. And this locality had been well chosen for its intended purpose.

There was a rush of the sea into the cove, which carried there large, drifting masses of seaweed, leaving them among the rocks when the tide was out. During the equinoctial winds[11] of the spring and autumn the supply would never fail; and even when the sea was calm, the long, soft, salt-bedewed, trailing masses of the weed could be gathered there when they could not be found elsewhere for miles along the coast. The task of getting the weed from the breakers[12] was often difficult and dangerous—so difficult that much of it was left to be carried away by the next incoming tide.

Mally doubtless did not gather half the crop that was there at her feet. What was taken by the returning waves she did not regret; but when <u>interlopers</u> came upon her cove, and gathered her wealth—her grandfather's wealth, beneath her eyes, then her heart was broken. It was this interloping, this intrusion, that drove poor Mally to the Camelford attorney. But, alas, though the Camelford attorney took Mally's money, he could do nothing for her, and her heart was broken!

She had an idea, in which no doubt her grandfather shared, that the path to the cove was, at any rate, their property. When she was told that the cove, and sea running into the cove, were not the freeholds[13] of her grandfather, she understood that the statement might be true. But what then as to the use of the path? Who had made the path what it was? Had she not painfully, wearily, with exceeding toil, carried up bits of rock with her own little hands, that her grandfather's donkey might have footing for his feet? Had she not scraped together crumbs of earth along the face of the cliff that she might make easier to the animal the track of that rugged way? And now, when she saw big farmer's lads coming down with other donkeys—and, indeed, there was one who came with a pony; no boy, but a young man, old enough to know better than rob a poor old man and a young girl—she reviled the whole human race, and swore that the Camelford attorney was a fool. ▶

Any attempt to explain to her that there was still weed enough for her was worse than useless. Was it not all hers and his, or, at any rate, was not the sole way to it his and hers? And was not her trade stopped and <u>impeded</u>? Had she not been forced to back her laden donkey down, twenty yards she said, but it had, in truth, been five, because Farmer Gunliffe's son had been in the way with his thieving pony? Farmer

130

140

150

interloper (ĭn′tər-lō′pər) *n.* intruder

CLARIFY

Why does Mally believe that her neighbors have no right to collect seaweed from the cove?

_____

_____

_____

_____

impede (ĭm-pēd′) *v.* to hinder or obstruct

---

11. **equinoctial** (ē′kwə-nŏk′shəl) **winds:** strong winds around the time of the spring or autumn equinox, when day and night are of equal length.
12. **breakers:** waves that break into foam when they hit the shore.
13. **freeholds:** land that is inherited or held for life.

Gunliffe had wanted to buy her weed at his own price, and because she had refused he had set on his thieving son to destroy her in this wicked
160　way.

"I'll hamstring[14] the beast the next time as he's down here!" said Mally to old Glos, while the angry fire literally streamed from her eyes.

Farmer Gunliffe's small homestead—he held about fifty acres of land—was close by the village of Tintagel, and not a mile from the cliff. The sea-wrack, as they call it, was pretty well the only manure within his reach, and no doubt he thought it hard that he should be kept from using it by Mally Trenglos and her obstinacy.

"There's heaps of other coves, Barty," said Mally to Barty Gunliffe, the farmer's son.

170　"But none so nigh,[15] Mally, nor yet none that fills 'emselves as this place."

Then he explained to her that he would not take the weed that came up close to hand. He was bigger than she was, and stronger, and would get it from the outer rocks, with which she never meddled. Then, with scorn in her eye, she swore that she could get it where he durst[16] not venture, and repeated her threat of hamstringing the pony. Barty laughed at her wrath, jeered her because of her wild hair, and called her a mermaid.

"I'll mermaid you!" she cried. "Mermaid, indeed! I wouldn't be a man to come and rob a poor girl and an old cripple. But you're no man, Barty Gunliffe! You're not half a man." ◀

180　Nevertheless, Bartholomew Gunliffe was a very fine young fellow as far as the eye went. He was about five feet eight inches high, with strong arms and legs, with light curly brown hair and blue eyes. His father was but in a small way as a farmer, but, nevertheless, Barty Gunliffe was well thought of among the girls around. Everybody liked Barty—excepting only Mally Trenglos, and she hated him like poison.

Barty, when he was asked why so good-natured a lad as he persecuted a poor girl and an old man, threw himself upon the justice of the thing. It wouldn't do at all, according to his view, that any single person should take upon himself to own that which God Almighty sent as the common
190　property of all. He would do Mally no harm, and so he had told her. But Mally was a vixen—a wicked little vixen; and she must be taught to have a civil tongue in her head. When once Mally would speak him civil as he

ANALYZE

Reread the boxed text. Underline portions of **dialogue** that give a **realistic** feeling to the story.

---

14. **hamstring:** to disable by cutting the hamstring, the large tendon found on the back of the leg in humans or on the hind leg in many quadrupeds.

15. **nigh** (nī): near.

16. **durst:** dare.

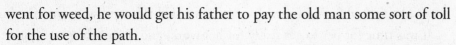

went for weed, he would get his father to pay the old man some sort of toll for the use of the path.

"Speak him civil?" said Mally. "Never; not while I have a tongue in my mouth!" And I fear old Glos encouraged her rather than otherwise in her view of the matter.

But her grandfather did not encourage her to hamstring the pony. Hamstringing a pony would be a serious thing, and old Glos thought it might be very awkward for both of them if Mally were put into prison. He suggested, therefore, that all manner of impediments should be put in the way of the pony's feet, surmising that the well-trained donkey might be able to work in spite of them. And Barty Gunliffe, on his next descent, did find the passage very awkward when he came near to Malachi's hut, but he made his way down, and poor Mally saw the lumps of rock at which she had labored so hard pushed on one side or rolled out of the way with a steady persistency of injury towards herself that almost drove her frantic. ▶

"Well, Barty, you're a nice boy," said old Glos, sitting in the doorway of the hut, as he watched the intruder.

"I ain't a doing no harm to none as doesn't harm me," said Barty. "The sea's free to all, Malachi."

"And the sky's free to all, but I mustn't get up on the top of your big barn to look at it," said Mally, who was standing among the rocks with a long hook in her hand. The long hook was the tool with which she worked in dragging the weed from the waves. "But you ain't got no justice, nor yet no sperrit,[17] or you wouldn't come here to vex an old man like he."

"I didn't want to vex him, nor yet to vex you, Mally. You let me be for a while, and we'll be friends yet."

"Friends!" exclaimed Mally. "Who'd have the likes of you for a friend? What are you moving them stones for? Them stones belongs to grandfather." And in her wrath she made a movement as though she were going to fly at him.

"Let him be, Mally," said the old man; "let him be. He'll get his punishment. He'll come to be drowned some day if he comes down here when the wind is in shore."

"That he may be drowned then!" said Mally, in her anger. "If he was in the big hole there among the rocks, and the sea running in at half tide, I wouldn't lift a hand to help him out."

"Yes, you would, Mally; you'd fish me up with your hook like a big stick of seaweed." ▶

---

17. **sperrit:** dialect for *spirit,* here meaning "courage" or "character."

CLARIFY

Reread lines 195–207. How does Mally's grandfather want her to respond to Barty's use of their path?

_____

_____

_____

_____

MAKE INFERENCES

Reread lines 198–230. How does Barty seem to feel about Mally? Explain.

_____

_____

_____

PAUSE & REFLECT

Based on what you know about Barty and Mally, what predictions would you make about their future? Why? *PREDICT*

_____

_____

_____

_____

FOCUS

Barty does not have Mally's experience in gathering seaweed. Read to find out what happens when he tries to compete with her.

garner (gär′nər) v. to gather up and store; to collect

desist (dĭ-sĭst′) v. to cease or stop

She turned from him with scorn as he said this, and went into the hut. It was time for her to get ready for her work, and one of the great injuries done her lay in this—that such a one as Barty Gunliffe should come and look at her during her toil among the breakers. **PAUSE & REFLECT**

It was an afternoon in April, and the hour was something after four o'clock. There had been a heavy wind from the northwest all the morning, with gusts of rain, and the seagulls had been in and out of the cove all the day, which was a sure sign to Mally that the incoming tide would cover the rocks with weed.

240 The quick waves were now returning with wonderful celerity[18] over the low reefs, and the time had come at which the treasure must be seized, if it was to be **garnered** on that day. By seven o'clock it would be growing dark, at nine it would be high water, and before daylight the crop would be carried out again if not collected. All this Mally understood very well, and some of this Barty was beginning to understand also.

As Mally came down with her bare feet, bearing her long hook in her hand, she saw Barty's pony standing patiently on the sand, and in her heart she longed to attack the brute. Barty at this moment, with a common three-pronged fork in his hand, was standing down on a large 250 rock, gazing forth towards the waters. He had declared that he would gather the weed only at places which were inaccessible to Mally, and he was looking out that he might settle where he would begin.

"Let 'un be, let 'un be," shouted the old man to Mally, as he saw her take a step towards the beast, which she hated almost as much as she hated the man.

Hearing her grandfather's voice through the wind, she **desisted** from her purpose, if any purpose she had had, and went forth to her work. As she passed down the cove, and scrambled in among the rocks, she saw Barty still standing on his perch; out beyond, the white-curling waves were 260 cresting and breaking themselves with violence, and the wind was howling among the caverns and abutments of the cliff.

Every now and then there came a squall[19] of rain, and though there was sufficient light, the heavens were black with clouds. A scene more beautiful might hardly be found by those who love the glories of the coast. The light for such objects was perfect. Nothing could exceed the grandeur of the colors—the blue of the open sea, the white of the breaking waves, the

---

18. **celerity** (sə-lĕr′ĭ-tē): swiftness of action; speed.
19. **squall** (skwôl): a brief, violent wind storm, usually accompanied by rain or snow.

yellow sands, or the streaks of red and brown which gave such richness to the cliff. ▶

But neither Mally nor Barty were thinking of such things as these. Indeed, they were hardly thinking of their trade after its ordinary forms. Barty was meditating how he might best accomplish his purpose of working beyond the reach of Mally's feminine powers, and Mally was resolving that wherever Barty went she would go farther.

And, in many respects, Mally had the advantage. She knew every rock in the spot, and was sure of those which gave a good foothold, and sure also of those which did not. And then her activity had been made perfect by practice for the purpose to which it was to be devoted. Barty, no doubt, was stronger than she, and quite as active. But Barty could not jump among the waves from one stone to another as she could do, nor was he as yet able to get aid in his work from the very force of the water as she could get it. She had been hunting seaweed in that cove since she had been an urchin of six years old, and she knew every hole and corner and every spot of vantage.[20] The waves were her friends, and she could use them. She could measure their strength, and knew when and where it would cease.

Mally was great down in the salt pools of her own cove—great, and very fearless. As she watched Barty make his way forward from rock to rock, she told herself, gleefully, that he was going astray. The curl of the wind as it blew into the cove would not carry the weed up to the northern buttresses of the cove; and then there was the great hole just there—the great hole of which she had spoken when she wished him evil. ▶

And now she went to work, hooking up the dishevelled hairs of the ocean, and landing many a cargo on the extreme margin of the sand, from whence she would be able in the evening to drag it back before the invading waters would return to reclaim the spoil.[21]

And on his side also Barty made his heap up against the northern buttresses of which I have spoken. Barty's heap became big and still bigger, so that he knew, let the pony work as he might, he could not take it all up that evening. But still it was not as large as Mally's heap. Mally's hook was better than his fork, and Mally's skill was better than his strength. And when he failed in some haul Mally would jeer him with a wild, weird laughter, and shriek to him through the wind that he was not half a man. At first he answered her with laughing words, but before long, as she boasted of her success and pointed to his failure, he became angry, and

20. **urchin** (ûr′chĭn) . . . **spot of vantage:** a mischievous youngster of six years old, who knew which places would give her the advantage (in her task).
21. **spoil:** treasure seized in battle; plunder or booty.

MALACHI'S COVE **213**

VISUALIZE

Reread lines 256–268. What details make this description of the **setting** seem **realistic** and **vivid**?

_____

_____

_____

_____

QUESTION

What would you like to find out about Mally's thoughts at this point in the story?

_____

_____

_____

_____

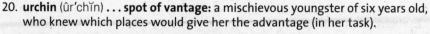

✋ PAUSE & REFLECT

What do Barty's and Mally's actions in this scene reveal about them? *MAKE INFERENCES*

_____

_____

_____

Ⓕ OCUS

Find out how a sudden, terrifying event becomes a test of Mally's character—and what she does as a result.

TESTSMART

What motivates Barty to try to harvest seaweed from the pool?

Ⓐ a sense of injustice

Ⓑ Mally's taunting

Ⓒ love of adventure

Ⓓ Barty's greed

TIP When a question asks about what **motivates** a character to take a certain action, the answer may not be directly stated in the text. To answer this question, look for clues in Barty's actions, thoughts, and feelings earlier in the scene.

then he answered her no more. He became angry with himself, in that he missed so much of the plunder before him.

The broken sea was full of the long straggling growth which the waves had torn up from the bottom of the ocean, but the masses were carried past him, away from him—nay, once or twice over him; and then Mally's weird voice would sound in his ear, jeering him. The gloom among the
310 rocks was now becoming thicker and thicker, the tide was beating in with increased strength, and the gusts of wind came with quicker and greater violence. But still he worked on. While Mally worked he would work, and he would work for some time after she was driven in. He would not be beaten by a girl. **✋ PAUSE & REFLECT**

The great hole was now full of water, but of water which seemed to be boiling as though in a pot. And the pot was full of floating masses—large treasures of seaweed which were thrown to and fro upon its surface, but lying there so thick that one would seem almost able to rest upon it without sinking.
320 Mally knew well how useless it was to attempt to rescue aught[22] from the fury of that boiling caldron. The hole went in under the rocks, and the side of it towards the shore lay high, slippery, and steep. The hole, even at low water, was never empty; and Mally believed that there was no bottom to it. Fish thrown in there could escape out to the ocean, miles away—so Mally in her softer moods would tell the visitors to the cove. She knew the hole well. Poulnadioul[23] she was accustomed to call it; which was supposed, when translated, to mean that this was the hole of the Evil One. Never did Mally attempt to make her own of weed which had found its way into that pot.
330 But Barty Gunliffe knew no better, and she watched him as he endeavoured to steady himself on the treacherously slippery edge of the pool. He fixed himself there and made a haul, with some small success. How he managed it she hardly knew, but she stood still for a while watching him anxiously, and then she saw him slip. He slipped, and recovered himself—slipped again, and again recovered himself. ◀

"Barty, you fool!" she screamed, "if you get yourself pitched in there, you'll never come out no more."

Whether she simply wished to frighten him, or whether her heart relented and she had thought of his danger with dismay, who shall say?

---

22. **aught** (ôt): anything.
23. **Poulnadioul** (pŭl'nä-jōōl'): Cornish for "pool of the devil."

340 She could not have told herself. She hated him as much as ever—but she could hardly have wished to see him drowned before her eyes.

"You go on, and don't mind me," said he, speaking in a hoarse, angry tone.

"Mind you—who minds you?" retorted the girl. And then she again prepared herself for her work.

But as she went down over the rocks with her long hook balanced in her hands, she suddenly heard a splash, and, turning quickly round, saw the body of her enemy tumbling amidst the **eddying** waves in the pool. The tide had now come up so far that every succeeding wave washed into
350 it and over it from the side nearest to the sea, and then ran down again back from the rocks, as the rolling wave receded, with a noise like the fall of a cataract.[24] And then, when the surplus water had retreated for a moment, the surface of the pool would be partly calm, though the fretting bubbles would still boil up and down, and there was ever a simmer on the surface, as though, in truth, the caldron were heated. But this time of comparative rest was but a moment, for the succeeding breaker would come up almost as soon as the foam of the preceding one had gone, and then again the waters would be dashed upon the rocks, and the sides would echo with the roar of the angry wave. ▶

360 Instantly Mally hurried across to the edge of the pool, crouching down upon her hands and knees for security as she did so. As a wave receded, Barty's head and face was carried round near to her, and she could see that his forehead was covered with blood. Whether he were alive or dead she did not know. She had seen nothing but his blood, and the light-colored hair of his head lying amidst the foam. Then his body was drawn along by the suction of the retreating wave; but the mass of water that escaped was not on this occasion large enough to carry the man out with it.

Instantly Mally was at work with her hook, and getting it fixed into his coat, dragged him towards the spot on which she was kneeling. During
370 the half minute of repose she got him so close that she could touch his shoulder. Straining herself down, laying herself over the long bending handle of the hook, she strove to grasp him with her right hand. But she could not do it; she could only touch him.

Then came the next breaker, forcing itself on with a roar, looking to Mally as though it must certainly knock her from her resting place and destroy them both. But she had nothing for it[25] but to kneel, and hold by her hook.

eddying (ĕd′ē-ĭng) *adj.*
moving in a whirlpool;
swirling **eddy** *v.*

TESTSMART

VOCABULARY
Which word below is related to the Latin word *cēdere*, which means "to go"?

Ⓐ cataract
Ⓑ receded
Ⓒ surplus
Ⓓ caldron

TIP Tests sometimes ask you to identify a vocabulary word related to a **Latin word**. Remember that words similar in spelling and structure are often related in meaning. In this case, look for the base of a word that is similar to *cēdere* and that describes a motion.

---

24. **cataract** (kăt′ə-răkt′): waterfall.

25. **had nothing for it:** had no alternative; could do nothing else.

What prayer passed through her mind at that moment for herself or for him, or for that old man who was sitting unconsciously[26] up at the cabin, 380 who can say? The great wave came and rushed over her as she lay almost prostrate, and when the water was gone from her eyes, and the tumult of the foam, and the violence of the roaring breaker had passed by her, she found herself at her length upon the rock, while his body had been lifted up, free from her hook, and was lying upon the slippery ledge, half in the water and half out of it. As she looked at him, in that instant, she could see that his eyes were open and that he was struggling with his hands.

"Hold by the hook, Barty," she cried, pushing the stick of it before him, while she seized the collar of his coat in her hands.

Had he been her brother, her lover, her father, she could not have clung 390 to him with more of the energy of despair. He did contrive to hold by the stick which she had given him, and when the succeeding wave had passed by, he was still on the ledge. In the next moment she was seated a yard or two above the hole, in comparative safety, while Barty lay upon the rocks with his still bleeding head resting upon her lap.

What could she do now? She could not carry him; and in fifteen minutes the sea would be up where she was sitting. He was quite insensible and very pale, and the blood was coming slowly—very slowly—from the wound on his forehead. Ever so gently she put her hand upon his hair to move it back from his face; and then she bent over his mouth to see if he 400 breathed, and as she looked at him she knew that he was beautiful. ◀

What would she not give that he might live? Nothing now was so precious to her as his life—as this life which she had so far rescued from the waters. But what could she do? Her grandfather could scarcely get himself down over the rocks, if indeed he could succeed in doing so much as that. Could she drag the wounded man backwards, if it were only a few feet, so that he might lie above the reach of the waves till further assistance could be procured?

She set herself to work and she moved him, almost lifting him. As she did so she wondered at her own strength, but she was very strong at that 410 moment. Slowly, tenderly, falling on the rocks herself so that he might fall on her, she got him back to the margin of the sand, to a spot which the waters would not reach for the next two hours.

Here her grandfather met them, having seen at last what had happened from the door.

"Dada," she said, "he fell into the pool yonder, and was battered against the rocks. See there at his forehead."

---

26. **unconsciously:** unaware of what was happening to Mally and Barty.

ANALYZE

Reread the boxed text. In what way does this passage establish Mally as a **complex character**?

_____

_____

_____

_____

List some of the traits Mally has displayed up to this point in the story.

_____

_____

_____

_____

"Mally, I'm thinking that he's dead already," said old Glos, peering down over the body.

"No, dada; he is not dead; but mayhap[27] he's dying. But I'll go at once up to the farm."

"Mally," said the old man, "look at his head. They'll say we murdered him."

"Who'll say so? Who'll lie like that? Didn't I pull him out of the hole?"

"What matters that? His father'll say we killed him."

It was manifest to Mally that whatever anyone might say hereafter, her present course was plain before her. She must run up the path to Gunliffe's farm and get necessary assistance. If the world were as bad as her grandfather said, it would be so bad that she would not care to live longer in it. But be that as it might, there was no doubt as to what she must do now. 🖐 **PAUSE & REFLECT**

So away she went as fast as her naked feet could carry her up the cliff. When at the top she looked round to see if any person might be within ken,[28] but she saw no one. So she ran with all her speed along the headland[29] of the cornfield which led in the direction of old Gunliffe's house, and as she drew near to the homestead she saw that Barty's mother was leaning on the gate. As she approached she attempted to call, but her breath failed her for any purpose of loud speech, so she ran on till she was able to grasp Mrs. Gunliffe by the arm.

"Where's himself?" she said, holding her hand upon her beating heart that she might husband her breath.

"Who is it you mean?" said Mrs. Gunliffe, who participated in the family feud against Trenglos and his granddaughter. "What does the girl clutch me for in that way?"

"He's dying then, that's all."

"Who is dying? Is it old Malachi? If the old man's bad, we'll send some one down."

"It ain't dada; it's Barty! Where's himself? where's the master?" But by this time Mrs. Gunliffe was in an agony of despair, and was calling out for assistance lustily. Happily Gunliffe, the father, was at hand, and with him a man from the neighboring village. ▶

---

27. **mayhap:** perhaps.
28. **within ken:** in view.
29. **headland:** a point of land extending out into a body of water.

🖐 **PAUSE & REFLECT**

What character traits does Mally reveal in her decision to tell Barty's parents what has happened? *MAKE INFERENCES*

_____

_____

_____

FOCUS

Read to find out what happens when Mally runs to Barty's farm for assistance.

ANALYZE

Underline **dialogue** in lines 439–447 that reflects the dialect spoken in the Cornish region where the story is set. ✏️

"Will you not send for the doctor?" said Mally. "Oh, man, you should send for the doctor!"

Whether any orders were given for the doctor she did not know, but in a very few minutes she was hurrying across the field again towards the path to the cove, and Gunliffe with the other man and his wife were following her.

As Mally went along she recovered her voice, for their step was not so quick as hers, and that which to them was a hurried movement allowed her to get her breath again. And as she went she tried to explain to the father
460 what had happened, saying but little, however, of her own doings in the matter. The wife hung behind listening, exclaiming every now and again that her boy was killed, and then asking wild questions as to his being yet alive. The father, as he went, said little. He was known as a silent, sober man, well spoken of for diligence and general conduct, but supposed to be stern and very hard when angered.

As they drew near to the top of the path the other man whispered something to him, and then he turned round upon Mally and stopped her.

"If he has come by his death between you, your blood shall be taken for his," said he.
470 Then the wife shrieked out that her child had been murdered, and Mally, looking round into the faces of the three, saw that her grandfather's words had come true. They suspected her of having taken the life, in saving which she had nearly lost her own.

She looked round at them with awe in her face, and then, without saying a word, preceded them down the path. What had she to answer when such a charge as that was made against her? If they chose to say that she pushed him into the pool and hit him with her hook as he lay amidst the waters, how could she show that it was not so?

Poor Mally knew little of the law of evidence, and it seemed to her
480 that she was in their hands. But as she went down the steep track with a hurried step—a step so quick that they could not keep up with her—her heart was very full—very full and very high. She had striven for the man's life as though he had been her brother. The blood was yet not dry on her own legs and arms, where she had torn them in his service. At one moment she had felt sure that she would die with him in that pool. And now they said that she had murdered him! It may be that he was not dead, and what would he say if ever he should speak again? Then she thought of that moment when his eyes had opened, and he had seemed to see her. She had no fear for herself, for her heart was very high. But it was full also—
490 full of scorn, disdain, and wrath. ◄

INTERPRET

How do you interpret the statement in line 489 that Mally's "heart was very high"?

_____

_____

_____

When she had reached the bottom, she stood close to the door of the hut waiting for them, so that they might precede her to the other group, which was there in front of them, at a little distance on the sand.

"He is there, and dada is with him. Go and look at him," said Mally.

The father and mother ran on stumbling over the stones, but Mally remained behind by the door of the hut.

Barty Gunliffe was lying on the sand where Mally had left him, and old Malachi Trenglos was standing over him, resting himself with difficulty upon a stick.

500 "Not a move he's moved since she left him," said he, "not a move. I put his head on the old rug as you see, and I tried 'un with a drop of gin, but he wouldn't take it—he wouldn't take it."

"Oh, my boy! my boy!" said the mother, throwing herself beside her son upon the sand.

"Haud[30] your tongue, woman," said the father, kneeling down slowly by the lad's head, "whimpering that way will do 'un no good."

Then having gazed for a minute or two upon the pale face beneath him, he looked up sternly into that of Malachi Trenglos.

The old man hardly knew how to bear this terrible inquisition.

510 "He would come," said Malachi; "he brought it all upon hisself."

"Who was it struck him?" said the father.

"Sure he struck hisself, as he fell among the breakers."

"Liar!" said the father, looking up at the old man.

"They have murdered him—they have murdered him!" shrieked the mother.

"Haud your peace, woman!" said the husband again. "They shall give us blood for blood." ▶

Mally, leaning against the corner of the hovel, heard it all, but did not stir. They might say what they liked. They might make it out to be
520 murder. They might drag her and her grandfather to Camelford gaol, and then to Bodmin,[31] and the gallows; but they could not take from her the conscious feeling that was her own. She had done her best to save him— her very best. And she had saved him!

She remembered her threat to him before they had gone down on the rocks together, and her evil wish. Those words had been very wicked; but since that she had risked her life to save his. They might say what they pleased of her, and do what they pleased. She knew what she knew.

---

30. **haud:** hold.
31. **to Camelford gaol** (jāl) . . . **Bodmin:** to Camelford jail and then to the county seat of Cornwall at Bodmin (for trial).

MAKE INFERENCES

What can you infer about Barty from his reaction to seeing Mally?

_____

_____

_____

_____

TESTSMART

VOCABULARY

The most likely meaning of the word *vindicated* (line 561) is

Ⓐ proved the innocence of

Ⓑ created doubt about

Ⓒ complicated the issue of

Ⓓ caused the triumph of

TIP If a test question asks you the likely meaning of an unfamiliar word, try using **context clues** to infer the meaning. In this case, an important context clue appears after the word *vindicated*. In lines 562–563, Mally says "I'm thinking they won't say anything more about our hurting him." What does this clue suggest about the meaning of *vindicated*?

Then the father raised his son's head and shoulders in his arms, and called on the others to assist him in carrying Barty towards the path. They raised him between them carefully and tenderly, and lifted their burden on towards the spot at which Mally was standing. She never moved, but watched them at their work; and the old man followed them, hobbling after them with his crutch.

When they had reached the end of the hut she looked upon Barty's face, and saw that it was very pale. There was no longer blood upon the forehead, but the great gash was to be seen there plainly, with its jagged cut, and the skin livid and blue round the <u>orifice</u>. His light brown hair was hanging back, as she had made it to hang when she had gathered it with her hand after the big wave had passed over them. Ah, how beautiful he was in Mally's eyes with that pale face, and the sad scar upon his brow! She turned her face away, that they might not see her tears; but she did not move, nor did she speak.

But now, when they had passed the end of the hut, shuffling along with their burden, she heard a sound which stirred her. She roused herself quickly from her leaning posture, and stretched forth her head as though to listen; then she moved to follow them. Yes, they had stopped at the bottom of the path, and had again laid the body on the rocks. She heard that sound again, as of a long, long sigh, and then, regardless of any of them, she ran to the wounded man's head.

"He is not dead," she said. "There; he is not dead."

As she spoke Barty's eyes opened, and he looked about him.

"Barty, my boy, speak to me," said the mother.

Barty turned his face upon his mother, smiled, and then stared about him wildly.

"How is it with thee, lad?" said his father. Then Barty turned his face again to the latter voice, and as he did so his eyes fell upon Mally.

"Mally!" he said, "Mally!" ◀

It could have wanted[32] nothing further to any of those present to teach them that, according to Barty's own view of the case, Mally had not been his enemy; and, in truth, Mally herself wanted no further triumph. That word had vindicated her, and she withdrew back to the hut.

"Dada," she said, "Barty is not dead, and I'm thinking they won't say anything more about our hurting him." ◀

Old Glos shook his head. He was glad the lad hadn't met his death there; he didn't want the young man's blood, but he knew what folk would say. The poorer he was the more sure the world would be to trample on

---

32. **wanted:** needed.

him. Mally said what she could to comfort him, being full of comfort herself. **PAUSE & REFLECT**

PAUSE & REFLECT

How does Mally react to the Gunliffes' accusations? *CLARIFY*

FOCUS
Read to find out what happens as Barty recovers.

570 She would have crept up to the farm if she dared, to ask how Barty was. But her courage failed her when she thought of that, so she went to work again, dragging back the weed she had saved to the spot at which on the morrow she would load the donkey. As she did this she saw Barty's pony still standing patiently under the rock, so she got a lock of fodder and threw it down before the beast.

It had become dark down in the cove, but she was still dragging back the seaweed, when she saw the glimmer of a lantern coming down the pathway. It was a most unusual sight, for lanterns were not common down in Malachi's Cove. Down came the lantern rather slowly—much more slowly than she was in the habit of descending, and then through the

580 gloom she saw the figure of a man standing at the bottom of the path. She went up to him, and saw that it was Mr. Gunliffe, the father.

"Is that Mally?" said Gunliffe.

"Yes, it is Mally; and how is Barty, Mr. Gunliffe?"

"You must come to 'un yourself, now at once," said the farmer. "He won't sleep a wink till he's seed you. You must not say but you'll come."

"Sure I'll come if I'm wanted," said Mally.

Gunliffe waited a moment, thinking that Mally might have to prepare herself, but Mally needed no preparation. She was dripping with salt water from the weed which she had been dragging, and her elfin locks were

590 streaming wildly from her head; but, such as she was, she was ready.

"Dada's in bed," she said, "and I can go now if you please."

Then Gunliffe turned round and followed her up the path, wondering at the life which this girl led so far away from all her sex. It was now dark night, and he had found her working at the very edge of the rolling waves by herself, in the darkness, while the only human being who might seem to be her protector had already gone to his bed.

When they were at the top of the cliff, Gunliffe took her by her hand and led her along. She did not comprehend this, but she made no attempt to take her hand from his. Something he said about falling on the cliffs,

600 but it was muttered so lowly that Mally hardly understood him. But in truth the man knew that she had saved his boy's life, and that he had injured her instead of thanking her. He was now taking her to his heart, and as words were wanting to him, he was showing his love after this silent fashion. He held her by the hand as though she were a child, and Mally tripped along at his side asking him no questions.

When they were at the farmyard gate he stopped there for a moment.

"Mally, my girl," he said, "he'll not be content till he sees thee, but thou must not stay long wi' him, lass. Doctor says he's weak like, and wants sleep badly."

610 Mally merely nodded her head, and then they entered the house. Mally had never been within it before, and looked about with wondering eyes at the furniture of the big kitchen. Did any idea of her future destiny flash upon her then, I wonder? But she did not pause here a moment, but was led up to the bedroom above stairs, where Barty was lying on his mother's bed.

"Is it Mally herself?" said the voice of the weak youth.

"It's Mally herself," said the mother, "so now you can say what you please."

"Mally," said he, "Mally, it's along of you[33] that I'm alive this moment."

620 "I'll not forget it on her," said the father, with his eyes turned away from her. "I'll never forget it on her."

"We hadn't a one but only him," said the mother, with her apron up to her face.

"Mally, you'll be friends with me now?" said Barty.

To have been made lady of the manor of the cove for ever, Mally couldn't have spoken a word now. It was not only that the words and presence of the people there cowed her and made her speechless, but the big bed, and the looking-glass, and the unheard-of wonders of the chamber, made her feel her own insignificance. But she crept up to Barty's

630 side, and put her hand upon his.

"I'll come and get the weed, Mally; but it shall all be for you," said Barty.

"Indeed, you won't then, Barty dear," said the mother; "you'll never go near the awesome place again. What would we do if you were took from us?"

"He mustn't go near the hole if he does," said Mally, speaking at last in a solemn voice, and imparting the knowledge which she had kept to herself while Barty was her enemy; "'specially not if the wind's any way from the nor'rard."

"She'd better go down now," said the father.

640 Barty kissed the hand which he held, and Mally, looking at him as he did so, thought that he was like an angel.

"You'll come and see us tomorrow, Mally?" said he.

To this she made no answer, but followed Mrs. Gunliffe out of the room. When they were down in the kitchen the mother had tea for her,

PREDICT

Reread lines 610–613. What "future destiny" do you think the narrator is referring to? What clues support your guess?

33. **along of you:** because of you.

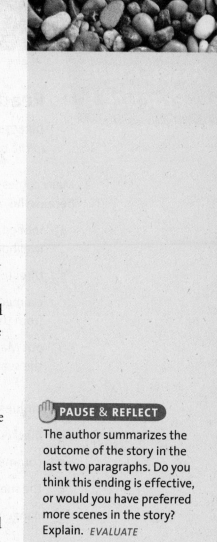

and thick milk, and a hot cake—all the delicacies which the farm could afford. I don't know that Mally cared much for the eating and drinking that night, but she began to think that the Gunliffes were good people—very good people. It was better thus, at any rate, than being accused of murder and carried off to Camelford prison.

650 "I'll never forget it on her—never," the father had said.

Those words stuck to her from that moment, and seemed to sound in her ears all the night. How glad she was that Barty had come down to the cove—oh, yes, how glad! There was no question of his dying now, and as for the blow on his forehead, what harm was that to a lad like him?

"But father shall go with you," said Mrs. Gunliffe, when Mally prepared to start for the cove by herself. Mally, however, would not hear of this. She could find her way to the cove whether it was light or dark.

"Mally, thou art my child now, and I shall think of thee so," said the mother, as the girl went off by herself.

660 Mally thought of this, too, as she walked home. How could she become Mrs. Gunliffe's child; ah, how?

I need not, I think, tell the tale any further. That Mally did become Mrs. Gunliffe's child, and how she became so the reader will understand; and in process of time the big kitchen and all the wonders of the farmhouse were her own. The people said that Barty Gunliffe had married a mermaid out of the sea; but when it was said in Mally's hearing I doubt whether she liked it; and when Barty himself would call her a mermaid she would frown at him, and throw about her black hair, and pretend to cuff him with her little hand.

670 Old Glos was brought up to the top of the cliff, and lived his few remaining days under the roof of Mr. Gunliffe's house; and as for the cove and the right of seaweed, from that time forth all that has been supposed to attach itself to Gunliffe's farm, and I do not know that any of the neighbors are prepared to dispute the right. ✋ **PAUSE & REFLECT**

✋ **PAUSE & REFLECT**

The author summarizes the outcome of the story in the last two paragraphs. Do you think this ending is effective, or would you have preferred more scenes in the story? Explain. *EVALUATE*

_____

_____

_____

_____

Big Question ?

Reread your response to the exercise on page 203. Which of the items you listed are most relevant to this story? Explain. *CONNECT*

_____

_____

_____

_____

Reading Comprehension

DIRECTIONS *Answer these questions about "Malachi's Cove" by filling
in the correct ovals.*

1. Mally comes to hate Barty Gunliffe
   because he

   (A) robbed her grandfather of his
   livelihood

   (B) threatened to teach her civility

   (C) claimed the right to harvest seaweed
   from the cove

   (D) put Mally out of business by hoarding
   the seaweed

2. Barty argues that Malachi's cove is

   (A) blocked by impediments

   (B) common property to all

   (C) the most beautiful cove

   (D) dangerous but profitable

3. Barty doesn't know the danger and futility
   of trying to

   (A) harvest seaweed in the rain

   (B) work in the breakers after dark

   (C) harvest seaweed with an ordinary
   fork

   (D) retrieve seaweed from "Poulnadioul"

4. In lines 488–489, "Molly had no fear for
   herself" because she knew that

   (A) she had done the right thing

   (B) evidence was on her side

   (C) Barty would not die

   (D) the Gunliffes were level-headed

5. Which aspect of lines 503–517 adds to the
   story's realism?

   (A) the seaside setting

   (B) the dialogue of daily life

   (C) fear of death

   (D) a conflict between characters

6. What motivates Gunliffe to take Mally by
   the hand in lines 597–598?

   (A) fear that she might fall from the cliffs

   (B) gratitude that she saved his son's life

   (C) concern that she might run away
   from him

   (D) feeling that she cannot take care of
   herself

7. The word *impediments* in line 201 means

   (A) rocks

   (B) obstacles

   (C) ramps

   (D) tools

8. As it is used in line 396, the word *insensible*
   means

   (A) imperceptible

   (B) lacking meaning

   (C) indifferent

   (D) unconscious

For help, use the **Test-Taker's Toolkit** below.

Responding in Writing

9. Short Response Many of the characters in "Malachi's Cove" change as a result of their experiences. Write a paragraph in which you describe the changes in two of the characters. End your paragraph by identifying the character who, in your opinion, goes through the greatest transformation. Explain why you chose that character.

_____

_____

_____

_____

_____

_____

TEST-TAKER'S TOOLKIT

GRAPHIC ORGANIZER Use the chart below to help you plan your response.

Character	How He or She Changes

One Rescuer Lives, One Drowns Saving Sisters in Rough Palm Beach Surf
NEWS ARTICLE

Use with "Malachi's Cove,"
p. 202

What's the Connection?

"Malachi's Cove" illustrates the profound change that can happen to a person as a result of risking life and limb to save another human being. The news article you are about to read explores the sometimes tragic side of being a Good Samaritan.

EMERGENCY! Imagine this scenario: You are sitting on a beach, enjoying the sunshine, when you hear a frantic call for help. Two children have been carried out into the deep water by the surf and are in danger of drowning. What should you do? With a group, discuss the possible courses of action you could take and the potential results, both positive and negative, of each. Record your ideas in the chart below.

Potential Course of Action	Possible Positive Result	Possible Negative Result
1.		
2.		
3.		

LEARN THE SKILL: ANALYZE CAUSE-AND-EFFECT RELATIONSHIPS

A **cause** is an event or action that directly results in another event or action. An **effect** is the direct or logical outcome of an event or action. The following information will help you analyze **cause-and-effect relationships:**

- A single cause can lead to a single effect.
- A cause can lead to multiple effects.
- Sometimes there are several causes for a single event.

For more on analyzing cause-and-effect relationships, see the Nonfiction Skills Handbook beginning on page R2.

One Rescuer Lives, One Drowns Saving Sisters in Rough Palm Beach Surf

by Rochelle E. B. Gilken

A stranger yelled for someone to help her drowning daughters, and Michael Sagaro bolted from his beach chair to the ocean. His best friend, Giankarlo Squicimari, stopped building a sand castle with Sagaro's 3-year-old and followed him.

Maybe 50 yards out, a desperate 12-year-old held out her hand and Sagaro grabbed it. Exhausted, he saw Squicimari a few yards away with the girl's sister. And then, Sagaro, of Fort Lauderdale, felt death coming. He couldn't get back.

"I'm kicking my feet, kicking my feet, kicking my feet," Sagaro said. "I'm trying to hold us together. The waves pull you and pull you. These riptides grab you and grab you." ▶

Sagaro didn't know it then, but his stronger best friend was enduring the same struggle.

"You're viewing death as it comes. Your body is saying there's nothing else to do. My legs couldn't hold anymore, the waves are flipping me under," said Sagaro.

Except he was saved.

Squicimari, 31, drowned. On a beautiful Sunday afternoon, behind the Four Seasons in Palm Beach, five people would walk his body out of the water.

Best friends. One lived. One died. They told Sagaro in the hospital after doctors got enough air in his lungs. And it took his breath away.

Sagaro grew up with Squicimari in Miami-Dade. Squicimari was planning to move from Southwest Miami-Dade to a town house in Fort Lauderdale.

"If there's one thing about him, he would've wanted to die this way," said Sagaro, 32. Squicimari held the girl out of the water long enough for another rescuer to get her. "He's a hero. He's one of those kids that would do it over and over again."

It was a Memorial Day weekend outing that brought strangers together for four rescues. Squicimari gave his life to save a little girl. Sagaro almost died holding another girl long enough

SPECIALIZED Vocabulary

The word *riptide* in line 21 is an informal variation of the term *rip current*, which refers to a current of water that flows rapidly away from the shore. Based on Michael Sagaro's description, what effect do rip currents have on swimmers? *WORD ANALYSIS*

An average of 465 people drown in Florida each year.

CAUSE AND EFFECT

Circle the event that **caused** Michael Sagaro to bolt from his beach chair into the ocean.

Put a star next to each of the **effects** that resulted from this cause.

60 for Lee Cooper to save them both. Others, unnamed, helped out. Another unnamed swimmer was saved. ◄

The water was rough for the life-long friends. But they were South Florida guys, they weren't scared, just enjoying a family weekend at the Four Seasons. Sagaro with his wife and two sons, 3 and 5.
70 Squicimari with the woman he was

engaged to marry in December, Sasha Herrera.

On Sunday afternoon, they were on the shore when they saw Tania Hernandez frantically pointing to the water. "When I look out, all I see is the little girl's hands waving," Sagaro said.

He couldn't tell how far she
80 was. Or how deep. But he kept going until he caught her. And he

struggled. Sagaro, all of 5-foot-3, was holding a 4-foot-6, 85-pound weight.

He was desperate when Lee Cooper put down his *Newsweek* and ran out in response to the screams. Cooper is a 44-year-old executive at General Electric corporate finance in Westport, Connecticut. He was a swimmer in high school. He didn't see anyone, but started swimming until he found the man and girl.

Screams were heard

The girl said, "I'm gonna die. I'm gonna drown."

Sagaro said, "Don't leave me. I need help. I can't make it."

Cooper tried, but couldn't pull them both. "I had to break him off. I said, 'I'm coming back, I'm coming back,'" Cooper said. Cooper swam off with the girl.

"Right there is when I thought I was gonna die," Sagaro said. "You're kicking for so long. You can't use your legs. I was just dying."

By the time Erika was safe on shore, Cooper was exhausted. "My husband was bent over, he couldn't breathe," Kim Cooper said. He told her he had to go back.

Sagaro, back at home in Fort Lauderdale with his wife, now counts the time he had left: Five, four, three, two . . .

"On my last breath, I started dropping underwater and some guy grabbed my right arm and pulled me to the shoreline. I don't remember everything. But I was lying there on the shore, and my little son was asking if I was dead. That stuck in my head," he said.

Cooper went in a third time, but other people already helped yet another potential rescuer who had almost drowned. An anonymous rescue. That person's name is not on the police report, but several witnesses saw it.

The girls who were rescued are back at home, safe in Miami. Their mother said she is grateful but trying not to think about it.

"I'm Praying"

"I'm praying for his soul. He was a person just trying to help someone else. . . . I'm terribly sorry. My heart is broken," said Hernandez. "It's terrible how in a minute everybody was drowning at the same time."

The water was rough, and there were no lifeguards on the beach. Several lifeguards came running down from nearby beaches. But they couldn't do it alone. ▶

Squicimari was an only child. He was born in Puerto Rico and grew up with Sagaro in Miami, where they went to school together. They played ball with future New York Yankee Alex Rodriguez. People called Squicimari "JC" because people assumed his name was Juan Carlos.

CAUSE AND EFFECT
What two circumstances caused an increase in danger at the beach that afternoon?

_____

_____

_____

Reading Comprehension

DIRECTIONS *Answer these questions about the two selections in this lesson by filling in the correct ovals.*

1. Michael Sagaro and Giankarlo Squicimari were both

   (A) lifeguards

   (B) Florida residents

   (C) tourists

   (D) reckless swimmers

2. What made Sagaro's attempt to rescue one of the girls more difficult?

   (A) He was an inexperienced swimmer.

   (B) His wife and sons were watching.

   (C) The girl's mother was screaming.

   (D) The girl was not much smaller than he was.

3. What caused Lee Cooper to go into the water a third time?

   (A) He had promised to come back for Sagaro.

   (B) He was trying to rescue Squicimari.

   (C) A third rescuer was drowning.

   (D) One of the girls was still in the water.

4. Which of the following statements sums up the effects of Lee Cooper's actions?

   (A) Two little girls were rescued.

   (B) One man lived and another man died.

   (C) Four rescues were attempted.

   (D) A girl and a man were saved.

5. Which character from "Malachi's Cove" performs a feat that is similar to Lee Cooper's actions in the news article?

   (A) Malachi

   (B) Mally

   (C) Barty

   (D) Mr. Gunliffe

6. Which of the following was an important factor in both "Malachi's Cove" and the incident described in the article?

   (A) rough water

   (B) a crowded beach

   (C) slippery rocks

   (D) stormy weather

7. The word *enduring* in lines 23–24 of the article means

   (A) overcoming

   (B) undergoing

   (C) avoiding

   (D) defeating

8. Which of the following is most similar in meaning to the word *desperate* in line 85?

   (A) hopeless

   (B) disoriented

   (C) fearful

   (D) irrational

Timed Writing Practice

PROMPT

Popular Victorian novelists such as Anthony Trollope created exciting plots to gain wide readership. <u>Write an analysis of the plot of "Malachi's Cove,"</u> examining how Trollope uses external and internal conflicts to move the plot forward and develop his characters. Discuss three conflicts that one or more of the characters experience. Use details and examples from the story to support your ideas.

BUDGET YOUR TIME

You have **45 minutes** to respond. Decide how much time to spend on each step.

Analyze _____

Plan _____

Write _____

Review _____

TEST-TAKER'S TOOLKIT

1. ANALYZE THE PROMPT

A. Underline key words and phrases that tell you what you are being asked to do. One phrase has been underlined for you.

B. Jot down a list of elements you need to include in your essay.

2. PLAN YOUR RESPONSE

A. **Make notes** Use a chart like the one shown to help you examine the story and plan your essay.

B. **Organize your information** Your chart can help you develop a five-paragraph essay. Your first paragraph should identify the topic of the essay and state your thesis. In each of the following three paragraphs, analyze one of the conflicts in your chart. Then write a conclusion in which you summarize your key points and explain how they deepen your understanding of the story.

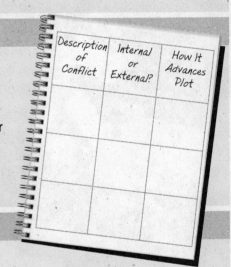

Description of Conflict	Internal or External?	How It Advances Plot

3. WRITE AND REVIEW

A. Your introduction should include a thesis statement that explains the significance of the conflicts you will discuss in the essay. To grab readers' attention, you might start off with an interesting quote from the story.

B. Be sure to leave time to check your spelling and grammar.

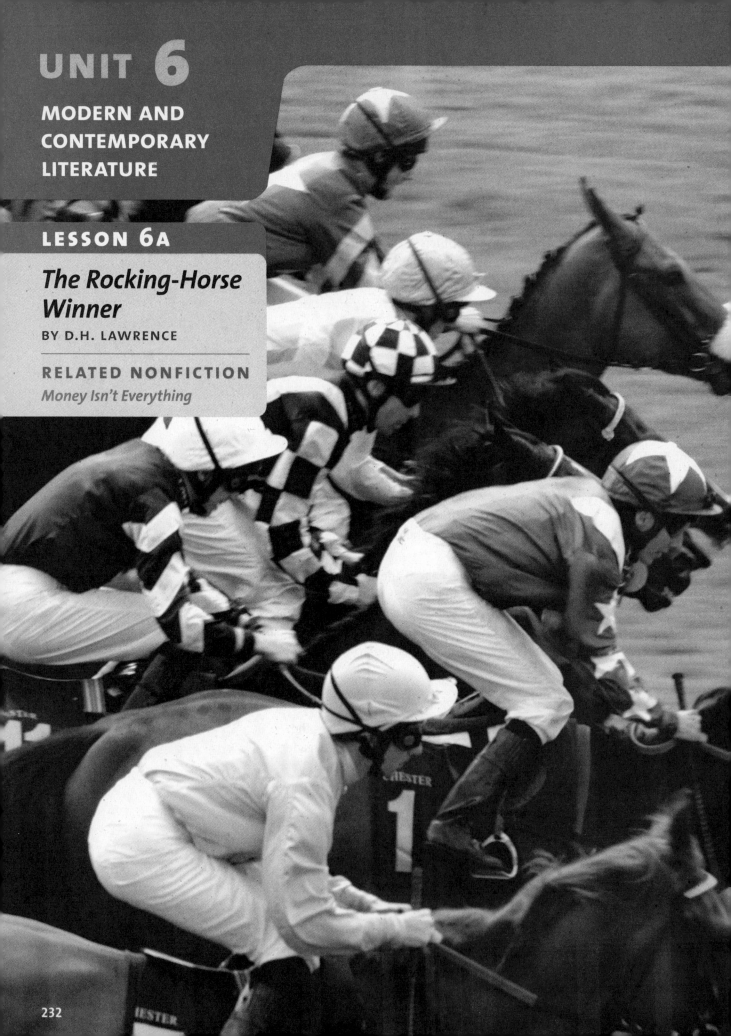

UNIT 6

MODERN AND CONTEMPORARY LITERATURE

LESSON 6A

The Rocking-Horse Winner

BY D.H. LAWRENCE

RELATED NONFICTION
Money Isn't Everything

Can money buy
HAPPINESS?

It's easy to imagine that unlimited wealth would lead to almost perfect happiness. With all financial concerns swept away, what else would there be to worry about? The story you're about to read explores the connection between money and happiness.

DISCUSS IT With a small group, discuss whether money is the key to contentment. Consider the questions in the chart, and use the space provided to jot down other group members' comments and opinions. After the discussion, write your own personal conclusions at the bottom of the chart.

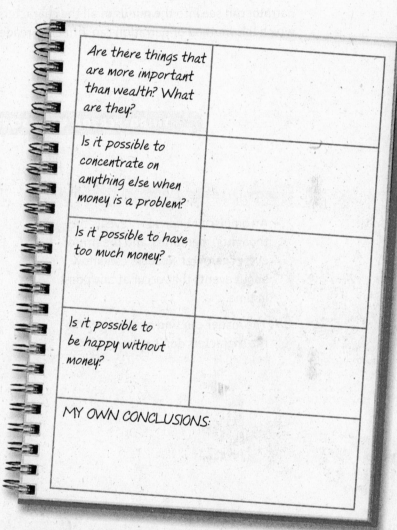

Are there things that are more important than wealth? What are they?	
Is it possible to concentrate on anything else when money is a problem?	
Is it possible to have too much money?	
Is it possible to be happy without money?	
MY OWN CONCLUSIONS:	

ASSESSMENT GOALS

By the end of this lesson, you will be able to . . .

- analyze omniscient point of view in a work of fiction
- use active reading strategies to comprehend text
- identify audience and purpose in a nonfiction work
- analyze a writing prompt and plan a persuasive essay

Omniscient Point of View

POINT OF VIEW refers to the perspective from which events in a story or novel are told. In the **THIRD-PERSON POINT OF VIEW**, events are narrated by a voice outside the action, not by one of the characters. A third-person narrator uses pronouns like *he*, *she*, and *they*. Some third-person narrators are **OMNISCIENT**, or all-knowing. An omniscient narrator can see into the minds of all the characters. Review the following ways in which this method of narration can influence readers' perception of a story.

THIRD-PERSON OMNISCIENT NARRATOR

ADVANTAGES

- An omniscient narrator reveals the thoughts, memories, and dreams of every character. Readers can know about events that occur at any point in time.

- The reader can find out things that the characters don't know.

DISADVANTAGE

- Because the narrator moves into and out of the thoughts of different characters, readers usually don't become as emotionally involved with any one character as they might be if the narrator were a character in the story or focused on one character.

The Rocking-Horse Winner

D. H. Lawrence

CLOSE READ

MARK IT UP

Use these marks to monitor your reading:

✱ This is important.

? I don't understand.

! This is a surprise.

When you see this pencil ✎, you'll be asked to mark up the text. You can also write in this book in any way you find useful.

BACKGROUND Two of the five great annual horseraces in England are the St. Leger Stakes and the Derby. Other notable English races mentioned in this story are the Grand National, the Ascot Gold Cup, and the Lincolnshire. Large sums of money are bet on horseraces. The amount a bettor can win depends on the odds. The odds on each horse are expressed as a ratio—3 to 1, for example—and are determined by what proportion of the total amount bet on the race is bet on that horse. The more money bet on a horse, the lower the odds and the lower the payoff.

FOCUS
The first part of the story introduces a family that seems perfect from the outside. Find out why the mother believes that they are unlucky.

There was a woman who was beautiful, who started with all the advantages, yet she had no luck. She married for love, and the love turned to dust. She had bonny[1] children, yet she felt they had been thrust upon her, and she could not love them. They looked at her coldly, as if they were finding fault with her. And hurriedly she felt she must cover up some fault in herself. Yet what it was that she must cover up she never knew. Nevertheless, when her children were present, she always felt the center of her heart go hard. This troubled her, and in her manner she was all the more gentle and anxious for her children, as if she loved them very
10 much. Only she herself knew that at the center of her heart was a hard little place that could not feel love, no, not for anybody. Everybody else said of her: "She is such a good mother. She adores her children." Only she herself, and her children themselves, knew it was not so. They read it in each other's eyes. ▶

There were a boy and two little girls. They lived in a pleasant house, with a garden, and they had discreet servants, and felt themselves superior to anyone in the neighborhood.

CLARIFY

Why does the mother behave so gently with her children?

_____

_____

1. **bonny:** pretty.

materialize (mə-tîr′ē-ə-līz)
v. to take form; to appear; to become fact

Although they lived in style, they felt always an anxiety in the house. There was never enough money. The mother had a small income, and the
20 father had a small income, but not nearly enough for the social position which they had to keep up. The father went into town to some office. But though he had good prospects, these prospects never <u>materialized</u>. There was always the grinding sense of the shortage of money, though the style was always kept up.

At last the mother said: "I will see if *I* can't make something." But she did not know where to begin. She racked her brains, and tried this thing and the other, but could not find anything successful. The failure made deep lines come into her face. Her children were growing up, they would have to go to school. There must be more money, there must be more
30 money. The father, who was always very handsome and expensive in his tastes, seemed as if he never *would* be able to do anything worth doing. And the mother, who had a great belief in herself, did not succeed any better, and her tastes were just as expensive. ◀

And so the house came to be haunted by the unspoken phrase: *There must be more money! There must be more money!* The children could hear it all the time, though nobody said it aloud. They heard it at Christmas, when the expensive and splendid toys filled the nursery. Behind the shining modern rocking-horse, behind the smart doll's house, a voice would start whispering: "There *must* be more money! There *must* be more
40 money!" And the children would stop playing, to listen for a moment. They would look into each other's eyes, to see if they had all heard. And each one saw in the eyes of the other two that they too had heard. "There *must* be more money! There *must* be more money!"

It came whispering from the springs of the still-swaying rocking-horse, and even the horse, bending his wooden, champing head, heard it. The big doll, sitting so pink and smirking in her new pram,² could hear it quite plainly, and seemed to be smirking all the more self-consciously because of it. The foolish puppy, too, that took the place of the teddy bear, he was looking so extraordinarily foolish for no other reason but that he heard the
50 secret whisper all over the house: "There *must* be more money!"

Yet nobody ever said it aloud. The whisper was everywhere, and therefore no one spoke it. Just as no one ever says: "We are breathing!" in spite of the fact that breath is coming and going all the time. ◀

"Mother," said the boy Paul one day, "why don't we keep a car of our own? Why do we always use uncle's, or else a taxi?"

"Because we're the poor members of the family," said the mother.

---

2. **pram:** baby carriage (a shortened form of *perambulator*).

MAKE INFERENCES

Reread lines 18–33. Why do you think the parents spend more money than they can afford?

_____

_____

_____

_____

_____

CLARIFY

What does the "whispering" in the house represent?

_____

_____

_____

"But why *are* we, mother?"

"Well—I suppose," she said slowly and bitterly, "it's because your father has no luck."

60   The boy was silent for some time.

"Is luck money, mother?" he asked, rather timidly.

"No, Paul. Not quite. It's what causes you to have money."

"Oh!" said Paul vaguely. "I thought when Uncle Oscar said *filthy lucker*, it meant money."

"*Filthy lucre*[3] does mean money," said the mother. "But it's lucre, not luck."

"Oh!" said the boy. "Then what *is* luck, mother?"

"It's what causes you to have money. If you're lucky you have money. That's why it's better to be born lucky than rich. If you're rich, you may lose
70 your money. But if you're lucky, you will always get more money." ▶

"Oh! Will you? And is father not lucky?"

"Very unlucky, I should say," she said bitterly.

    The boy watched her with unsure eyes.

"Why?" he asked.

"I don't know. Nobody ever knows why one person is lucky and another unlucky."

"Don't they? Nobody at all? Does *nobody* know?"

"Perhaps God. But He never tells."

"He ought to, then. And aren't you lucky either, mother?"

80 "I can't be, if I married an unlucky husband."

"But by yourself, aren't you?"

"I used to think I was, before I married. Now I think I am very unlucky indeed."

"Why?"

"Well—never mind! Perhaps I'm not really," she said.

    The child looked at her to see if she meant it. But he saw, by the lines of her mouth, that she was only trying to hide something from him.

"Well, anyhow," he said stoutly,[4] "I'm a lucky person."

"Why?" said his mother, with a sudden laugh.

90   He stared at her. He didn't even know why he had said it.

"God told me," he asserted, brazening it out. ▶

"I hope He did, dear!" she said, again with a laugh, but rather bitter.

---

3. *filthy lucre* (lōō′kər): money, especially when obtained through fraud or greed. The term comes from the King James Bible (Titus 1:11) and has passed into familiar usage.

4. **stoutly**: bravely; firmly.

EVALUATE

Do you agree with the mother's definition of luck? Explain why or why not.

_____

_____

_____

_____

TESTSMART

VOCABULARY

The most likely meaning of the word *brazening* in line 91 is

(A) pitifully whining

(B) brashly facing

(C) finally figuring

(D) sadly shouting

TIP If a test question asks you the meaning of a word that looks unfamiliar, **try thinking of a related word** that might give you a clue. You may know that the word *brazen* can mean "bold and shameless." Based on this, what is the likely meaning of *brazening*?

PAUSE & REFLECT

How would you characterize the parents' marriage? Explain. **DRAW CONCLUSIONS**

_____

_____

_____

_____

FOCUS

Paul is determined to be lucky. Find out how he tries to make this happen.

career (kə-nîr´) _v._ to move at full speed; to rush wildly

steed (stēd) _n._ a horse, especially a high-spirited riding horse

ANALYZE

Reread the boxed text. Underline the other characters' thoughts and feelings about Paul's riding. ✏

What does the **omniscient point of view** help you understand in this passage?

_____

_____

_____

_____

_____

_____

"He did, mother!"

"Excellent!" said the mother, using one of her husband's exclamations.

The boy saw she did not believe him; or rather, that she paid no attention to his assertion. This angered him somewhere, and made him want to compel her attention. **PAUSE & REFLECT**

He went off by himself, vaguely, in a childish way, seeking for the clue to "luck." Absorbed, taking no heed of other people, he went about with a sort of stealth, seeking inwardly for luck. He wanted luck, he wanted it, he wanted it. When the two girls were playing dolls in the nursery, he would sit on his big rocking-horse, charging madly into space, with a frenzy that made the little girls peer at him uneasily. Wildly the horse <u>careered</u>, the waving dark hair of the boy tossed, his eyes had a strange glare in them. The little girls dared not speak to him.

When he had ridden to the end of his mad little journey, he climbed down and stood in front of his rocking-horse, staring fixedly into its lowered face. Its red mouth was slightly open, its big eye was wide and glassy-bright.

"Now!" he would silently command the snorting <u>steed</u>. "Now, take me to where there is luck! Now take me!"

And he would slash the horse on the neck with the little whip he had asked Uncle Oscar for. He _knew_ the horse could take him to where there was luck, if only he forced it. So he would mount again and start on his furious ride, hoping at last to get there. He knew he could get there.

"You'll break your horse, Paul!" said the nurse.

"He's always riding like that! I wish he'd leave off!" said his elder sister Joan.

But he only glared down on them in silence. Nurse gave him up. She could make nothing of him. Anyhow, he was growing beyond her. ◀

One day his mother and his Uncle Oscar came in when he was on one of his furious rides. He did not speak to them.

"Hallo, you young jockey! Riding a winner?" said his uncle.

"Aren't you growing too big for a rocking-horse? You're not a very little boy any longer, you know," said his mother.

But Paul only gave a blue glare from his big, rather close-set eyes. He would speak to nobody when he was in full tilt.[5] His mother watched him with an anxious expression on her face.

_____

5. **in full tilt:** moving at full speed.

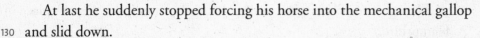

At last he suddenly stopped forcing his horse into the mechanical gallop and slid down.

"Well, I got there!" he announced fiercely, his blue eyes still flaring, and his sturdy long legs straddling apart.

"Where did you get to?" asked his mother.

"Where I wanted to go," he flared back at her.

"That's right, son!" said Uncle Oscar. "Don't you stop till you get there. What's the horse's name?"

"He doesn't have a name," said the boy.

"Gets on without all right?" asked the uncle.

"Well, he has different names. He was called Sansovino last week."

"Sansovino, eh? Won the Ascot.[6] How did you know his name?"

"He always talks about horse races with Bassett," said Joan.

The uncle was delighted to find that his small nephew was posted with all the racing news. Bassett, the young gardener, who had been wounded in the left foot in the war and had got his present job through Oscar Cresswell, whose batman[7] he had been, was a perfect blade of the "turf."[8] He lived in the racing events, and the small boy lived with him. ▶

Oscar Cresswell got it all from Bassett.

"Master Paul comes and asks me, so I can't do more than tell him, sir," said Bassett, his face terribly serious, as if he were speaking of religious matters.

"And does he ever put anything on a horse he fancies?"

"Well—I don't want to give him away—he's a young sport,[9] a fine sport, sir. Would you mind asking him himself? He sort of takes a pleasure in it, and perhaps he'd feel I was giving him away, sir, if you don't mind."

Bassett was serious as a church.

The uncle went back to his nephew and took him off for a ride in the car.

"Say, Paul, old man, do you ever put anything on a horse?" the uncle asked.

The boy watched the handsome man closely.

"Why, do you think I oughtn't to?" he parried.

"Not a bit of it! I thought perhaps you might give me a tip for the Lincoln."

MAKE INFERENCES

Reread the boxed text. How does Oscar's attitude contrast with Paul's?

_____

_____

_____

What does this contrast suggest about how important the races—and luck—are to each character?

_____

_____

_____

---

6. **Won the Ascot:** won at the famous horse races held on Ascot Heath, a horsetrack southwest of London.
7. **batman:** in Britain, a soldier who acts as an officer's servant.
8. **blade of the "turf":** someone very knowledgeable about horseracing.
9. **sport:** good fellow.

The car sped on into the country, going down to Uncle Oscar's place in Hampshire.

"Honor bright?"[10] said the nephew.

"Honor bright, son!" said the uncle.

"Well, then, Daffodil."

"Daffodil! I doubt it, sonny. What about Mirza?"

170 "I only know the winner," said the boy. "That's Daffodil."

"Daffodil, eh?"

There was a pause. Daffodil was an obscure horse comparatively.

"Uncle!"

"Yes, son?"

"You won't let it go any further, will you? I promised Bassett."

"Bassett be damned, old man! What's he got to do with it?"

"We're partners. We've been partners from the first. Uncle, he lent me my first five shillings,[11] which I lost. I promised him, honor bright, it was only between me and him; only you gave me that ten-shilling note I

180 started winning with, so I thought you were lucky. You won't let it go any further, will you?"

The boy gazed at his uncle from those big, hot, blue eyes, set rather close together. The uncle stirred and laughed uneasily.

"Right you are, son! I'll keep your tip private. Daffodil, eh? How much are you putting on him?"

"All except twenty pounds,"[12] said the boy. "I keep that in reserve."

The uncle thought it a good joke.

"You keep twenty pounds in reserve, do you, you young romancer? What are you betting, then?"

190 "I'm betting three hundred," said the boy gravely. "But it's between you and me, Uncle Oscar! Honor bright?"

The uncle burst into a roar of laughter.

"It's between you and me all right, you young Nat Gould,"[13] he said, laughing. "But where's your three hundred?"

"Bassett keeps it for me. We're partners."

"You are, are you! And what is Bassett putting on Daffodil?"

"He won't go quite as high as I do, I expect. Perhaps he'll go a hundred and fifty." ◄

SUMMARIZE

Summarize Paul's conversation with Uncle Oscar in lines 158–198.

_____

_____

_____

_____

_____

Underline details in the text that show that Oscar doubts Paul's story. ✏

10. **Honor bright:** an expression meaning "on your (or my) honor."
11. **shillings:** former British coins worth 1/20 of a pound.
12. **twenty pounds:** the equivalent of about a thousand dollars in today's money. (In the mid-1920s, a pound was worth about five dollars, and the purchasing power of a dollar was about ten times what it is now.)
13. **Nat Gould:** a well-known British horseracing authority and writer.

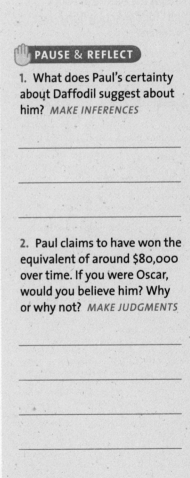

"What, pennies?" laughed the uncle.

200 "Pounds," said the child, with a surprised look at his uncle. "Bassett keeps a bigger reserve than I do."

Between wonder and amusement Uncle Oscar was silent. He pursued the matter no further, but he determined to take his nephew with him to the Lincoln races.

"Now, son," he said, "I'm putting twenty on Mirza, and I'll put five on for you on any horse you fancy. What's your pick?"

"Daffodil, uncle."

"No, not the fiver on Daffodil!"

"I should if it was my own fiver," said the child.

210 "Good! Good! Right you are! A fiver for me and a fiver for you on Daffodil."

The child had never been to a race-meeting before, and his eyes were blue fire. He pursed his mouth tight and watched. A Frenchman just in front had put his money on Lancelot. Wild with excitement, he flayed his arms up and down, yelling *"Lancelot! Lancelot!"* in his French accent.

Daffodil came in first, Lancelot second, Mirza third. The child, flushed and with eyes blazing, was curiously serene. His uncle brought him four five-pound notes, four to one.

"What am I to do with these?" he cried, waving them before the boy's
220 eyes.

"I suppose we'll talk to Bassett," said the boy. "I expect I have fifteen hundred now; and twenty in reserve; and this twenty."

His uncle studied him for some moments.

"Look here, son!" he said. "You're not serious about Bassett and that fifteen hundred, are you?"

"Yes, I am. But it's between you and me, uncle. Honor bright?"

"Honor bright all right, son! But I must talk to Bassett."

"If you'd like to be a partner, uncle, with Bassett and me, we could all be partners. Only, you'd have to promise, honor bright, uncle, not
230 to let it go beyond us three. Bassett and I are lucky, and you must be lucky, because it was your ten shillings I started winning with. . . ."

✋ **PAUSE & REFLECT**

Uncle Oscar took both Bassett and Paul into Richmond Park for an afternoon, and there they talked.

"It's like this, you see, sir," Bassett said. "Master Paul would get me talking about racing events, spinning yarns, you know, sir. And he was always keen on knowing if I'd made or if I'd lost. It's about a year since,

✋ **PAUSE & REFLECT**

1. What does Paul's certainty about Daffodil suggest about him? *MAKE INFERENCES*

_____

_____

_____

2. Paul claims to have won the equivalent of around $80,000 over time. If you were Oscar, would you believe him? Why or why not? *MAKE JUDGMENTS*

_____

_____

_____

_____

Ⓕ**OCUS**
Do you think Paul really does have a special ability to predict horse-race winners? Read on to find out.

now, that I put five shillings on Blush of Dawn for him: and we lost. Then the luck turned, with that ten shillings he had from you: that we put on Singhalese. And since that time, it's been pretty steady, all things considering. What do you say, Master Paul?"

"We're all right when we're sure," said Paul. "It's when we're not quite sure that we go down."

"Oh, but we're careful then," said Bassett.

"But when are you *sure?*" smiled Uncle Oscar.

"It's Master Paul, sir," said Bassett in a secret, religious voice. "It's as if he had it from heaven. Like Daffodil, now, for the Lincoln. That was as sure as eggs."[14] ◄

"Did you put anything on Daffodil?" asked Oscar Cresswell.

"Yes, sir. I made my bit."

"And my nephew?"

Bassett was obstinately silent, looking at Paul.

"I made twelve hundred, didn't I, Bassett? I told uncle I was putting three hundred on Daffodil."

"That's right," said Bassett, nodding.

"But where's the money?" asked the uncle.

"I keep it safe locked up, sir. Master Paul he can have it any minute he likes to ask for it."

"What, fifteen hundred pounds?"

"And twenty! And *forty*, that is, with the twenty he made on the course."

"It's amazing!" said the uncle.

"If Master Paul offers you to be partners, sir, I would, if I were you: if you'll excuse me," said Bassett.

Oscar Cresswell thought about it.

"I'll see the money," he said.

They drove home again, and, sure enough, Bassett came round to the garden-house with fifteen hundred pounds in notes. The twenty pounds reserve was left with Joe Glee, in the Turf Commission deposit.[15]

"You see, it's all right, uncle, when I'm *sure!* Then we go strong, for all we're worth. Don't we, Bassett?"

"We do that, Master Paul."

"And when are you sure?" said the uncle, laughing.

---

14. **as sure as eggs:** absolutely certain; shortened from the expression "as sure as eggs is eggs."

15. **Turf Commission deposit:** a bank in which bettors keep money for future bets.

"Oh, well, sometimes I'm *absolutely* sure, like about Daffodil," said the boy; "and sometimes I have an idea; and sometimes I haven't even an idea, have I, Bassett? Then we're careful, because we mostly go down."

"You do, do you! And when you're sure, like about Daffodil, what makes you sure, sonny?"

"Oh, well, I don't know," said the boy uneasily. "I'm sure, you know, uncle; that's all." ▶

"It's as if he had it from heaven, sir," Bassett **reiterated**.

280   "I should say so!" said the uncle.

But he became a partner. And when the Leger was coming on Paul was "sure" about Lively Spark, which was a quite inconsiderable horse. The boy insisted on putting a thousand on the horse, Bassett went for five hundred, and Oscar Cresswell two hundred. Lively Spark came in first, and the betting had been ten to one against him. Paul had made ten thousand.

"You see," he said, "I was absolutely sure of him."

Even Oscar Cresswell had cleared two thousand.

"Look here, son," he said, "this sort of thing makes me nervous."

"It needn't, uncle! Perhaps I shan't be sure again for a long time."

290   "But what are you going to do with your money?" asked the uncle.

"Of course," said the boy, "I started it for mother. She said she had no luck, because father is unlucky, so I thought if I was lucky, it might stop whispering."

"What might stop whispering?"

"Our house. I *hate* our house for whispering."

"What does it whisper?"

"Why—why"—the boy fidgeted—"why, I don't know. But it's always short of money, you know, uncle."

"I know it, son, I know it."

300   "You know people send mother writs,[16] don't you, uncle?"

"I'm afraid I do," said the uncle.

"And then the house whispers, like people laughing at you behind your back. It's awful, that is! I thought if I was lucky—"

"You might stop it," added the uncle.

The boy watched him with big blue eyes, that had an **uncanny** cold fire in them, and he said never a word.

"Well, then!" said the uncle. "What are we doing?"

"I shouldn't like mother to know I was lucky," said the boy.

"Why not, son?"

310   "She'd stop me."

MAKE INFERENCES

Reread lines 275–278. What can you infer from the way Paul responds to Uncle Oscar's question? Underline a word or phrase that supports your inference.

_____

_____

_____

reiterate (rē-ĭt′ə-rāt′) *v.* to repeat

uncanny (ŭn-kăn′ē) *adj.* strange or mysterious in a way that causes unease; eerie

---

16. **writs:** legal documents, in this case demanding payment of debts.

PAUSE & REFLECT

1. Why do you think Paul's uncle feels "nervous" about the winnings? *MAKE INFERENCES*

_____

_____

_____

_____

2. Uncle Oscar not only allows Paul to continue gambling, but he also becomes a partner in the venture. What does this tell you about Oscar's character? *MAKE JUDGMENTS*

_____

_____

_____

_____

FOCUS

Read on to find out if Paul's gift to his mother makes the house stop whispering.

MAKE INFERENCES

Reread the boxed text. In what way does this passage reflect the narrator's **omniscient point of view?**

_____

_____

_____

_____

Underline examples that support your answer.

"I don't think she would."

"Oh!"—and the boy writhed in an odd way—"I *don't* want her to know, uncle."

"All right, son! We'll manage it without her knowing."

They managed it very easily. Paul, at the other's suggestion, handed over five thousand pounds to his uncle, who deposited it with the family lawyer, who was then to inform Paul's mother that a relative had put five thousand pounds into his hands, which sum was to be paid out a thousand pounds at a time, on the mother's birthday, for the next five years.

320 "So she'll have a birthday present of a thousand pounds for five successive years," said Uncle Oscar. "I hope it won't make it all the harder for her later." **PAUSE & REFLECT**

Paul's mother had her birthday in November. The house had been "whispering" worse than ever lately, and, even in spite of his luck, Paul could not bear up against it. He was very anxious to see the effect of the birthday letter, telling his mother about the thousand pounds.

When there were no visitors, Paul now took his meals with his parents, as he was beyond the nursery control. His mother went into town nearly every day. She had discovered that she had an odd knack of 330 sketching furs and dress materials, so she worked secretly in the studio of a friend who was the chief "artist" for the leading drapers.[17] She drew the figures of ladies in furs and ladies in silk and sequins for the newspaper advertisements. This young woman artist earned several thousand pounds a year, but Paul's mother only made several hundreds, and she was again dissatisfied. She so wanted to be first in something, and she did not succeed, even in making sketches for drapery advertisements.

She was down to breakfast on the morning of her birthday. Paul watched her face as she read her letters. He knew the lawyer's letter. As his mother read it, her face hardened and became more expressionless. Then 340 a cold, determined look came on her mouth. She hid the letter under the pile of others, and said not a word about it.

"Didn't you have anything nice in the post for your birthday, mother?" said Paul.

"Quite moderately nice," she said, her voice cold and absent.

She went away to town without saying more.

---

17. **drapers:** British term for a dealer in cloth and dry goods.

But in the afternoon Uncle Oscar appeared. He said Paul's mother had had a long interview with the lawyer, asking if the whole five thousand could not be advanced at once, as she was in debt. ▶

"What do you think, uncle?" said the boy.

350 "I leave it to you, son."

"Oh, let her have it, then! We can get some more with the other," said the boy.

"A bird in the hand is worth two in the bush, laddie!" said Uncle Oscar.

"But I'm sure to *know* for the Grand National; or the Lincolnshire; or else the Derby.[18] I'm sure to know for *one* of them," said Paul.

So Uncle Oscar signed the agreement, and Paul's mother touched[19] the whole five thousand. Then something very curious happened. The voices in the house suddenly went mad, like a chorus of frogs on a spring evening. There were certain new furnishings, and Paul had a tutor. He was

360 *really* going to Eton, his father's school, in the following autumn. There were flowers in the winter, and a blossoming of the luxury Paul's mother had been used to. And yet the voices in the house, behind the sprays of mimosa and almond-blossom, and from under the piles of **iridescent** cushions, simply trilled and screamed in a sort of ecstasy: "There *must* be more money! Oh-h-h; there *must* be more money. Oh, now, now-w! Now-w-w—there *must* be more money!—more than ever! More than ever!" ▶

It frightened Paul terribly. He studied away at his Latin and Greek with his tutor. But his intense hours were spent with Bassett. The Grand National had gone by: he had not "known," and had lost a hundred

370 pounds. Summer was at hand. He was in agony for the Lincoln. But even for the Lincoln he didn't "know," and he lost fifty pounds. He became wild-eyed and strange, as if something were going to explode in him.

"Let it alone, son! Don't you bother about it!" urged Uncle Oscar. But it was as if the boy couldn't really hear what his uncle was saying.

"I've got to know for the Derby! I've got to know for the Derby!" the child reiterated, his big blue eyes blazing with a sort of madness.

His mother noticed how **overwrought** he was.

"You'd better go to the seaside. Wouldn't you like to go now to the seaside, instead of waiting? I think you'd better," she said, looking down at

380 him anxiously, her heart curiously heavy because of him.

But the child lifted his uncanny blue eyes.

---

18. **Grand National . . . Derby:** three major English horse races held annually. The Derby is England's best-known flat-track race.

19. **touched:** took.

QUESTION

What questions do you have about the way Paul's mother's reacts to the lawyer's letter?

_____

_____

_____

iridescent (ĭr′ĭ-dĕs′ənt) *adj.* shining with a rainbow-like display of colors

MAKE INFERENCES

Why do you think that the sudden influx of cash has made the house whisper louder than ever?

_____

_____

_____

overwrought (ō′vər-rôt′) *adj.* very nervous or excited

"I couldn't possibly go before the Derby, mother!" he said. "I couldn't possibly!"

"Why not?" she said, her voice becoming heavy when she was opposed. "Why not? You can still go from the seaside to see the Derby with your Uncle Oscar, if that's what you wish. No need for you to wait here. Besides, I think you care too much about these races. It's a bad sign. My family has been a gambling family, and you won't know till you grow up how much damage it has done. But it has done damage. I shall have to send Bassett
390 away, and ask Uncle Oscar not to talk racing to you, unless you promise to be reasonable about it: go away to the seaside and forget it. You're all nerves!"

"I'll do what you like, mother, so long as you don't send me away till after the Derby," the boy said.

"Send you away from where? Just from this house?"

"Yes," he said, gazing at her.

"Why, you curious child, what makes you care about this house so much, suddenly? I never knew you loved it."

He gazed at her without speaking. He had a secret within a secret,
400 something he had not divulged, even to Bassett or to his Uncle Oscar.

But his mother, after standing undecided and a little bit sullen for some moments, said:

"Very well, then! Don't go to the seaside till after the Derby, if you don't wish it. But promise me you won't let your nerves go to pieces. Promise you won't think so much about horse-racing and *events,* as you call them!"

"Oh no," said the boy casually. "I won't think much about them, mother. You needn't worry. I wouldn't worry, mother, if I were you."

"If you were me and I were you," said his mother, "I wonder what we *should* do!"
410 "But you know you needn't worry, mother, don't you?" the boy repeated.

"I should be awfully glad to know it," she said wearily.

"Oh, well, you *can,* you know. I mean, you *ought* to know you needn't worry," he insisted.

"Ought I? Then I'll see about it," she said.

Paul's secret of secrets was his wooden horse, that which had no name. Since he was emancipated from a nurse and a nursery-governess, he had had his rocking-horse removed to his own bedroom at the top of the house.

"Surely you're too big for a rocking-horse!" his mother had remonstrated.

"Well, you see, mother, till I can have a *real* horse, I like to have *some*
420 sort of animal about," had been his quaint answer.

"Do you feel he keeps you company?" she laughed.

PREDICT

What do you think Paul's "secret within a secret" (line 399) will turn out to be?

_____

_____

_____

"Oh yes! He's very good, he always keeps me company, when I'm there," said Paul.

So the horse, rather shabby, stood in an arrested prance in the boy's bedroom. **PAUSE & REFLECT**

The Derby was drawing near, and the boy grew more and more tense. He hardly heard what was spoken to him, he was very frail, and his eyes were really uncanny. His mother had sudden strange **seizures** of uneasiness about him. Sometimes, for half an hour, she would feel a
430   sudden anxiety about him that was almost anguish. She wanted to rush to him at once, and know he was safe.

Two nights before the Derby, she was at a big party in town, when one of her rushes of anxiety about her boy, her first-born, gripped her heart till she could hardly speak. She fought with the feeling, might and main,[20] for she believed in common sense. But it was too strong. She had to leave the dance and go downstairs to telephone to the country. The children's nursery-governess was terribly surprised and startled at being rung up in the night.

"Are the children all right, Miss Wilmot?"
440   "Oh yes, they are quite all right."

"Master Paul? Is he all right?"

"He went to bed as right as a trivet.[21] Shall I run up and look at him?"

"No," said Paul's mother reluctantly. "No! Don't trouble. It's all right. Don't sit up. We shall be home fairly soon." She did not want her son's privacy intruded upon.

"Very good," said the governess.

It was about one o'clock when Paul's mother and father drove up to their house. All was still. Paul's mother went to her room and slipped off her white fur cloak. She had told her maid not to wait up for her. She
450   heard her husband downstairs, mixing a whisky and soda.

And then, because of the strange anxiety at her heart, she stole upstairs to her son's room. Noiselessly she went along the upper corridor. Was there a faint noise? What was it? ▶

She stood, with arrested muscles, outside his door, listening. There was a strange, heavy, and yet not loud noise. Her heart stood still. It was a soundless noise, yet rushing and powerful. Something huge, in violent,

---

20. **might and main:** with all her strength.
21. **as right as a trivet:** in fine condition.

PAUSE & REFLECT

Do you think Paul's mother was wrong to let him stay in the house? Why or why not? *MAKE JUDGMENTS*

_____

_____

_____

seizure (sē'zhər) *n.* a sudden attack; a fit

FOCUS
As the story continues, Paul's obsession with the Derby intensifies. Read on to find out what his obsession ultimately leads to.

TESTSMART

Which passage could only have been written in the omniscient point of view?

Ⓐ lines 426–431
Ⓑ lines 439–441
Ⓒ lines 442–445
Ⓓ lines 447–450

TIP A passage that reflects an **omniscient point of view** presents the thoughts and feelings of more than one character. Reread each set of lines and look for a passage that tells what more than one character thinks and feels.

hushed motion. What was it? What in God's name was it? She ought to know. She felt that she knew the noise. She knew what it was.

Yet she could not place it. She couldn't say what it was. And on and on
460 it went, like a madness.

Softly, frozen with anxiety and fear, she turned the door handle.

The room was dark. Yet in the space near the window, she heard and saw something plunging to and fro. She gazed in fear and amazement.

Then suddenly she switched on the light, and saw her son, in his green pajamas, madly surging on the rocking-horse. The blaze of light suddenly lit him up, as he urged the wooden horse, and lit her up, as she stood, blonde, in her dress of pale green and crystal, in the doorway.

"Paul!" she cried. "Whatever are you doing?"

"It's Malabar!" he screamed in a powerful, strange voice. "It's Malabar!" ◀
470 His eyes blazed at her for one strange and senseless second, as he ceased urging his wooden horse. Then he fell with a crash to the ground, and she, all her tormented motherhood flooding upon her, rushed to gather him up.

But he was unconscious, and unconscious he remained, with some brain-fever. He talked and tossed, and his mother sat stonily by his side.

"Malabar! It's Malabar! Bassett, Bassett, I *know*! It's Malabar!"

So the child cried, trying to get up and urge the rocking-horse that gave him his inspiration.

"What does he mean by Malabar?" asked the heart-frozen mother.

"I don't know," said the father stonily.
480 "What does he mean by Malabar?" she asked her brother Oscar.

"It's one of the horses running for the Derby," was the answer.

And, in spite of himself, Oscar Cresswell spoke to Bassett, and himself put a thousand on Malabar: at fourteen to one.

The third day of the illness was critical: they were waiting for a change. The boy, with his rather long, curly hair, was tossing ceaselessly on the pillow. He neither slept nor regained consciousness, and his eyes were like blue stones. His mother sat, feeling her heart had gone, turned actually into a stone.

In the evening, Oscar Cresswell did not come, but Bassett sent a
490 message, saying could he come up for one moment, just one moment? Paul's mother was very angry at the intrusion, but on second thoughts she agreed. The boy was the same. Perhaps Bassett might bring him to consciousness.

The gardener, a shortish fellow with a little brown mustache and sharp little brown eyes, tiptoed into the room, touched his imaginary cap to Paul's mother, and stole to the bedside, staring with glittering, smallish eyes at the tossing, dying child.

CLARIFY

What has Paul been doing, and what is the outcome?

_____

_____

_____

_____

"Master Paul!" he whispered. "Master Paul! Malabar came in first all right, a clean win. I did as you told me. You've made over seventy thousand pounds, you have; you've got over eighty thousand.[22] Malabar came in all right, Master Paul."

"Malabar! Malabar! Did I say Malabar, mother? Did I say Malabar? Do you think I'm lucky, mother? I knew Malabar, didn't I? Over eighty thousand pounds! I call that lucky, don't you, mother? Over eighty thousand pounds! I knew, didn't I know I knew? Malabar came in all right. If I ride my horse till I'm sure, then I tell you, Bassett, you can go as high as you like. Did you go for all you were worth, Bassett?"

"I went a thousand on it, Master Paul."

"I never told you, mother, that if I can ride my horse, and *get there,* then I'm absolutely sure—oh, absolutely! Mother, did I ever tell you? I *am* lucky!"

"No, you never did," said his mother.

But the boy died in the night.

And even as he lay dead, his mother heard her brother's voice saying to her: "My God, Hester, you're eighty-odd thousand to the good, and a poor devil of a son to the bad. But, poor devil, poor devil, he's best gone out of a life where he rides his rocking-horse to find a winner."

---

22. **eighty thousand:** the equivalent of about $4 million in today's dollars.

Reading Comprehension

DIRECTIONS *Answer these questions about "The Rocking-Horse Winner" by filling in the correct ovals.*

1. Paul's parents consider their family to be superior to other families because they have

   (A) wealthy friends and relatives

   (B) pride in their accomplishments

   (C) expensive tastes and fine things

   (D) more money than other families

2. Why does Paul only know the name of the winning horse?

   (A) His rocking-horse rides only reveal the winner's name.

   (B) Bassett will not tell him the other horses' names.

   (C) The winner's name is the only lucky one.

   (D) He forgets the other horses' names.

3. When Paul's mother receives a letter informing her of an anonymous birthday gift, her reaction suggests that she feels

   (A) grateful   (C) dissatisfied

   (B) curious   (D) happy

4. Which passage could only have been narrated from the omniscient point of view?

   (A) lines 286–293

   (B) lines 315–319

   (C) lines 346–352

   (D) lines 373–380

5. Paul's "secret within a secret" (lines 399–400) is that

   (A) he rides his rocking horse to find the winners

   (B) his luck is better than his family's luck

   (C) Uncle Oscar, Bassett, and he bet on horseraces

   (D) he has won more than 1,500 pounds

6. A third-person omniscient narrator is

   (A) an all-knowing character in a story

   (B) an all-knowing outside observer

   (C) a narrator who focuses on one character

   (D) a narrator who misleads the reader

7. The word *assertion* (line 96) means

   (A) polite request

   (B) timid suggestion

   (C) bold statement

   (D) sincere apology

8. The most likely meaning of the word *remonstrated* (line 418) is

   (A) heartily agreed

   (B) suggested politely

   (C) questioned intently

   (D) forcefully objected

Responding in Writing

9. Short Response Imagine that Paul himself is narrating "The Rocking-Horse Winner." Choose a short scene from the story (other than the last scene) that you would like to retell from Paul's point of view. Rewrite the scene using the first-person point of view, putting Paul in the storyteller's chair.

_____

_____

_____

_____

_____

_____

TEST-TAKER'S TOOLKIT

⊗ **ACADEMIC VOCABULARY** Remember that a **first-person** narrator refers to himself or herself as *I*.

⊗ **GRAPHIC ORGANIZER** Reread the scene you have selected to help you remember the details. Then use the chart below to help you plan your response.

The scene I have chosen: _____

page: _____ lines: _____

Paul would think: _____

_____

He would feel: _____

_____

He would say: _____

_____

What's the Connection?

"The Rocking-Horse Winner" portrays a family plagued by out-of-control spending and financial anxiety. In the newspaper article "Money Isn't Everything," you will read about how these problems affect many people in our society.

INTERPRET QUOTATIONS Money is a favorite topic for writers of all kinds. With a group of classmates, discuss the quotations below. Write the meaning of each quote in the space provided. Put a check next to the quote you agree with most.

Quotes About Money	What the Quotes Mean
We can tell our values by looking at our checkbook stubs. —Gloria Steinem	
I cannot afford to waste my time making money. —Louis Agassiz	
When I have money, I get rid of it quickly, lest it find a way into my heart. —John Wesley	
Money is much more exciting than anything it buys. —Mignon McLaughlin	

LEARN THE SKILL: IDENTIFY AUDIENCE AND PURPOSE

When you read nonfiction, look for clues about the **author's purpose** for writing and about the **audience** for which the piece is intended.

- Scan the title, any subheadings, and the first paragraph to get a sense of what the text is about.

- Consider why the author might have written the text—for example, to inform, to entertain, to express feelings, or to persuade. Sometimes an author has more than one purpose.

- Think about what sort of audience the language and style of the text would be appropriate for. Also consider who might be interested in the topic.

For more on identifying audience and purpose, see the Author's Purpose entry in the Nonfiction Skills Handbook beginning on page R2.

Money Isn't Everything

by Charles A. Jaffe
from
The Boston Globe

We've all heard that the pursuit of money is the root of all evil, but nowhere is that more true than when it comes to your personal and family life, self-esteem, and well-being. . . . The stresses in life that push

10 people to their limits often revolve around money.

Fighting over money is the top cause for divorce in this country. Many crimes are all about money. And general money-related troubles—from debts to emergencies to simple fear

20 of running out of money—are high on the nation's list of stress points.

Moreover, most people believe those kinds of troubles could become serious only for someone else. ▶

"Many people are out of control about their money emotionally, yet they don't look at it that way," says

30 George Kinder, a Cambridge financial planner and author of *The Seven Stages of Money Maturity*.

"They don't have a good relationship with money and deep down they know it—they spend too much, they go on shopping sprees they can't control, they don't feel in control of their future—but they don't admit it. And then some-

40 thing happens and that's when the problems become visible." . . .

A little unemployment, a setback in the stock market that wipes out a chunk of savings, an unexpectedly large car repair or tax bill, a few debts drawing the notice of bill collectors, a family health crisis for

AUDIENCE

Underline clues in lines 1–26 about the article's intended audience. ✎

CLARIFY

What two ideas about money does the author express in lines 27–70?

1. _____

_____

_____

_____

2. _____

_____

_____

_____

AUDIENCE

Reread lines 76–104. What does the language and style of the writing suggest about the intended audience? Explain.

_____

_____

_____

_____

which you are uninsured—any or all of these things could force you to focus first on money.

"People don't realize how close to the edge they are," says Jeffrey Heisler, a professor at Boston University who studies behavioral finance. "They talk themselves into 'I can handle this' and 'No, it won't be a problem.' Then something happens and it is a problem, and they don't know how to handle it."

Experts who study behavioral finance normally look at issues around investment patterns, not mental health. Yet they acknowledge that too many people have their self-worth tied up in their net worth, and that such behavior can become self-destructive and make someone unhappy, regardless of how much money he actually has. ◀

With that in mind, here are four questions experts suggest asking—and answering honestly—to help determine if your attitudes about money are balanced and stable.

1. What do I want from life? Am I pursuing my aspirations?

Money is a means to an end, not an end itself. Your happiness revolves more around lifestyle issues than cash.

For example, Kinder asks people what their life would be like if they had all the money they could ever need. Most people answer with a list of what they would buy and where they would go and how they would spend.

At that point, Kinder asks what they would have missed out on in life if they had only 24 hours to live. And the answers change from being money-related to peace-of-mind issues. The value of time spent not working, of time out from the rat race becomes a little more clear; the supposed benefits from pushing yourself unhappily toward some nebulous goal are diminished.

No one gets to the end of his life and says: "Gee, I wish I had put in a few more hours at work." . . . ◀

2. Do I have a practical plan for achieving my aspirations?

This does not necessarily have to be a financial plan, but there has to be enough strategy here so that you can see where you are on the road to success.

For example, many people worry about running out of money in retirement, even when they have enough money to live out their lives comfortably. Part of the problem comes from not knowing how much they actually need; instead of having set a concrete financial goal and feeling a sense of achievement when they cross that finish line, they are in a constant state of worry that maybe they have not made it.

Knowing what you want to do with your life and your money is not enough. You have to come up with a way of pursuing those goals.

130 3. How do I sabotage myself from reaching those goals?

Remember, many personal aspirations have more to do with your personal life than your pocketbook. Yet money and your habits sometimes get in the way.

Many people who claim to be trying to get ahead and secure their future find ways to put them-140 selves back in the hole. They feel entitled to, say, a new car, because they work so hard, when what they really need is less car and more financial freedom. To maintain what they outwardly consider a great lifestyle, they booby-trap their finances. Not surprisingly, they then feel more obligated to work and are more likely to 150 feel pressure as debts linger or mount. . . .

4. Are you too busy counting your money? Do you share it?

Charity and generosity are personal things and shouldn't be forced on anyone. Plenty of people need to accumulate money and gain control of their lives before they can share with others. Still, 160 generosity of spirit around money is considered a healthy attitude.

"If someone really has enough, but acts like they don't, there is a bit of an illness there in the person's relationship with money," says Jeff Halvorsen of Psychological Motivations, a Dobbs Ferry, New York, firm that studies consumer behavior. "Some people get too 170 involved in counting their money, in seeing what it can do for them and what they can buy. They get so wrapped up in keeping track of what they have and making it get bigger and bigger and bigger that they lose sight of what's important to them."

All of the experts I talked with noted that money stresses can be 180 solved. Obviously, some of that change comes from finding a way to improve your financial position so that the problems dissipate or disappear. But the change can also happen if you simply change your attitude about money.

Says Kinder: "You need to learn to tolerate the anxiety and understand the emotions involved. It's important 190 to keep perspective; money should not be running your life." ▶

Reading Comprehension

DIRECTIONS *Answer these questions about the two selections in this lesson by filling in the correct ovals.*

1. According to "Money Isn't Everything," which of the following statements reflects a healthy attitude toward money?

   (A) I will never have enough money to retire!

   (B) It feels good to give some of my money away.

   (C) My credit card debt is no problem.

   (D) I work hard—I deserve a new SUV!

2. The mistake described in lines 42–60 of "Money Isn't Everything" is

   (A) giving too many charitable donations

   (B) refusing to prepare for the unexpected

   (C) out-of-control spending

   (D) being uninsured during a health crisis

3. Which sentence best sums up the advice the author gives in lines 76–104?

   (A) Escape from the rat race.

   (B) Avoid nebulous goals.

   (C) Remember what's important in life.

   (D) Don't quit, no matter what.

4. Which two purposes would you identify in "Money Isn't Everything"?

   (A) to inform and entertain

   (B) to express feelings and inform

   (C) to entertain and persuade

   (D) to persuade and inform

5. The family in "The Rocking-Horse Winner" is most aptly described in which lines of the news article?

   (A) lines 27–41

   (B) lines 89–100

   (C) lines 112–124

   (D) lines 154–161

6. Which characters from "The Rocking-Horse Winner" would benefit most from reading "Money Isn't Everything"?

   (A) Uncle Oscar and Bassett

   (B) Paul and his sisters

   (C) the gamblers at the track

   (D) Paul's mother and father

7. The word *nebulous* is used in line 99 of "Money Isn't Everything" to describe a goal that is

   (A) perpetual

   (B) distant

   (C) vague

   (D) unattainable

8. Using context clues in lines 180–184 of "Money Isn't Everything," you can tell that the word *dissipate* means

   (A) remain stable

   (B) intensify

   (C) fade away

   (D) accumulate

Timed Writing Practice

PROMPT

What do you consider to be a healthy attitude toward money? Write a (persuasive essay) in which you try to convince readers to make one change in their thinking or behavior that will help them feel more secure about their financial situation. Provide at least three reasons and one or two examples to support each reason. Draw examples from your own experiences and observations as well as from the two selections you have read.

TEST-TAKER'S TOOLKIT

1. ANALYZE THE PROMPT

A. Underline the question in the prompt and circle key words in the sentences that follow the question. The writing form has been circled for you.

B. Jot down a list of the key elements you need to include in your persuasive essay.

2. PLAN YOUR RESPONSE

A. **Make notes** In the chart, list three good reasons for your opinion and examples to support your reasons.

B. **Organize your information** In your introduction, identify the topic of your essay and present a thesis statement that clearly identifies the claim you are making. Then you can write a paragraph for each reason you noted in the chart. Use your examples to support each reason. Be sure to include a conclusion in which you wrap up your ideas.

Reason 1:	Example(s):
Reason 2:	Example(s):
Reason 3:	Example(s):

3. WRITE AND REVIEW

A. You might use a quote to help you craft a memorable ending. Here is an example:

Author Alexandre Dumas said that money "is a good servant but a bad master." Don't let money rule your life!

B. Be sure to leave time to check your spelling and grammar.

UNIT **6**

**MODERN AND
CONTEMPORARY
LITERATURE**

LESSON 6B

*Shooting an
Elephant*
BY GEORGE ORWELL

RELATED NONFICTION
Myanmar

How important is it to
"SAVE FACE"?

George Orwell once said, "An autobiography is only to be trusted when it reveals something disgraceful." Most people have done something that they regret or about which they feel ashamed. Sometimes people make the wrong decision in order to avoid looking foolish. Character flaws are difficult to admit, and people often go to great lengths—even compromising their values—to protect their reputation.

QUICKWRITE Recall a time when you did something you later regretted in order to "save face." Write a short description of the incident on the notebook. Tell what you might do differently if you encountered a similar situation today.

What I did to "save face":
_____

_____

_____

_____

_____

_____

What I might do differently today: _____

_____

_____

_____

_____

_____

ASSESSMENT GOALS

By the end of this lesson, you will be able to . . .

- analyze a reflective essay
- use active reading strategies to comprehend text
- analyze characteristics of an encyclopedia article
- analyze a writing prompt and plan a personal narrative

Reflective Essay

In a **REFLECTIVE ESSAY**, the writer makes a connection between a **PERSONAL OBSERVATION** and a **UNIVERSAL IDEA**—such as love, honor, or freedom. Review the characteristics of a reflective essay in the graphic below.

In "Shooting an Elephant," George Orwell reflects on a specific incident from his time as a young police officer in British-ruled Burma during the 1920s. As you read the essay, notice how Orwell uses his personal experience in the British Empire to convey a message about colonialism.

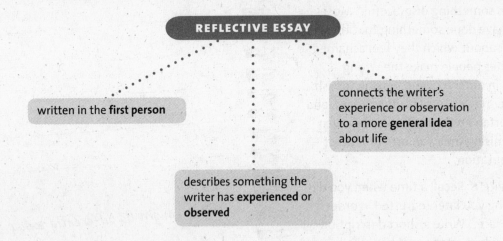

REFLECTIVE ESSAY

written in the **first person**

describes something the writer has **experienced** or **observed**

connects the writer's experience or observation to a more **general idea** about life

Shooting an Elephant

George Orwell

MARK IT UP

Use these marks to monitor your reading:

* This is important.

? I don't understand.

! This is a surprise.

When you see this pencil ✏, you'll be asked to mark up the text. You can also write in this book in any way you find useful.

BACKGROUND Orwell's essay is set in Burma, a Southeast Asian country now known as Myanmar. In a series of wars in the 19th century, the British gained control of Burma and made it a province of British India. The Burmese resented British rule, under which they endured poverty and a lack of political and religious freedom. Like many of his fellow British officers, Orwell was inexperienced in police work when he arrived in Burma at age 19.

FOCUS
As you read the first part of the essay, find out what internal conflict Orwell experienced as he tried to do his job.

I n Moulmein, in Lower Burma,[1] I was hated by large numbers of people—the only time in my life that I have been important enough for this to happen to me. I was subdivisional police officer of the town, and in an aimless, petty kind of way anti-European feeling was very bitter. No one had the guts to raise a riot, but if a European woman went through the bazaars alone somebody would probably spit betel juice[2] over her dress. As a police officer I was an obvious target and was baited whenever it seemed safe to do so. When a nimble Burman tripped me up on the football[3] field and the referee (another Burman) looked the other way, the
10 crowd yelled with hideous laughter. This happened more than once. In the end the sneering yellow faces of young men that met me everywhere, the insults hooted after me when I was at a safe distance, got badly on my nerves. The young Buddhist priests were the worst of all. There were

---

1. **Moulmein** (mōōl-mān′), **in Lower Burma:** the main city of British-controlled Burma, now the independent Asian nation of Myanmar. Moulmein is now usually called Mawlamyine.

2. **betel** (bēt′l) **juice:** the saliva created when chewing a mixture of betel palm nuts, betel palm leaves, and lime.

3. **football:** soccer.

SUMMARIZE

Summarize the experiences
Orwell describes in lines
1–15 and the effects these
experiences have on him.

_____

_____

_____

imperialism
(ĭm-pîr′ē-ə-lĭz′əm) *n.*
the policy of forming and
maintaining an empire,
especially in the quest for raw
materials and more markets

cowed (koud) *adj.* made timid
and submissive through fear
or awe **cow** *v.*

supplant (sə-plănt′) *v.* to take
the place of

prostrate (prŏs′trāt′) *adj.*
completely submissive

TESTSMART

Orwell's observation of
the "dirty work of Empire"
suggests that imperialism is

(A) evil

(B) temporary

(C) unclean

(D) necessary

TIP This question asks you
to link a specific observation
to a more general
statement. To answer,
reread Orwell's **personal
observations** about the
British rule of its colonies
in lines 16–38. Ask yourself
what general point Orwell is
making about the British.

despotic (dĭ-spŏt′ĭk) *adj.*
ruling absolutely without
allowing any dissent;
tyrannical

several thousands of them in the town and none of them seemed to have anything to do except stand on street corners and jeer at Europeans. ◄

All this was perplexing and upsetting. For at that time I had already made up my mind that **imperialism** was an evil thing and the sooner I chucked up[4] my job and got out of it the better. Theoretically—and secretly, of course—I was all for the Burmese and all against their
20 oppressors, the British. As for the job I was doing, I hated it more bitterly than I can perhaps make clear. In a job like that you see the dirty work of Empire at close quarters. The wretched prisoners huddling in the stinking cages of the lock-ups, the gray, **cowed** faces of the long-term convicts, the scarred buttocks of the men who had been flogged with bamboos—all these oppressed me with an intolerable sense of guilt. But I could get nothing into perspective. I was young and ill-educated and I had had to think out my problems in the utter silence that is imposed on every Englishman in the East. I did not even know that the British Empire is dying, still less did I know that it is a great deal better than the
30 younger empires that are going to **supplant** it. All I knew was that I was stuck between my hatred of the empire I served and my rage against the evil-spirited little beasts who tried to make my job impossible. With one part of my mind I thought of the British Raj[5] as an unbreakable tyranny, as something clamped down, *in saecula saeculorum,*[6] upon the will of **prostrate** peoples; with another part I thought that the greatest joy in the world would be to drive a bayonet into a Buddhist priest's guts. Feelings like these are the normal by-products of imperialism; ask any Anglo-Indian official, if you can catch him off duty. ◄

One day something happened which in a roundabout way was
40. enlightening. It was a tiny incident in itself, but it gave me a better glimpse than I had had before of the real nature of imperialism—the real motives for which **despotic** governments act. Early one morning the subinspector at a police station the other end of the town rang me up on the phone and said that an elephant was ravaging the bazaar. Would I please come and do something about it? I did not know what I could do, but I wanted to see what was happening and I got on to a pony and started out. I took my rifle, an old .44 Winchester and much too small to kill an elephant, but I thought the noise might be useful *in terrorem.*[7]

---

4. **chucked up:** threw off; gave up.
5. **British Raj:** India and adjoining areas (such as Burma) controlled by Britain in the 19th and early 20th centuries. *Raj* is the word for "kingdom" or "rule" in Hindi, a chief language of India.
6. *in saecula saeculorum* (ĭn sĕk′yə-lə sĕk-yə-lôr′əm) *Latin:* forever and ever.
7. *in terrorem* (ĭn tĕ-rôr′əm) *Latin:* for terror.

Various Burmans stopped me on the way and told me about the elephant's
doings. It was not, of course, a wild elephant, but a tame one which had
gone "must."[8] It had been chained up as tame elephants always are when
their attack of "must" is due, but on the previous night it had broken
its chain and escaped. Its mahout,[9] the only person who could manage
it when it was in that state, had set out in pursuit, but had taken the
wrong direction and was now twelve hours' journey away, and in the
morning the elephant had suddenly reappeared in the town. The Burmese
population had no weapons and were quite helpless against it. It had
already destroyed somebody's bamboo hut, killed a cow and raided some
fruit-stalls and devoured the stock; also it had met the municipal rubbish
van, and, when the driver jumped out and took to his heels, had turned
the van over and inflicted violences upon it. ▶

    The Burmese subinspector and some Indian constables[10] were waiting
for me in the quarter where the elephant had been seen. It was a very poor
quarter, a labyrinth of squalid bamboo huts, thatched with palm-leaf,
winding all over a steep hillside. I remember that it was a cloudy stuffy
morning at the beginning of the rains. We began questioning the people
as to where the elephant had gone, and, as usual, failed to get any definite
information. That is invariably the case in the East; a story always sounds
clear enough at a distance, but the nearer you get to the scene of events the
vaguer it becomes. Some of the people said that the elephant had gone in
one direction, some said that he had gone in another, some professed not
even to have heard of any elephant. I had almost made up my mind that
the whole story was a pack of lies, when we heard yells a little distance
away. There was a loud, scandalized cry of "Go away, child! Go away this
instant!" and an old woman with a switch in her hand came round the
corner of a hut, violently shooing away a crowd of naked children. Some
more women followed, clicking their tongues and exclaiming; evidently
there was something there that the children ought not to have seen. I
rounded the hut and saw a man's dead body sprawling in the mud. He was
an Indian, a black Dravidian coolie,[11] almost naked, and he could not have
been dead many minutes. The people said that the elephant had come
suddenly upon him round the corner of the hut, caught him with its trunk,
put its foot on his back and ground him into the earth. This was the rainy

---

8. **gone "must":** had an attack of must, a dangerous frenzy that periodically seizes
   male elephants.
9. **mahout** (mə-hout′): an elephant keeper.
10. **constables:** police officers.
11. **Dravidian** (drə-vĭd′ē-ən) **coolie:** a dark-skinned menial laborer from the south of
    India.

PREDICT

Reread lines 39–61. Underline
the sentence that suggests
that the essay leads up to
the realization of a **universal
idea.** ✎

Based on what you have read
so far, what do you think this
greater truth will involve?

_____

_____

_____

labyrinth (lăb′ə-rĭnth′) *n.* an
intricate structure of winding
passages; a maze

PAUSE & REFLECT

1. What conflicted feelings about his role in Burma does Orwell describe? **CLARIFY**

_____

_____

_____

2. Do you think that Orwell is well-suited to his job? Why or why not? **MAKE JUDGMENTS**

_____

_____

_____

_____

FOCUS
Read on to find out what Orwell decides to do after he locates the elephant—and why he feels he must carry out his decision whether it is right or not.

season and the ground was soft, and his face had scored a trench a foot deep and a couple of yards long. He was lying on his belly with arms crucified and head sharply twisted to one side. His face was coated with mud, the eyes wide open, the teeth bared and grinning with an expression of unendurable agony. (Never tell me, by the way, that the dead look peaceful. Most of the corpses I have seen looked devilish.) The friction of the great beast's foot had stripped the skin from his back as neatly as one skins a rabbit. As soon as I saw the dead man I sent an orderly[12] to a friend's house nearby to borrow an elephant rifle. I had already sent back the pony, not wanting it to go mad with fright and throw me if it smelled the elephant. **PAUSE & REFLECT**

The orderly came back in a few minutes with a rifle and five cartridges, and meanwhile some Burmans had arrived and told us that the elephant was in the paddy fields[13] below, only a few hundred yards away. As I started forward practically the whole population of the quarter flocked out of the houses and followed me. They had seen the rifle and were all shouting excitedly that I was going to shoot the elephant. They had not shown much interest in the elephant when he was merely ravaging their homes, but it was different now that he was going to be shot. It was a bit of fun to them, as it would be to an English crowd; besides, they wanted the meat. It made me vaguely uneasy. I had no intention of shooting the elephant—I had merely sent for the rifle to defend myself if necessary—and it is always unnerving to have a crowd following you. I marched down the hill, looking and feeling a fool, with the rifle over my shoulder and an ever-growing army of people jostling at my heels. At the bottom, when you got away from the huts, there was a metalled road and beyond that a miry waste of paddy fields a thousand yards across, not yet ploughed but soggy from the first rains and dotted with coarse grass. The elephant was standing eighty yards from the road, his left side towards us. He took not the slightest notice of the crowd's approach. He was tearing up bunches of grass, beating them against his knees to clean them and stuffing them into his mouth.

I had halted on the road. As soon as I saw the elephant I knew with perfect certainty that I ought not to shoot him. It is a serious matter to shoot a working elephant—it is comparable to destroying a huge and costly piece of machinery—and obviously one ought not to do it if it can

12. **orderly:** a military aid.
13. **paddy fields:** rice fields.

120 possibly be avoided. And at that distance, peacefully eating, the elephant looked no more dangerous than a cow. I thought then and I think now that his attack of "must" was already passing off; in which case he would merely wander harmlessly about until the mahout came back and caught him. Moreover, I did not in the least want to shoot him. I decided that I would watch him for a little while to make sure that he did not turn savage again, and then go home.

But at that moment I glanced round at the crowd that had followed me. It was an immense crowd, two thousand at the least and growing every minute. It blocked the road for a long distance on either side. I looked
130 at the sea of yellow faces above the **garish** clothes—faces all happy and excited over this bit of fun, all certain that the elephant was going to be shot. They were watching me as they would watch a conjurer about to perform a trick. They did not like me, but with the magical rifle in my hands I was momentarily worth watching. And suddenly I realized that I should have to shoot the elephant after all. The people expected it of me and I had got to do it; I could feel their two thousand wills pressing me forward, irresistibly. And it was at this moment, as I stood there with the rifle in my hands, that I first grasped the hollowness, the futility of the white man's dominion in the East. Here was I, the white man with
140 his gun, standing in front of the unarmed native crowd—seemingly the leading actor of the piece; but in reality I was only an absurd puppet pushed to and fro by the will of those yellow faces behind. I perceived in this moment that when the white man turns tyrant it is his own freedom that he destroys. He becomes a sort of hollow, posing dummy, the conventionalized figure of a sahib.[14] For it is the condition of his rule that he shall spend his life in trying to impress the "natives," and so in every crisis he has got to do what the "natives" expect of him. He wears a mask, and his face grows to fit it. I had got to shoot the elephant. I had committed myself to doing it when I sent for the rifle. A sahib has got to
150 act like a sahib; he has got to appear resolute, to know his own mind and do definite things. To come all that way, rifle in hand, with two thousand people marching at my heels, and then to trail feebly away, having done nothing—no, that was impossible. The crowd would laugh at me. And my whole life, every white man's life in the East, was one long struggle not to be laughed at. ▶

garish (gârʹĭsh) *adj.* too bright or showy; gaudy; glaring

ANALYZE

Reread the boxed text. What connection does Orwell draw between his **personal experience** and British colonialism?

_____

_____

_____

_____

Underline the part of the text that expresses the realization of a larger, more **universal idea.** ✎

14. **sahib** (säʹĭb): a title of respect formerly used by native Indians to address a European gentleman.

But I did not want to shoot the elephant. I watched him beating his bunch of grass against his knees, with that preoccupied grandmotherly air that elephants have. It seemed to me that it would be murder to shoot him. At that age I was not squeamish about killing animals, but I had never shot an elephant and never wanted to. (Somehow it always seems worse to kill a *large* animal.) Besides, there was the beast's owner to be considered. Alive, the elephant was worth at least a hundred pounds; dead, he would only be worth the value of his tusks—five pounds, possibly. But I had got to act quickly. I turned to some experienced-looking Burmans who had been there when we arrived, and asked them how the elephant had been behaving. They all said the same thing: he took no notice of you if you left him alone, but he might charge if you went too close to him.

It was perfectly clear to me what I ought to do. I ought to walk up to within, say, twenty-five yards of the elephant and test his behavior. If he charged I could shoot, if he took no notice of me it would be safe to leave him until the mahout came back. But also I knew that I was going to do no such thing. I was a poor shot with a rifle and the ground was soft mud into which one would sink at every step. If the elephant charged and I missed him, I should have about as much chance as a toad under a steam-roller. But even then I was not thinking particularly of my own skin, only of the watchful yellow faces behind. For at that moment, with the crowd watching me, I was not afraid in the ordinary sense, as I would have been if I had been alone. A white man mustn't be frightened in front of "natives"; and so, in general, he isn't frightened. The sole thought in my mind was that if anything went wrong those two thousand Burmans would see me pursued, caught, trampled on and reduced to a grinning corpse like that Indian up the hill. And if that happened it was quite probable that some of them would laugh. That would never do. There was only one alternative. I shoved the cartridges into the magazine and lay down on the road to get a better aim. ◄

The crowd grew very still, and a deep, low, happy sigh, as of people who see the theater curtain go up at last, breathed from innumerable throats. They were going to have their bit of fun after all. The rifle was a beautiful German thing with cross-hair sights. I did not then know that in shooting an elephant one should shoot to cut an imaginary bar running from ear-hole to ear-hole. I ought, therefore, as the elephant was sideways on, to have aimed straight at his ear-hole; actually I aimed several inches in front of this, thinking the brain would be further forward.

PREDICT

What effect will shooting the elephant have on Orwell's public reputation? What effect will it have on his own self-image?

When I pulled the trigger I did not hear the bang or feel the kick—one never does when a shot goes home—but I heard the devilish roar of glee that went up from the crowd. In that instant, in too short a time, one would have thought, even for the bullet to get there, a mysterious, terrible change had come over the elephant. He neither stirred nor fell, but every line of his body had altered. He looked suddenly stricken, shrunken, immensely old, as though the frightful impact of the bullet had paralyzed him without knocking him down. At last, after what seemed a long time—it might have been five seconds, I dare say—he sagged flabbily to his knees. His mouth slobbered. An enormous **senility** seemed to have settled upon him. One could have imagined him thousands of years old. I fired again into the same spot. At the second shot he did not collapse but climbed with desperate slowness to his feet and stood weakly upright, with legs sagging and head drooping. I fired a third time. That was the shot that did for him. You could see the agony of it jolt his whole body and knock the last remnant of strength from his legs. But in falling he seemed for a moment to rise, for as his hind legs collapsed beneath him he seemed to tower upwards like a huge rock toppling, his trunk reaching skyward like a tree. He trumpeted, for the first and only time. And then down he came, his belly towards me, with a crash that seemed to shake the ground even where I lay.

I got up. The Burmans were already racing past me across the mud. It was obvious that the elephant would never rise again, but he was not dead. He was breathing very rhythmically with long rattling gasps, his great mound of a side painfully rising and falling. His mouth was wide open—I could see far down into caverns of pale pink throat. I waited a long time for him to die, but his breathing did not weaken. Finally I fired my two remaining shots into the spot where I thought his heart must be. The thick blood welled out of him like red velvet, but still he did not die. His body did not even jerk when the shots hit him, the tortured breathing continued without a pause. He was dying, very slowly and in great agony, but in some world remote from me where not even a bullet could damage him further. I felt that I had got to put an end to that dreadful noise. It seemed dreadful to see the great beast lying there, powerless to move and yet powerless to die, and not even to be able to finish him. I sent back for my small rifle and poured shot after shot into his heart and down his throat. They seemed to make no impression. The tortured gasps continued as steadily as the ticking of a clock. ▶

senility (sĭ-nĭl′ĭ-tē) *n.* the mental deterioration that sometimes comes with old age

MAKE INFERENCES

What are some likely reasons why Orwell fired so many shots into the elephant?

_____

_____

_____

_____

TestSmart

VOCABULARY

The word *pretext* (line 244) means

Ⓐ permission

Ⓑ prior reason

Ⓒ message

Ⓓ premonition

TIP If a test question asks you to choose the meaning of a word, you can use the **process of elimination** to find the right answer. To answer this question, substitute each answer choice for the word *pretext* in line 244. Eliminate the ones that don't make sense, given the overall story context.

 PAUSE & REFLECT

What do you think the shooting of the elephant symbolizes for Orwell? *ANALYZE*

_____

_____

_____

Big Question ?

Does Orwell seem to feel that he made the right choice by shooting the elephant to "save face"? Explain your response. *DRAW CONCLUSIONS*

_____

_____

_____

_____

In the end I could not stand it any longer and went away. I heard later that it took him half an hour to die. Burmans were arriving with dahs[15] and baskets even before I left, and I was told they had stripped his body almost to the bones by the afternoon.

Afterwards, of course, there were endless discussions about the shooting of the elephant. The owner was furious, but he was only an Indian and could do nothing. Besides, legally I had done the right thing, for a mad elephant has to be killed, like a mad dog, if its owner fails to control it.
240 Among the Europeans opinion was divided. The older men said I was right, the younger men said it was a damn shame to shoot an elephant for killing a coolie, because an elephant was worth more than any damn Coringhee[16] coolie. And afterwards I was very glad that the coolie had been killed; it put me legally in the right and it gave me a sufficient pretext for shooting the elephant. I often wondered whether any of the others grasped that I had done it solely to avoid looking a fool. ◀

PAUSE & REFLECT

---

15. **dahs:** large knives.
16. **Coringhee:** coming from a port in southeastern India.

Reading Comprehension

DIRECTIONS *Answer these questions about "Shooting an Elephant" by filling in the correct ovals.*

1. The incident with the elephant made Orwell realize that he was

   Ⓐ a poor shot with a rifle

   Ⓑ fighting for the wrong side

   Ⓒ capable of violating his conscience

   Ⓓ more powerful than he imagined

2. Orwell's observation of the crowd of Burmese following him (lines 127–155) suggests that oppressed people

   Ⓐ are always unhappy

   Ⓑ develop a cruel streak

   Ⓒ find cruelty humorous

   Ⓓ have power over their oppressors

3. What universal truth is expressed in lines 139–147?

   Ⓐ Those who imprison others imprison themselves.

   Ⓑ Man is a hollow, posing dummy.

   Ⓒ British rule is mostly about impressing native peoples.

   Ⓓ An unarmed native crowd can be menacing.

4. For the Burmese onlookers, the shooting of the elephant is

   Ⓐ a violation

   Ⓑ a revelation

   Ⓒ entertainment

   Ⓓ legal justice

5. Why did Orwell feel that he had to shoot the elephant?

   Ⓐ to maintain his reputation

   Ⓑ to remove a public danger

   Ⓒ to follow the law

   Ⓓ to show off his marksmanship

6. Which phrase *best* sums up the attitude of the Burmese toward the British?

   Ⓐ impatient tolerance

   Ⓑ simmering bitterness

   Ⓒ overt and violent hostility

   Ⓓ sorrowful resignation

7. The most likely meaning of the word *conjurer* (line 132) is

   Ⓐ emperor

   Ⓑ magician

   Ⓒ hunter

   Ⓓ marksman

8. Based on context clues in lines 184–185, you can tell that a *magazine* is the

   Ⓐ part of a gun that ejects a bullet

   Ⓑ place where the British store their rifles

   Ⓒ cross-hairs on a German rifle

   Ⓓ compartment from which bullets are fed into the firing chamber

GO ON →

For help, use the **Test-Taker's Toolkit** below.

Responding in Writing

9. Short Response Write a paragraph in which you evaluate George Orwell's decision to shoot the elephant. Explain why the decision was so difficult for him, and discuss whether you would have taken the same action.

_____

_____

_____

_____

_____

_____

TEST-TAKER'S TOOLKIT

⊗ **GRAPHIC ORGANIZER** Use the chart below to help you plan your response.

Why the decision was so difficult:
My opinion about Orwell's decision:
Why I feel that way:

What's the Connection?

"Shooting an Elephant" recounts a dramatic incident that took place in the early 1900s during British colonial rule in Burma. "Myanmar" is an excerpt from an encyclopedia article about Myanmar—the country formerly known as Burma.

ASK QUESTIONS Life in Myanmar has greatly changed since the days when George Orwell wrote about his experiences there. Yet some things have remained the same. Write five questions that you would like to have answered about Myanmar, past and present. After you have read the encyclopedia article excerpt, revisit your questions to see which ones were answered.

Myanmar
ENCYCLOPEDIA ARTICLE

Use with "Shooting an Elephant," p. 258

Questions About Myanmar

1. _____

2. _____

3. _____

4. _____

5. _____

LEARN THE SKILL: ANALYZE CHARACTERISTICS OF AN ENCYCLOPEDIA ARTICLE

Encyclopedia articles present general information on subjects in every field of knowledge. They often include photographs, maps, graphics, bibliographies, and references to articles on related topics. When reading an encyclopedia article, it can be helpful to note the following:

- The articles are arranged alphabetically.
- They present information in a **neutral tone.**
- **Boldfaced headings** and **subheadings** help you to locate the **topics** and **subtopics** you are looking for.
- Encyclopedia articles are usually organized into **categories** such as *Geography, Climate, People, History,* and so on.
- **Pronunciations** are often provided for unfamiliar words.

For more on analyzing characteristics of an encyclopedia article, see the Text Features entry in the Nonfiction Skills Handbook beginning on page R2.

SET A PURPOSE

_____

_____

_____

ENCYCLOPEDIA ARTICLE

To identify the **topics** and **subtopics** that will be covered in the article, circle the **main headings** and underline the **subheadings**. 🖉

MONITOR

The first three paragraphs present an overview of Myanmar. Put a _G_ beside the paragraph that tells about Myanmar's geography. Put a _P_ beside the paragraph that tells about Myanmar's people. Put an _H_ beside the paragraph that tells about Myanmar's history.

Myanmar

from World Book ◀

Myanmar, (*myahn MAHR*), formerly called Burma, is a country in Southeast Asia. It lies along the Bay of Bengal. Mountains border Myanmar on the west, north, and east. They enclose the Irrawaddy River Valley. The Irrawaddy River empties into the Bay of Bengal
10 through many mouths, forming a delta. Yangon, Myanmar's largest city, lies on the delta. Yangon is also spelled *Rangoon*. Naypyidaw Myodaw, in central Myanmar, is the capital.

The people of Myanmar are called the Burmese. The great majority of them are Buddhists and live in villages on the delta
20 and in the Irrawaddy Valley. They make a bare living farming the land.

People have lived in what is now Myanmar since prehistoric times. Several kingdoms arose and fell in the region from the A.D. 1000's to the 1800's, when the United Kingdom conquered the country. The nation won its
30 independence with the name Burma in 1948. In 1989, the military government announced that it had changed the official name of the country from the Union of Burma to the Union of Myanmar. The United States and the United Kingdom oppose the military regime and still refer to the country as Burma. . . . ◀

40 ## PEOPLE

Religion. About 85 percent of Myanmar's people belong to the Theravada school of Buddhism. Buddhism, which teaches that people can find happiness only by freeing themselves of worldly desires, strongly influences family and community life. Other religious groups in
50 Myanmar include Christians, Hindus, and Muslims.

Way of Life. The majority of Myanmar's people live in farm villages. Most villages consist of about 50 to 100 bamboo houses with thatch roofs. The houses are built on poles above the ground for protection against floods and wild animals. Most villages have
60 a Buddhist monastery, which is the center of much social as well as religious activity. Boys spend from a few days to several months in the monastery after an adulthood ceremony called *shin-pyu*. In the ceremony, the boys' heads are shaved to symbolize

Myanmar

GEOGRAPHY
Capital: Naypyidaw Myodaw
Total Area: 261,970 sq. mi.
Population: 50,519,000

ECONOMY
Imports: machinery, chemicals, fuels, food
Exports: food, fuels, wood

CULTURE
Language: Burmese
Religions: Buddhism, traditional beliefs, Christianity, Islam, Hinduism

their temporary rejection of the world. Girls mark their entry into adulthood with an earlobe-piercing ceremony called *nahtwin*, after which they receive their first pair of earrings.

In towns and cities, many people live in small brick or concrete buildings and work for the government or in trade or industry. City life has more leisure and cultural activities than rural life and moves at a faster pace. But most city people keep close ties with their family and ethnic group, and religion remains important to them. . . .

HISTORY

Early days. The first known people to live in what is now Myanmar were the Mon. They shared a culture with the Khmer, a people who lived in what is now Cambodia. The Mon moved into the Myanmar region as early as 3000 B.C. and settled near the mouths of the Salween and Sittang rivers. The peoples who came later migrated from an area in central Asia that is now southwestern China. The Pyu arrived in the A.D. 600's. The Burmans, Chin, Kachin, Karen, and Shan came during the 800's. Most of these peoples lived apart from one another and kept their own cultures.

In 1044, a Burman ruler named Anawrahta united the region and founded a kingdom that lasted nearly 250 years. The kingdom's capital, Pagan, lay on the Irrawaddy River in the central part of the country. The Burmans adopted features of the Mon and Pyu cultures, including Theravada Buddhism. Mongol invaders led by Kublai Khan captured Pagan in 1287, shattering the kingdom. A new Burman kingdom arose at Toungoo during the 1500's. It was brought down by a Mon rebellion in 1752.

ENCYCLOPEDIA ARTICLE

What does the graphic add to your understanding of Myanmar?

_____

_____

_____

MAKE INFERENCES

Underline the names of the groups of people who came to live in what is now Myanmar.

What problems might have arisen as a result of their keeping their cultures separate?

_____

_____

_____

_____

British conquest and rule.
The last Burman kingdom was
founded by Alaungpaya after
the Mon rebellion. Three wars
with the British—triggered by
Burmese resistance to the United
Kingdom's commercial and
130 territorial ambitions—led to the
kingdom's collapse. The first war
was fought from 1824 to 1826,
the second in 1852, and the
third in 1885. In these wars, the
British gradually conquered all of
what was then called Burma.

After the third war with the
United Kingdom, Burma became
a province of India, which the
140 British ruled. Under British
control, Burma's population
and economy grew rapidly. But
educated Burmese called for
Burma's separation from India
and eventual independence. The
Burmese protests led the United
Kingdom to set up a legislature
in the 1920's that gave the people
a small role in the government.

150 Protests against British rule
continued, however. During the
early 1930's, a former Buddhist
monk named Saya San led
thousands of peasants in an
unsuccessful rebellion. At the
same time, university students
founded the All-Burma Students'
Union to work for independence.
The students called one another
160 *Thakin* (Master), a title of respect
that had been used before only in
addressing the British. Leaders of
the movement included Thakin
Nu and Thakin Aung San.
They organized a student strike

in 1936. The United Kingdom
separated Burma from India
in 1937 and gave the Burmese
partial self-government. But the
170 struggle for full independence
continued.

World War II (1939–1945).
In 1942, Japan conquered
Burma. The Thakins had
formed the Burma Independence
Army, which helped the Japanese
drive the British out of Burma.
The Japanese declared Burma
independent in 1943, but
180 they actually controlled the
government. The Burmese
disliked Japanese rule even more
than British rule. To fight the
Japanese, the Thakins formed
the Anti-Fascist People's Freedom
League (AFPFL), led by General
Aung San. The AFPFL helped
the United Kingdom and other
Allied powers regain Burma
190 in 1945.

Independence. Following
Japan's defeat, the British returned
to power in Burma. The AFPFL
had become a strong political
party, however, and it challenged
British control. The British could
not govern the country without
AFPFL support. They decided in
1947 to name AFPFL President
200 Aung San prime minister of
Burma, but he was assassinated
before independence came. U Nu,
who had been vice president
of the AFPFL, became the
party's president, and the British
appointed him prime minister.
Burma won full independence on
January 4, 1948. ◀

TESTSMART

When did Burma finally
achieve full independence?

(A) 1752

(B) 1945

(C) 1948

(D) 1951

TIP If a test question asks
you to locate a specific bit of
information, use **headings**
and **subheadings** to help
you quickly locate the
answer. The question above
asks about a specific date
relating to Burma's history.
Locate that **category**, then
circle the subheading that
tells you where to look for
the answer. 🖉

Reading Comprehension

DIRECTIONS *Answer these questions about the two selections in this lesson by filling in the correct ovals.*

1. The time span covered in the encyclopedia article excerpt is

   (A) A.D. 1000 to 1800

   (B) 2000 B.C. to A.D. 1948

   (C) 1000 B.C. to A.D. 1948

   (D) 3000 B.C. to A.D. 1989

2. The main religion in Myanmar is

   (A) Christianity

   (B) Buddhism

   (C) Hinduism

   (D) Islam

3. Which subheading would you look under to find out about childhood in Myanmar?

   (A) PEOPLE

   (B) Way of Life

   (C) Independence

   (D) HISTORY

4. Which group of people ruled what is now Myanmar during much of the 1800s?

   (A) the British

   (B) the Mon

   (C) the Thakin

   (D) the Japanese

5. Which of the following information from "Myanmar" is *not* connected with the time period described in "Shooting an Elephant?"

   (A) Most people live in farm villages.

   (B) There were protests against British rule.

   (C) Anawrahta united the region.

   (D) Buddhism is the main religion.

6. "Shooting an Elephant" is different from "Myanmar" because it

   (A) mentions the prevalence of Buddhism

   (B) is written in a neutral tone

   (C) describes the people and culture of Myanmar/Burma

   (D) gives personal opinions about the British in Myanmar/Burma

7. The meaning of *commercial* in line 129 of "Myanmar" is

   (A) paid for by advertisers

   (B) related to land disputes

   (C) having to do with trade or commerce

   (D) designed for mass appeal

8. *Territorial ambitions* (line 130 of "Myanmar") are carried out by

   (A) peasant farmers

   (B) imperialistic outsiders

   (C) political freedom fighters

   (D) Buddhist monks

GO ON

Timed Writing Practice

PROMPT

Think of an incident or event in your life that you can connect to a more <u>universal idea such as love, freedom, or courage</u>. Write a (personal narrative) in which you use your personal experience to discuss one of life's great truths. Remember to use the first-person point of view.

TEST-TAKER'S TOOLKIT

1. ANALYZE THE PROMPT

A. Read the prompt twice. Underline the phrases that tell what your narrative should include.

B. Circle the key elements you will need to include. The writing form has been circled for you.

C. Restate the prompt in your own words.

2. PLAN YOUR RESPONSE

A. **Make notes** Use the key elements you circled in the prompt to take notes. Organize your notes into a graphic organizer like the one shown.

B. **Organize your information** Because a narrative is the retelling of a story, the events are usually told in sequence. Knowing this can help you organize your narrative.

> Personal experience I will write about: _____
>
> What happened: _____
>
> When it happened: _____
>
> Why I remember it: _____
>
> How it connects to a universal idea: _____

3. WRITE AND REVIEW

A. Use vivid language and precise descriptions to help give your narrative emotional impact. Here is an example of how careful word choice can improve a sentence:

ORIGINAL:
Once I went to my uncle's farm and watched him kill a pig for food.

REVISED:
Visiting my uncle's farm had always been a treat—until the traumatic day when I watched him slaughter, skin, and prepare a pig for our family dinner.

B. Write your narrative, using your notes to guide you. Be sure to leave enough time to reread your narrative carefully, correct any errors, and make sure you have met all the requirements of the prompt.

Student Handbooks

Nonfiction Skills Handbook

Test-Taking Handbook

Argument

ACADEMIC VOCABULARY

argument: speaking or writing that expresses a position on an issue and supports it with reasons and evidence

claim: the writer's position on an issue or problem in an argument

counterargument: an argument made to oppose another argument

evidence: a fact, example, or quotation that supports a claim

fallacy: an error in reasoning

generalization: a general principle derived from evidence

inductive reasoning: logically reasoning from specific observation to arrive at a general conclusion or principle

logic: system of reasoning. Good logic finds a valid or reasonable connection between two things. Faulty logic creates a mistaken or unreasonable connection between two things.

reasons: declarations that explain or justify an action, decision, or belief

STEP 1 **Identify the claim.** Ask yourself: What assertion or opinion is expressed in the argument? Write the claim as a complete statement.

STEP 2 **Look for reasons and evidence to support the claim.** *Reasons* explain or justify an opinion or action. They usually appeal to logic or common sense. *Evidence* is factual support, such as facts, statistics, examples, and quotations from experts.

STEP 3 **Check that reasons make sense and are logical.** Take note of sound reasons. Question or reject others.

STEP 4 **Check that evidence is AAA: accurate, appropriate, adequate.** Ask yourself: Is the supporting evidence *accurate*—correct (documented), and not distorted or exaggerated? Is the supporting evidence *appropriate*—relevant to the particular claim? Is it *adequate*—or enough—to prove the claim?

STEP 5 **Check that there is no faulty reasoning.** Look for errors in judgment or logic. How logical is the argument? Does it make sense or are there errors or fallacies in the reasoning? Is it slanted to gain political power as in propaganda?

STEP 6 **Look for counterarguments.** Raising opposing viewpoints and countering them firmly but respectfully can strengthen an argument.

STEP 7 **Evaluate.** Decide if the argument is weak or strong. Is the argument free of loaded language, attacks on people, and emotional appeals that mislead?

Author's Craft

STEP 1 Examine the choice of details. What details does the writer include to support his or her ideas? What do these details tell you about the writer's overall purpose?

STEP 2 Look at the language. Examine the language the writer uses. Focus on:

- **tone**—what are the writer's feelings toward this subject? Is the tone angry, happy, humorous? What words convey the tone?
- **figurative language**—does the writer include any similes or metaphors? Does the use of figurative language make the writing vivid and interesting?
- **imagery**—does the writer use language that appeals to the senses? What effect does this language have on the writing?
- **quotations**—if the writer has included quotations, how does the language and content of the quotations affect you as a reader?

STEP 3 Study the pattern of organization. Has the writer chosen an organizational pattern that supports the ideas? If the writer wants a "you are there" feeling, has he or she written about events in the order they happened? If the writer wants readers to understand the causes of an event, has he or she used a clear cause-and-effect order?

Author's Purpose

STEP 1 **Learn common purposes.** Keep the four common author purposes in mind as you read:

- **to explain or inform**
- **to persuade**
- **to entertain**
- **to express emotion and ideas**

STEP 2 **Identify clues to author's purpose.** As you read a text, look for clues in the work's title, subject, and **tone;** the choice of details and words; the context, or intended **audience;** the effects on you as a reader; and the pattern of organization, or **structure.**

- Tone is an especially helpful clue to the author's purpose. For example, because a political speech is usually meant to persuade, the author may include words and phrases that establish a forceful or inspiring tone.
- There are some common match-ups between text structure and purpose, but be aware that there are no firm rules.

EXAMPLE

Sequence, cause-effect, or **main idea and details** are often used to explain or to inform.

Problem-solution, proposition-support, or **compare-contrast order** may signal that the author's purpose is to persuade.

Chronological order is often used in dramatic histories or storytelling and may signal that the purpose is to entertain.

Order of degree or **spatial order** may be used to express emotion.

STEP 3 **Determine the audience.** Is the text intended for children, for informed adults, for undecided voters, or for some other audience? The intended audience will influence the writer's choice of words, the structure, the explanations, and many other elements of the writing.

STEP 4 **Use purpose to understand and evaluate work.** Use the author's purpose to guide how you read. Take notes on an informational piece, or jot down arguments or opinions about a persuasive piece. Entertainment may come through better if you relax. Evaluate the piece in light of the author's purpose: How well or poorly did the passage achieve the goal? How well were you entertained, informed, persuaded, or instructed?

Author's Perspective

ACADEMIC VOCABULARY

background: facts about an author's experience and knowledge

bias: an author's preference or slant on a particular topic

personal essay: writing that combines an author's insights on a topic with details from his or her own life

perspective: the way an author looks at a topic

selective details: information an author includes—and decides not to include—in a text

word choice: the words an author uses to create a specific effect on readers

STEP 1 **Identify the author.** Look for the author's name and any additional information about the person. This usually can be found at the beginning or end of a text, sometimes set off as a separate feature. Ask the following questions for clues about the author's experiences, values, and beliefs:

- What does the author's name suggest about the person's sex and possibly nationality?
- What is the author's education? How has that education or lack of it, affected the author's life?
- What do the author's activities, responsibilities, and publications say about his or her reliability?
- What social and cultural values have influenced the author?

STEP 2 **Examine the text for clues to the author's point of view.** Carefully read the text, looking for indications of the author's point of view. Focus on:

- **word choice**—words with strong positive or negative emotional associations, or connotations
- **selective details**—facts and opinions that support a specific point of view
- **biased language**—statements that reveal a one-sided belief
- **direct statements**—clear admissions of point of view, often beginning with the words "I believe" or "In my opinion"

STEP 3 **Identify the author's perspective.** Review the evidence you have discovered and ask yourself, "What does this information tell me about the author's point of view on the topic?" Then write a sentence describing that point of view. Finally, read through the text again, keeping the author's perspective in mind. Write down questions, comments, or counterevidence that occurs to you as you read. Take this information into account as you evaluate the reliability or usefulness of the text.

Cause-and-Effect Order

ACADEMIC VOCABULARY

cause-and-effect order: a method of organizing ideas and information in an essay that shows causal relationships

cause: why something happens

effect: a result; what happened as an outcome of the cause

STEP 1 **Look for effects.** Ask: "What was the outcome?" Check for multiple effects.

EXAMPLE

Because Harry left the cage open, <u>the canary escaped</u> and <u>flew around the room</u>.

STEP 2 **Look for causes.** Ask: "Why did it happen?" Check for multiple causes.

EXAMPLE

<u>Because Harry left the cage open</u> and <u>never noticed</u>, the canary escaped.

STEP 3 **Check for cause-effect chains.** A cause can lead to an effect that then causes another effect, and so on. A series of such linked events is a cause-effect chain.

EXAMPLE

Harry left the <u>cage open</u>, allowing the <u>canary to escape</u>. As a result, <u>Harry chased the bird</u> around the room for an hour.

STEP 4 **Find signal words.** Signal words and phrases for cause and effect include: *because, since, as a result, therefore,* and *due to.*

EXAMPLE

I forgot to study, and <u>as a result</u>, I didn't do very well on the quiz.

STEP 5 **Use a graphic organizer.** Arrange ideas in a cause-and-effect diagram or chain.

EXAMPLE

| Cause: | | Effect: |
| Angel oversleeps. | → | Angel misses bus. |

STEP 6 **Check your logic.** The cause must spark, or set in motion the result. They do not have to be presented in sequence. In many sentences, the effect appears first.

EXAMPLE

Angel missed the bus <u>due to</u> oversleeping.

Charts and Other Graphic Aids

ACADEMIC VOCABULARY

bar graph: a coordinate grid with shaded bars, used to compare amounts or levels in various categories

chart: a table, displaying information in rows and columns or in boxes

diagram: a sketch or plan designed to explain how something works or to show the relationship of parts to the whole

illustration: usually a drawing designed to explain a concept or to show relationships of parts to the whole

line graph: connected points on a coordinate grid, showing change over time

map: a drawing of a region of the earth, showing the location of places

pie chart/circle graph: a circle divided into sliced sections, measured to represent percentages of a whole

STEP 1 **Read the title.** Ask yourself: What information does the graphic aid display? Does the title include time periods, locations, ages, or other details about the subject?

STEP 2 **Study the data.** Use these tips to analyze various charts and graphs:

- **Line Graph:** Check what's being measured on the vertical axis and the horizontal axis. Study the slant of the line. The steeper the line, the faster the rate of change.
- **Bar Graph:** Check what's being measured on the vertical axis and the horizontal axis. Check the range of numbers: small differences can look big if the range is small.
- **Pie Chart/Circle Graph:** Determine what the "whole" is and what the "parts" are. Then look at the relative size of the slices to understand the percentage of the whole.
- **Chart:** Read down the outside column and across the top. Note the headings. Make sure you understand what data are being shown and any abbreviations or terms. To find specific data, run your finger down the outside column to the correct row. Then move across that row to a specific column. Compare the information in the rows and columns to get an idea of any similarities, differences, or patterns.

STEP 3 **Draw conclusions.** Decide why the information in the graphic aid is useful and how it could be used. Ask yourself:

- What can I conclude from the information in the graphic aid?
- Which data allow me to make that conclusion?
- What further information would be helpful?
- What new questions arise from learning this data?

Chronological Order

ACADEMIC VOCABULARY

chronological order: organization in order of occurrence, forward in time, usually used to tell stories, to report events, or to record histories

sequence order: the order in which events should, may, or usually occur; sequence order is used to give directions or to show steps or events in a process

STEP 1 Look for times, dates, or numbers that show order. Clue words such as *first, second,* and so on indicate sequence of information. Numerals (*1, 2, 3, . . .*) or dates and times may give order of events.

STEP 2 Organize information in a graphic. Based on any time-order clue words, place the events in a graphic organizer. The organizer can be a numbered list. Or you can create a left-to-right series of boxes and arrows to track information.

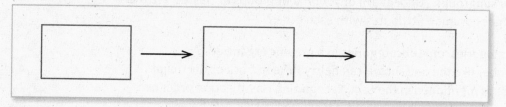

STEP 3 Look for words and phrases that show duration or sequence. Certain signal words and phrases help structure both chronological and sequential texts: *then, next, before, after, during, finally,* and so on.

STEP 4 Infer the author's purpose. The author may want to explain how to carry out a task or report a story about how events unfolded in time. Ask yourself: Why does the author arrange details in this way? What is he or she trying to achieve?

Classification Order

STEP 1 Look for words and phrases that signal groups. Words and phrases writers use to indicate a subject's class include *group, category, kind, set, type, class, classification, division, divided into,* and *common characteristics.* Notice how many groups there are.

STEP 2 Look for how classes or groups are defined. What do each of these objects, ideas, or facts have in common? What qualities or attributes unite the items in each group?

STEP 3 Look for subgroups. Under each of your major groups or classes, are there other items that share common attributes with each other?

STEP 4 Write categories and subcategories in a graphic organizer. A classification organizer like the one shown can help you keep track of the major groups and subgroups mentioned in the text. Recognizing classification order can help you understand the relationships between ideas and details and help you remember important information.

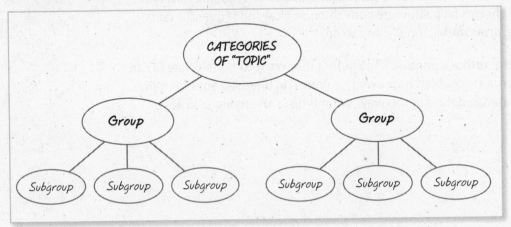

Connect Texts

ACADEMIC VOCABULARY

fiction: writing that contains imaginary elements. Although fiction can be inspired by real events and people, it usually springs from writers' imaginations.

nonfiction: writing that tells about real people, places, and events

theme: the underlying message about life or human nature that a writer wants the reader to understand

treatment: the way a topic is handled, includes the form a writer uses, the writer's purpose, and tone

STEP 1 Identify the topic or theme you wish to examine. Choose a topic or theme that is specific and narrow enough to find several texts that examine it.

STEP 2 Find related texts. If your topic or theme is clear and specific, you are more likely to find texts that cover it or you may already be studying two texts that have been presented together.

STEP 3 Examine how the texts treat the subject. Make a note of the tone of each text. Does one writer seem more serious than the other, for example? Does one writer include more facts and the other include more anecdotes? If the texts are fiction, what are the differences in approach?

STEP 4 What ideas are covered? Do the writers share some ideas or are the ideas very different? Note the major ideas of each text.

STEP 5 Identify contradictory ideas. Do the two writers contradict each other? If so, you may have to do further reading. What have you learned from connecting these texts that you wouldn't learn from one text alone?

Critical Essays

STEP 1 Identify the writer's tone. What are the writer's feelings toward this subject? Is the tone sarcastic, understanding, measured, or bitter, for example? What words convey the tone?

STEP 2 Identify the conclusions the writer makes. What is the writer saying about this topic? What critical conclusions are expressed? Make sure you understand exactly what the writer is saying about the topic.

STEP 3 Examine the evidence. Now that you are clear about the interpretations the writer is making, what evidence supports those conclusions? Focus on:

- **facts**—does the writer include any facts as support?
- **quotations**—does the writer choose relevant quotations from the work to back up the ideas?
- **examples**—are the examples the writer uses relevant to the ideas?
- **explanations**—does the writer explain the ideas clearly with relevant details?
- **personal experiences**—if the writer includes some personal experiences as support, are the experiences relevant to the ideas?

Evaluate Evidence

ACADEMIC VOCABULARY

evaluate evidence: determine the strength and quality of the facts, statistics, reasons, examples, and sources that support a position or claim

evidence: a reason, fact, statistic, example, or expert opinion that supports a proposition or claim

fact: a statement that can be proved

objective: not influenced by emotions or personal prejudices; factual

opinion: a statement that cannot be proved, such as a personal feeling or belief

proposition or claim: the writer's position on an issue or problem

subjective: personal to a given person; existing only in the mind

STEP 1 **Look for opinions to be sure they are supported.** No one can check whether an opinion is true or false. So a writer must support any claims, positions, or personal opinions with examples, facts, and reasons. For any expert opinions, be sure that sources are clearly identified. Don't accept vague language, such as "experts agree."

STEP 2 **Look for facts–statistics, examples, and expert opinions.** Part of a writer's job is to present enough facts to support each claim. Facts include quotations from experts, anecdotes and examples, and definitions, as well as **statistics** (mathematical data). Decide whether there is enough evidence. Decide if the evidence is up to date. If there are no data to back up the ideas, don't accept the claim.

STEP 3 **Look for ways in which sources are documented.** Writers should name the source of their facts. Look for sources that are **objective** and **credible,** like an encyclopedia, rather than **subjective** and **biased** like a personal blog. Good documentation includes the *who, where,* and *when* of each source, so readers can check it.

STEP 4 **Weigh the evidence.** After evaluating the support, the hard data, and the documentation, a reader can decide whether to accept or agree with the writer's position or not. You can also weigh how reasonable, valuable, or useful the writer's ideas are to you.

Main Ideas and Supporting Details

STEP 1 **Identify the topic.** Ask yourself: What is this passage or paragraph about?

STEP 2 **Think about the main idea.** Ask yourself: What idea does the writer express?

STEP 3 **Look for a topic sentence.** The topic sentence is usually either the first or last sentence in a paragraph, although it can occur anywhere. In some paragraphs, the main idea is not stated directly, but is implied by the supporting details.

STEP 4 **Identify the supporting details.** Writers use different types of details to support different purposes and main ideas. Sensory details describe, examples illustrate, reasons persuade, and facts and statistics explain.

STEP 5 **Use a graphic organizer.** A chart can help you take notes on the main idea and supporting details in a paragraph. List a main idea, then note all the details that support it.

Main Idea	Supporting Details

Narrative Nonfiction

ACADEMIC VOCABULARY

characters: the individuals who participate in the action

conflict: a struggle between opposing forces

feature article: in-depth coverage of human-interest or lifestyle topics found in newspapers or magazines

figurative language: language that communicates meanings beyond the literal meanings of words

historical narrative: a nonfiction story about an event in history

narrative: a story with characters, settings, and events

pacing: the speed at which events in the story unfold. Writers choose a rapid or leisurely pace depending on the purpose the writing serves.

plot events: the actions of the story

setting: the time and place of the action of a story

tone: the attitude the writer takes toward the subject

STEP 1 **Identify the author's purpose.** Does the writer want to inform, entertain, describe, persuade? What evidence leads you to your conclusion?

STEP 2 **Examine the narrative devices.** What devices does the writer use to make the narrative appealing? Look for colorful characters, dramatic plot events, figurative language, and strong conflicts.

STEP 3 **Evaluate accuracy.** Although the events and characters may sound fictional, a nonfiction narrative tells about true people and events. Even though the narrative style reads like a story, the writer must take care to present an accurate picture of what happened. What support does the writer provide to back up his or her version of the events?

Patterns of Organization

STEP 1 **Get a general sense of the organization.** To form an initial impression of how a text is organized, skim it quickly, asking yourself, "Am I learning about:

- time sequence?"
- relation in space?"
- relative ranking?"
- membership in a category?"
- causes and effects?"
- similarities and differences?"
- the solution to a problem?"

STEP 2 **Look for clues to the organization.** Each organizational pattern uses a variety of signal words and structural patterns.

Cause-and-Effect Order

- Look for signal words like *because, therefore, since, as a result, the effect of,* and *consequently.*
- Look for answers to the question, "What happens next?"
- Study the text for clues to implied causes and effects.

Chronological Order

- Look for signal words like *first, next, then, afterward,* and *before.*
- Study the text for times, dates, or numbers that show order.

Classification

- Look for words or phrases that signal groups: *group, category, kind, set, type, class, classification, division, divided into, common characteristics.*
- Look for definitions of the groups used in the text. What do each of these objects, ideas, or facts have in common?
- Look for subgroups under the major groups.

Comparison-Contrast Order

- Signal words for this pattern are *similarly, also, both, like, neither, unlike, instead,* and *in contrast.*
- Identify the subjects being compared or contrasted. The subjects usually have similar characteristics.
- Look for the pattern. Does the text compare each subject in turn, or does it compare each subject feature by feature?

Problem-Solution Order

- Look for words like *problem, solution, pros, cons,* and *recommendation.*
- Examine the text for a clear statement of the problem, an analysis of the problem, and a proposed solution.
- Look for a discussion of the causes and effects of the problem.

Spatial Order

- Look for signal words such as *in front of, behind, under, above, left, right, top,* and *bottom.*
- Identify the specific way in which the spatial details are organized. A writer usually arranges spatial details in a certain order such as front to back, near to far, low to high, and so on.

STEP 3 **Determine the most important ideas and supporting details.** Once you have determined how the text is organized, focus on the main ideas the author is presenting and the support that he/she provides. Making an informal outline like the one below can help you understand how the organizational pattern helps convey an author's message.

Organizational pattern _____

  I. Main idea

    A. Supporting detail

    B. Supporting detail

  II. Main idea related to first idea by _____

    A. Supporting detail

    B. Supporting detail

  III. Main idea related to first and second ideas by _____

    A. Supporting detail

    B. Supporting detail

Persuasion

STEP 1 Recognize persuasive messages. Notice the writer's purpose. Is the message addressed to a specific audience? What does the writer want readers to do? These messages often appear in speeches, ads, and editorials.

STEP 2 Look for words that stir positive and negative emotions. Does the writer talk about people who are "foolish dreamers" or about those who are "courageous visionaries"? Look carefully at the writer's word choices throughout.

STEP 3 Identify emotional appeals. In addition to using language with strong positive and negative emotions, writers may appeal to readers' sense of fair play or desire to join a group of other smart people, or other strategies. Be critical of such appeals.

STEP 4 Recognize logical fallacies. Look for reasons and examples that offer only two choices, such as "Either we build a new soccer field or our students will not get adequate exercise." Watch for statements that claim that "all" or "everyone" will "always" do something. These statements signal an overgeneralization. Also, watch for statements with claims such as "All you need to know is . . ." or "It is just a question of . . . ." These are oversimplifications.

Primary Sources

ACADEMIC VOCABULARY

eyewitness account: an account written by someone who was present at the event. An eyewitness could be an observer or a participant. Such an account has the advantage of being on the scene, but it can also be incomplete or influenced by the eyewitness's opinions and background.

observer: someone who is watching an event

participant: someone who is part of the action, such as a soldier in battle

primary source: information supplied by an eyewitness to events. Letters, diaries, autobiographies, speeches, and photographs are examples of primary sources.

secondary source: records of events created by writers who were not directly involved. Encyclopedias, textbooks, biographies, and most newspaper and magazine articles are examples of secondary sources.

STEP 1 **Identify the writer.** Ask yourself questions such as these about the writer.

- What is the writer's age and gender?
- What can you tell about the writer's background? You might try to determine the author's educational background or country of origin, for example.
- Was the writer an observer or a participant in the events?
- How might the writer's background influence what he or she writes?

STEP 2 **Determine the author's purpose.** Read the text carefully to determine why the author is writing this material. Some possible questions to ask:

- Does the writer want to provide a full, factual account of the events?
- Does the writer seem to want to explain his or her own behavior or the behavior of others?
- Is the writer trying to persuade you to believe in his or her own version of the events?

STEP 3 **Examine the details.** Look at the details the author includes. Think about any other information that might have been included but was not. Question the reason for any missing information.

Problem-Solution Order

ACADEMIC VOCABULARY

problem-solution order: presents a problem, explores various solutions, and identifies a solution, or outcome

STEP 1 Identify the problems or problems. To signal a **problem,** writers may use words and phrases like *problem, difficulty, issue, conflict,* and *need for change.*

STEP 2 Look for solutions. Signal words and phrases can help you.

- **solutions**—words like *solution, answer, approach, method, way, option, remedy, alternative*
- **outcomes**—words and phrases like *but, however, can lead to, would result in, most likely, might also, on the other hand*
- **preferred solution**—words and phrases like *best, most effective, useful, helpful, valuable*

STEP 3 Use a graphic organizer. Use a chart like the one shown to keep track of the problem, solutions, and possible outcomes.

State Problem	

Solution 1	Pros • • •
	Cons • • •
Solution 2	Pros • • •
	Cons • • •

Decision	

Speeches

ACADEMIC VOCABULARY

audience: the people for whom the speech is intended

message: the idea the speaker wants to convey

purpose: the speaker may want to persuade, to inform, to entertain, or to express emotion or ideas

rhetorical devices: techniques writers and speakers use to enhance their arguments. Common rhetorical devices include repetition, rhetorical questions, and others.

speech: a talk or public address

tone: the attitude the speaker takes toward the subject. The tone reflects the feelings of the speaker such as anger, scorn, or pleading.

STEP 1 **Determine the audience.** Who is listening? Do the audience members already know the subject, or do they need background information? Is the speaker addressing a friendly audience or one that is opposed to the proposed ideas? Answers to these questions will give you better understanding of the speech.

STEP 2 **Identify the purpose.** Is the speaker trying to persuade the audience to accept his or her ideas? Or does the speaker have another purpose? What tone does the speaker take? If a speaker is pleading or heaping scorn on another person or idea, the tone will affect the audience in various ways.

STEP 3 **What is the message?** What idea does the speaker want to convey? Does the speaker give relevant reasons and examples to support his or her message? Examining the evidence the speaker uses will help you decide if you can agree with the ideas.

STEP 4 **Examine rhetorical devices.** What devices does the speaker use to get you to pay attention and to agree with the ideas? A speaker may use repetition to make his or her point. Dr. Martin Luther King's "I Have a Dream" speech uses repetition with great effect. Another device is to ask a question that the audience must answer for themselves.

Summarize and Paraphrase

ACADEMIC VOCABULARY

main idea: the most important idea in a paragraph or essay

paraphrase: to restate information in simpler language. A paraphrase is about the same length as the original text. It includes all the details of the original but is written in simpler language.

scan: to read quickly to find specific information. Scanning involves letting your eyes sweep across a page looking for key words that may lead you to the information you want.

skim: to read quickly to get the general idea of a text. Skimming involves reading only the title, headings, graphic aids, highlighted words, and the first sentence of each paragraph in addition to the introduction, conclusion, or summary.

summarize: to retell the main ideas of a piece of writing in your own words. A summary is usually shorter than the original text.

topic sentence: the main idea of a paragraph. All details in the paragraph provide supporting details. A topic sentence may be stated or implied.

STEP 1 **Skim the text before summarizing.** Skim to find the main ideas. These ideas will be the focus of your summary. Note the stated or implied topic of each paragraph. Leave out details and information that are not essential for understanding the writer's key ideas.

STEP 2 **Paraphrase difficult passages.** Writing a paraphrase may help you understand any difficult main ideas. Use your own words to restate the author's ideas in simpler language. This process will help you clarify main ideas for a summary.

STEP 3 **Identify key details.** The title may give you a clue to the overall main idea, or you may have identified it in another way. Scan the text to find key words related to that idea. Determine which details the author provides are essential for understanding the main idea and which details simply provide additional information. Note the essential details.

STEP 4 **Prepare a summary.** Restate the main ideas and the essential details you have identified. Writing a summary or a paraphrase is a good way to preview for tests.

Synthesize

> **ACADEMIC VOCABULARY**
>
> **synthesize:** to combine individual ideas, influences, or materials to create a new product or idea
>
> **synthesizing information:** drawing from a variety of research materials, combining new ideas with prior knowledge, and applying the information to some new work or creation

STEP 1 **Determine the message in each source.** Decide what is most memorable or important about each work you are using. Then look for details the writers use to support these main ideas.

STEP 2 **Paraphrase the main ideas.** You will find the main ideas easier to work with after you have rephrased them in your own words. You should also paraphrase difficult concepts and wording in each selection to improve your understanding.

STEP 3 **Compare sources in light of author's purpose and audience.** Determine whether each selection was written to explain, inform, express an opinion, persuade, tell a story, or express emotion. You may interpret information in different ways depending on its purpose and audience.

STEP 4 **Ask questions about your sources.** The right questions will help you view your subject from different perspectives. Ask questions starting with *who, what, when, where, why, how,* and even *what if*. For example:

- How do the sources differ?
- What approach has the author of each work taken?
- Whose perspective is, or is *not*, represented?
- Who is the intended audience?
- Why is the message important to the author? to me?
- When and where is the writing set? When and where was it created?

STEP 5 **Connect to other sources, or your own experiences.** Look for ways that key ideas relate to other works on the same subject, or to your prior knowledge of the subject. Use your imagination to find connections that may not seem obvious at first. Ask yourself:

- How does the information confirm or refute other material?
- How does the information relate to my life or to world affairs?

STEP 6 **Synthesize.** After reviewing your sources as a group, piece the information together to create something new—an essay, story, poem, research paper, map, poster, or other work. Be sure to offer your own original insights about the topic.

Text Features

text features: design elements that highlight the organization and especially important information in a text

boldface type: thicker, darker type, often used for key terms

bulleted list: each listed item is signaled with a dot or "bullet"

caption: written information about an illustration, photograph, or graphic

footnote: a numbered note placed at the bottom of a page that provides additional or source information

graphic aid: a visual tool (a photograph, table, graph, or other illustration)

head *or* heading: title that identifies the topic of the content that follows it

key word: important term, may be italicized, boldfaced, or highlighted

numbered or lettered list: each listed item begins with a numeral or a letter of the alphabet to show a sequence or an order of importance

review questions: help readers focus or assess their understanding

sidebar: additional information set in a box or otherwise apart from the main text

subhead *or* subheading: signals the beginning of a new topic or section under a more general heading

title: the name given to a book, chapter, play, film, or poem

---

STEP 1 **Before you read, identify the text features.** Knowing the kinds of features that a text contains can help you find information.

STEP 2 **Next, preview the text features carefully.** Follow these steps:

- **Read the heads and subheads** to get an overview of the material and to determine which details go with which main ideas.
- **Scan for boldfaced terms,** other key words, and lists for important details.
- **Glance at the graphic aids and corresponding captions** to see what kind of data the text offers besides words.
- **Locate any sidebars.** Familiarize yourself with the kind of material that is covered in the sidebars, but don't read them yet.

STEP 3 **Now read the text and organize information.** As you read, paragraph by paragraph, work in the graphic aids and sidebars as convenient. Use the text features to help your note taking, outlining, summarizing, and questioning.

Transitions and Other Text Clues

ACADEMIC VOCABULARY

demonstrative pronouns: words like *this, these,* and *those* that refer to people, places, and things and clarify relationships between ideas

synonyms: words with similar meanings that help define and elaborate on ideas

transitions: signal words that indicate how ideas relate to each other, such as *but* and *however* for contrast; *like* and *similarly* for comparison; *first, then,* and *next* for sequence, and *so* and *because* for cause

STEP 1 **Scan the text for an overall impression.** As you skim the title, subheads, graphics, and first few paragraphs, ask yourself:

- What is this text about?
- What is the author's purpose?
- Who is the intended audience?
- What is the author's tone?

STEP 2 **Preview the text clues.** Look for words that signal relationships between the ideas and list them in a three-column chart like this one.

Demonstrative Pronouns	Synonyms	Transitions

Then add the following information for each entry:

- **demonstrative pronouns**—the word each refers to
- **synonyms**—the meaning (using a dictionary if necessary)
- **transitions**—the type of relationship each transition word signals—comparison, contrast, sequence, or some other connection

STEP 3 **Analyze the flow of ideas.** Then read the text carefully, using your chart to help you understand the main ideas and how they relate to each other. Make an informal outline as you read or summarize the information afterward to make sure you understand the author's point.

Treatment, Organization, and Scope of Ideas

ACADEMIC VOCABULARY

organization: a particular arrangement, or pattern, of ideas in a text

scope: the focus of a text; the depth and breadth of detail included

tone: the writer's attitude toward his or her subject

treatment: the way a topic is handled; includes the form a writer uses, the writer's purpose, and tone

STEP 1 **Identify and compare treatment.** Look for differences and similarities in form, purpose, and tone between two works. Ask yourself:

- **What is the form, or genre, of each text?** Examples of forms include news reports, summaries, editorials, interviews, and reviews.
- **What is the writer's purpose?** Is it to inform, persuade, instruct, advise, warn, critique, promote, amuse, or inspire readers?
- **What is the tone of the writing?** Is it serious? comical? angry? fearful?

STEP 2 **Identify and compare organization.** Some common patterns of organization include:

- **Chronological order** arranges events from earliest to latest in time. Reverse chronological order starts with recent events.
- **Deductive order** begins with a general statement, followed by facts and evidence, building toward a specific conclusion.
- **Main idea and supporting details** begins with the main idea, followed by reasons, facts, and examples that strengthen the reader's understanding of it.
- **Cause-effect organization** shows that a certain event, idea, or trend causes a change. The writing may begin with the cause or begin with the effects.

STEP 3 **Identify and compare scope.** Two texts about one subject may each have a different focus, such as an overview versus a close-up look. Ask:

- **What is the topic?** This may appear in the title or first sentence.
- **What aspects of the topic are covered?** Scan headings or topic sentences throughout the work to see what the focus is.
- **How much and what sort of details are used?** In articles with wide scope, facts and statistics are given and background is provided. A narrow piece covers personal anecdotes and minor incidents.

TEST-TAKING
HANDBOOK

Successful Test Taking

You can prepare for tests in several ways. First, study and understand the content that will be on the test. Second, learn as many test-taking techniques as you can. These techniques will help you better understand the questions and how to answer them. Following are some general suggestions for preparing for and taking tests. Starting on page R32, you'll find more detailed suggestions and test-taking practice.

 ## Study Content Throughout the Year

1. **Master the content of your language arts class.** The best way to study for tests is to read, understand, and review the content of your language arts class. Read your daily assignments carefully. Study the notes that you have taken in class. Participate in class discussions. Work with classmates in small groups to help one another learn. You might trade writing assignments and comment on your classmates' work.

2. **Use your textbook for practice.** Your textbook includes many different types of questions. Some may ask you to talk about a story you just read. Others may ask you to figure out what's wrong with a sentence or how to make a paragraph sound better. Try answering these questions out loud and in writing. This type of practice can make taking a test much easier.

3. **Learn how to understand the information in charts, maps, and graphic organizers.** One type of test question may ask you to look at a graphic organizer, such as a spider map, and explain something about the information you see there. Another type of question may ask you to look at a map to find a particular place. You'll find charts, maps, and graphic organizers to study in your literature textbook. You'll also find charts, maps, and graphs in your science, mathematics, and social studies textbooks. When you look at these, ask yourself, What information is being presented and why is it important?

4. **Practice taking tests.** Use copies of tests you have taken in the past or in other classes for practice. Every test has a time limit, so set a timer for 15 or 20 minutes and then begin your practice. Try to finish the test in the time you've given yourself.

5. **Talk about test-taking experiences.** After you've taken a classroom test or quiz, talk about it with your teacher and classmates. Which types of questions were the hardest to understand? What made them difficult? Which questions seemed easiest, and why? When you share test-taking techniques with your classmates, everyone can become a successful test taker.

Use Strategies During the Test

1. **Read the directions carefully.** You can't be a successful test taker unless you know exactly what you are expected to do. Look for key words and phrases, such as *circle the best answer, write a paragraph,* or *choose the word that best completes each sentence.*

2. **Learn how to read test questions.** Test questions can sometimes be difficult to figure out. They may include unfamiliar language or be written in an unfamiliar way. Try rephrasing the question in a simpler way using words you understand. Always ask yourself, What type of information does this question want me to provide?

3. **Pay special attention when using a separate answer sheet.** If you accidentally skip a line on an answer sheet, all the rest of your answers may be wrong! Try one or more of the following techniques:

   - Use a ruler on the answer sheet to make sure you are placing your answers on the correct line.

   - After every five answers, check to make sure you're on the right line.

   - Each time you turn a page of the test booklet, check to make sure the number of the question is the same as the number of the answer line on the answer sheet.

   - If the answer sheet has circles, fill them in neatly. A stray pencil mark might cause the scoring machine to count the answer as incorrect.

4. **If you're not sure of the answer, make your best guess.** Unless you've been told that there is a penalty for guessing, choose the answer that you think is likeliest to be correct.

5. **Keep track of the time.** Answering all the questions on a test usually results in a better score. That's why finishing the test is important. Keep track of the time you have left. At the beginning of the test, figure out how many questions you will have to answer by the halfway point in order to finish in the time given.

Understand Types of Test Questions

Most tests include two types of questions: multiple-choice and open-ended. Specific strategies will help you understand and correctly answer each type of question.

A **multiple-choice question** has two parts. The first part is the question itself, called the stem. The second part is a series of possible answers. Usually four possible answers are provided, and only one of them is correct. Your task is to choose the correct answer. Here are some strategies to help you do just that.

1. Read and think about each question carefully before looking at the possible answers.

2. Pay close attention to key words in the question. For example, look for the word *not,* as in "Which of the following is *not* a cause of the conflict in this story?"

3. Read and think about all of the possible answers before making your choice.

4. Reduce the number of choices by eliminating any answers you know are incorrect. Then, think about why some of the remaining choices might also be incorrect.

   - If two of the choices are pretty much the same, both are probably wrong.

   - Answers that contain any of the following words are usually incorrect: *always, never, none, all,* and *only.*

5. If you're still unsure about an answer, see if any of the following applies:

   - When one choice is longer and more detailed than the others, it is often the correct answer.

   - When a choice repeats a word that is in the question, it may be the correct answer.

   - When two choices are direct opposites, one of them is likely the correct answer.

   - When one choice includes one or more of the other choices, it is often the correct answer.

   - When a choice includes the word *some* or *often,* it may be the correct answer.

   - If one of the choices is *All of the above,* make sure that at least two of the other choices seem correct.

   - If one of the choices is *None of the above,* make sure that none of the other choices seems correct.

An **open-ended test item** can take many forms. It might ask you to write a word or phrase to complete a sentence. You might be asked to create a chart, draw a map, or fill in a graphic organizer. Sometimes, you will be asked to write one or more paragraphs in response to a writing prompt. Use the following strategies when reading and answering open-ended items:

1. If the item includes directions, read them carefully. Take note of any steps required.

2. Look for key words and phrases in the item as you plan how you will respond. Does the item ask you to identify a cause-and-effect relationship or to compare and contrast two or more things? Are you supposed to provide a sequence of events or make a generalization? Does the item ask you to write an essay in which you state your point of view and then try to persuade others that your view is correct?

3. If you're going to be writing a paragraph or more, plan your answer. Jot down notes and a brief outline of what you want to say before you begin writing.

4. Focus your answer. Don't include everything you can think of, but be sure to include everything the item asks for.

5. If you're creating a chart or drawing a map, make sure your work is as clear as possible.

Functional Reading Test

DIRECTIONS *Study the warranty statement below. Then answer the questions that follow.*

READING STRATEGIES FOR ASSESSMENT

Identify the purpose. Circle the statement that tells what this warranty offers consumers.

Note type style and content. Why is this paragraph written in capital letters? How do *incidental and consequential damages* differ from *defects in material or workmanship*?

_____

_____

ANSWER STRATEGIES

Note the conditions of the warranty stated in the title and in the first and second paragraphs. You can eliminate choice C because the warranty is only good for five years and D because there is no mention of a refund of the purchase price.

This question asks you to identify damages the warranty will *not* cover. You can eliminate damages that the warranty does cover or conditions that it does not mention.

The warranty clearly states that its coverage does not include *any other warranties made by any other person, including authorized distributors of our products.*

Littleton Electronics Full Five-Year Warranty

Coverage: For five years from the date of original consumer purchase of this product, we promise, without charge, to repair or replace, at our option, any defects in material or workmanship. Warranty coverage does not include defects due to lack of care (see accompanying instructions for guidance) or any other warranties made by any other person, including authorized distributors of our products.

ALL INCIDENTAL AND CONSEQUENTIAL DAMAGES ARE EXCLUDED FROM WARRANTY COVERAGE. SOME STATES DO NOT ALLOW THE EXCLUSION OR LIMITATION OF INCIDENTAL OR CONSEQUENTIAL DAMAGES, SO THE ABOVE EXCLUSION MAY NOT APPLY TO YOU. THIS WARRANTY GIVES YOU SPECIFIC LEGAL RIGHTS, AND YOU MAY ALSO HAVE OTHER RIGHTS THAT VARY FROM STATE TO STATE.

Warranty Service Procedure: When warranty service is needed, deliver or send the product, insured and properly packaged, freight prepaid, with a description of the apparent defect and the means to ascertain the date of original consumer purchase (such as a copy of your receipt or canceled check) to the factory service center listed below. If at any time you are not satisfied with our warranty service, contact Vice President, Service and Distribution, 7777 Eastgate Rd., Wesley, OR 97777.

1. What promise does this warranty offer buyers of the company's product?
- **A** to replace the product if the buyer is not satisfied
- **B** to repair or replace a defective product
- **C** to repair the product for as long as the buyer owns it
- **D** to refund the buyer's money if the product is returned within five years

2. This warranty will *not* cover damages
- **E** due to mishandling or improper use of the product in certain states
- **F** noticed after the product is purchased in every state
- **G** due to defects in workmanship in certain states
- **H** made by persons other than the buyers in every state

3. How will a lifetime extended warranty offered by a store that sells Littleton Electronics products affect this warranty?
- **A** It will cancel out and replace this warranty.
- **B** It will take effect after this five-year warranty expires.
- **C** It will extend this warranty for the lifetime of the product.
- **D** It will have no effect under the terms of this warranty.

Functional Reading Test

DIRECTIONS *Study the following warning label from a can of insect spray. Circle the information you think is most important. Then answer the multiple-choice questions that follow.*

PRECAUTIONARY STATEMENTS

Hazards to Humans and Domestic Animals

CAUTION: Harmful if swallowed or absorbed through the skin. Avoid breathing spray mist. Avoid contact with skin or clothing. Wash thoroughly with soap and water after using. Provide adequate ventilation of area being treated. Do not apply to humans, plants, or pets, or contaminate feed, foodstuffs, dishes, or utensils. Cover and avoid spraying fish aquariums. Cover or remove exposed food, dishes, utensils, and food-handling equipment. Keep out of reach of children.

Practical Treatment

If swallowed: Do not induce vomiting. Call a physician or Poison Control Center immediately. If in eyes: Flush with plenty of water.

If on skin: Wash promptly with soap and water. Get medical attention if irritation develops.

If inhaled: Remove victim to fresh air. Apply artificial respiration if indicated.

NOTE TO PHYSICIAN: Product contains petroleum distillate (aspiration hazard).

Physical or Chemical Hazards

FLAMMABLE. CONTENTS UNDER PRESSURE. Keep away from heat, sparks, open flame, or pilot lights. Do not puncture or incinerate container. Exposure to temperatures above 130° F may cause bursting.

Questions or comments: Call (888) BUG-SPRAY

---

1. What should you do if you accidentally touch an area that has just been sprayed with this product?

    (A) Call 911.

    (B) Call (888) BUG-SPRAY.

    (C) Get medical attention immediately.

    (D) Wash your hands with lots of soap and water.

2. Why does the warning label include a note to physicians?

    (E) so the manufacturer of the spray will not be legally responsible for injuries

    (F) because physicians use more insect sprays than other groups of people do

    (G) to give them information that will help them treat victims of inhalation

    (H) to reassure users that the label has been approved by physicians

3. What might cause the bug spray can to burst?

   (A) shaking it too hard

   (B) placing it near gardening tools

   (C) exposing it to high temperatures

   (D) dropping it

4. When using this product in the home, what are you advised to do?

   (E) Allow air to move through the area during and after treatment.

   (F) Drain fish tanks and then refill with fresh water.

   (G) Wash all dishes and utensils thoroughly after spraying.

   (H) Throw away all foodstuffs that were purchased before spraying the area.

Revising-and-Editing Test

DIRECTIONS *Read the following paragraph carefully. Then answer the multiple-choice questions that follow. After answering the questions, read the material in the side column to check your answer strategies.*

¹ Tashi Wangchuk Tenzing an Austrian travel agent was a tired but happy man in May 1997, when he scaled Mount Everest. ² Much of his familys' history has involved mountain climbing. ³ In fact, one of his grandfathers, Tenzing Norgay, have the honor of being among the first climbers to reach the top of Mount Everest. ⁴ With this feat, he becomes the third generation of his family to successfully reach the summit. ⁵ Statistics in the record books for his climb. ⁶ Though many people have applauded this accomplishment, they're is a chance that his mountain-climbing days are over. ⁷ He is not among the climbers who are planning to return to the peak. ⁸ Does this surprise you? ⁹ It should. ¹⁰ More than 90 percent of the 700 people who have made it to the top of Everest try to scale the mighty mountain again.

1. Which of the following is the correct way to rewrite the first part of sentence 1?
   - (A) Tashi Wangchuk Tenzing an Austrian travel agent,
   - (B) Tashi Wangchuk Tenzing an Austrian, travel agent,
   - (C) Tashi Wangchuk Tenzing, an Austrian travel agent,
   - (D) Tashi Wangchuk Tenzing, an Austrian, travel agent

2. What is the correct spelling of *familys'* in sentence 2?
   - (E) families'
   - (F) family's
   - (G) familys
   - (H) families

3. Which sentence in the paragraph is a fragment?
   - (A) sentence 5
   - (B) sentence 8
   - (C) sentence 9
   - (D) sentence 10

4. What is the correct way to rewrite the main verb in sentence 3?
   - (E) has
   - (F) have had
   - (G) will have
   - (H) have been

READING STRATEGIES FOR ASSESSMENT

Watch for common errors. Revising-and-editing test questions often focus on typical errors such as mistakes in punctuation, spelling, and capitalization; incomplete sentences; and missing or misplaced information. Circle or underline these errors.

ANSWER STRATEGIES

Commas Use commas to set off appositives.

Possessive Nouns The phrase *familys' history* shows possession. Therefore, the correct spelling must include an apostrophe. Also note that *family* is a singular noun.

Complete Sentences A sentence must express a complete thought.

Subject-Verb Agreement Note that the subject of the sentence is *one*. The verb must agree in person and number with this subject.

5. Which phrase should replace *he* in sentence 4 to clarify its meaning?

(A) his grandfather

(B) Tashi Wangchuk Tenzing's grandfather

(C) Tenzing Norgay

(D) Tashi Wangchuk Tenzing

6. What is the best way to rewrite sentence 5?

(E) Statistics for his climb have been entered in the record books.

(F) Statistics have for his climb been entered in the record books.

(G) Statistics have been entered for his climb in the record books.

(H) Statistics have been for his climb entered in the record books.

7. Which of the following changes should be made in sentence 6?

(A) Change *they're* to *there*.

(B) Change *they're* to *their*.

(C) Delete the hyphen in *mountain-climbing*.

(D) Change *Though* to *However*.

8. Where in the paragraph would you add details about why Tenzing does not plan to climb Everest again?

(E) between sentences 1 and 2

(F) between sentences 6 and 7

(G) between sentences 7 and 8

(H) between sentences 8 and 9

Revising-and-Editing Test

DIRECTIONS *Read the following paragraph carefully. As you read, circle each error you find and identify the error in the side column—for example, you might write* misspelled word *or* not a complete sentence. *When you have finished, fill in the letter of the correct choice for each question that follows.*

¹ How good is your memory? ² Are you able to recall names, dates, and places effortlessly? ³ If you can, you probably have a memory that is more sharper than average. ⁴ Even so it is probably difficult for you to recall entire pages of text. ⁵ That was not the case for the British author and adventurer T. E. Lawrence he accomplished an extraordinary act of memory. ⁶ Toiling long and hard over his book *Seven Pillars of Wisdom*, an account of his Arabian adventures, he took the manuscript to his trusted adviser. ⁷ Following their discussion, Lawrence put the manuscript in a briefcase and headed home. ⁸ The briefcase had been given to him by his grandfather. ⁹ While changing trains, the briefcase was lost. ¹⁰ Lawrence didn't have no choice but to rewrite the manuscript from memory. ¹¹ Yes, that's exactly what he did!

1. Which sentence in this paragraph should be deleted?
   - (A) sentence 1
   - (B) sentence 5
   - (C) sentence 8
   - (D) sentence 11

2. What is the correct form of the comparative adjective in sentence 3?
   - (E) sharper
   - (F) most sharp
   - (G) most sharper
   - (H) more sharpest

3. Which sentence in the paragraph is a run-on?
   - (A) sentence 3
   - (B) sentence 5
   - (C) sentence 6
   - (D) sentence 10

4. Which change should be made to sentence 4?
   - (E) Add a comma after *so*.
   - (F) Add a comma after *is*.
   - (G) Add commas after *even* and *so*.
   - (H) Add commas before and after *probably*.

5. Which transitional word or phrase should be inserted at the beginning of sentence 6?

(A) As a result of

(B) Meanwhile,

(C) After

(D) On the other hand,

6. Which of the following is the *best* way to rewrite sentence 9?

(E) While changing trains, Lawrence lost the briefcase.

(F) The briefcase was lost while changing trains.

(G) While changing trains, the briefcase was lost by Lawrence.

(H) While the briefcase was lost, Lawrence changed trains.

7. What change, if any, should be made in sentence 10?

(A) Change *didn't have* to *had*.

(B) Change *no* to *some*.

(C) Change *choice* to *choices*.

(D) No change is necessary.

8. In sentence 11, what is the antecedent of *that?*

(E) changing trains

(F) no choice

(G) the manuscript

(H) to rewrite the manuscript from memory

ACKNOWLEDGMENTS

UNIT 1A

Penguin Group (USA) Inc.: Excerpt from *Beowulf* translated by Burton Raffel. Copyright © 1963, renewed 1991 by Burton Raffel. Used by permission of Dutton Signet, a division of Penguin Group (USA) Inc.

The Gazette: Excerpt from "The Years of the Dragon" by Bill Reed, from *The Gazette* April 14, 2007. Copyright © 2007 by The Gazette. Reprinted by permission of The Gazette, Colorado Springs (Freedom Colorado Information, Inc.).

UNIT 1B

University of Chicago Press: Excerpts from *Sir Gawain and the Green Knight*, translated by John Gardner. Copyright © 1965 by the University of Chicago. Reprinted by permission of the University of Chicago Press.

UNIT 2A

Margot Starr Kernan: Excerpt from "She Said Yes! She Said Yes! She Said Yes!" by Michael Kernan, from *Smithsonian,* Volume 27, #11. Copyright © 1997 by Michael Kernan. Reprinted by permission of the Estate of Michael Kernan.

UNIT 2B

Simon & Schuster: Excerpt from "Love Is Blind," from *Love Lessons: Twelve Real-Life Love Stories* by Lois Smith Brady. Copyright © 1999 by Lois Smith Brady. Reprinted by permission of Simon & Schuster Adult Publishing Group.

UNIT 3A

The Associated Press: Excerpt from "Children sink to the bottom – Forced from homes, thousands in Haiti subsist on nation's leavings" by Ian James, from the Associated Press, December 15, 2002. Copyright © 2002 by the Associated Press. Reprinted by permission of the Associated Press.

UNIT 3B

New York University Press: Excerpt from *Fight Like a Girl: How to Be a Fearless Feminist* by Megan Seely. Copyright © 2007 by New York University. Reprinted by permission of New York University Press.

UNIT 4B

Cathy Johnson: "Collecting Leaves: Tips for gathering, preserving, and appreciating autumn's brilliant foliage" by Cathy Johnson, from *Country Living*, September 1996. Copyright © 1996 by Cathy Johnson. Reprinted courtesy of Cathy Johnson, artist and writer.

UNIT 5B

Palm Beach Post: "One rescuer lives, one drowns saving sisters in rough Palm Beach surf" by Rochelle E. Gilken, Palm Beach Post staff writer, from the *Palm Beach Post*, May 30, 2007. Copyright © 2007 by the Palm Beach Post. Reprinted by permission of the Palm Beach Post.

UNIT 6A

Penguin Group (USA) Inc.: "The Rocking-Horse Winner," from *The Complete Stories of D. H. Lawrence* by D. H. Lawrence. Copyright © 1933 by the Estate of D. H. Lawrence, renewed 1961 by Angelo Ravagli and C. M. Weekley, Executors of the Estate of Frieda Lawrence Ravagli. Used by permission of Viking Penguin, a division of Penguin Group (USA) Inc.

Globe Newspaper Company: Excerpt from "Money Isn't Everything" by Charles A. Jaffe from the *Boston Globe*, August 16, 1999. Copyright © 1999 by the Globe Newspaper Company. Reprinted by permission of the Globe Newspaper Company.

UNIT 6B

Harcourt, Inc.: "Shooting an Elephant," from *Shooting an Elephant and Other Essays* by George Orwell. Copyright © 1950 by Sonia Brownell Orwell and renewed 1978 by Sonia Pitt-Rivers. Reprinted by permission of Harcourt, Inc.

World Book, Inc.: Excerpts from "Myanmar," from the *World Book Encyclopedia*. Copyright © 2008 by the World Book Encyclopedia. Reprinted by permission of World Book, Inc.

FRONT MATTER

ix *Rainy Embankment* (1929), Fox Photos. © Hulton Archive/Getty Images; **x** *Just Starve Us. Tell Ah! Tell Us, Can Aught be Worse?...Great Overseer,* Isaac Robert Cruikshank. British Library, London. Photo © The Bridgeman Art Library; **xiii** © Jupiterimages Corporation; **xiv–xxi** © Alex Staroseltsev/ShutterStock; **xxiv** *Just Starve Us. Tell Ah! Tell Us, Can Aught be Worse?...Great Overseer,* Isaac Robert Cruikshank. British Library, London. Photo © The Bridgeman Art Library; **xxv** © Thony Belizaire/AFP/Getty Images; **xxvi** Map by GeoNova LLC; **xxvii** © Shaul Schwarz/Getty Images.

UNIT 1A

2 © Vasile Tiplea/ShutterStock; **5** © Wally Stemberger/ShutterStock; **6–31** © DLW-Designs/ShutterStock; **34** © Vasile Tiplea/ShutterStock; **35** © William Casey/ShutterStock.

UNIT 1B

40 © Robert H. Creigh/ShutterStock; **42** © Topal/ShutterStock; **43** © Jo Ann Snover/ShutterStock; **44–56** © Mityukhin Oleg Petrovich/ShutterStock; **59** © Robert H. Creigh/ShutterStock; **60** © Robert Inglis/ShutterStock; **61** © LockStockBob/ShutterStock; **63** © Tatiana Morozova/ShutterStock.

UNIT 2A

66 © Kevin Eaves/ShutterStock; **68** *Mousehold Heath,* John Crome. Tate Gallery, London. Photo © Sally Chappell/Tate Gallery, London/The Art Archive; **70–72** © Kevin Eaves/ShutterStock; **75** © Kevin Eaves/ShutterStock; **76** Illustration by Lucy Kirchner.

UNIT 2B

82 Detail of *Francesca da Rimini* (1837), William Dyce. Oil on canvas, 142 cm × 176 cm. National Gallery of Scotland, Edinburgh. © National Gallery of Scotland, Edinburgh/ The Bridgeman Art Library; **85** © Jupiterimages Corporation; **86–88** © Robert O. Brown Photography/ShutterStock; **91** Detail of *Francesca da Rimini* (1837), William Dyce. Oil on canvas, 142 cm × 176 cm. National Gallery of Scotland, Edinburgh. © National Gallery of Scotland, Edinburgh/The Bridgeman Art Library; **92** © Joan Loitz/ShutterStock.

UNIT 3A

98 *Just Starve Us. Tell Ah! Tell Us, Can Aught be Worse?...Great Overseer,* Isaac Robert Cruikshank. British Library, London. Photo © The Bridgeman Art Library; *background* © Alex Staroseltsev/ShutterStock; **101** © Jupiterimages Corporation; **102–109** © Alex Staroseltsev/ShutterStock; **112** *Just Starve Us. Tell Ah! Tell Us, Can Aught be Worse?... Great Overseer,* Isaac Robert Cruikshank. British Library, London. Photo © The Bridgeman Art Library; *background* © Alex Staroseltsev/ShutterStock; **113** © Thony Belizaire/AFP/Getty Images; **114** Map by GeoNova LLC; **115** © Shaul Schwarz/Getty Images.